# Contextuality of Healthcare Choices in Pakistan

# Contextuality of Healthcare Choices in Pakistan

Edited by Saman Nazir

LEXINGTON BOOKS
*Lanham • Boulder • New York • London*

Published by Lexington Books
An imprint of The Rowman & Littlefield Publishing Group, Inc.
4501 Forbes Boulevard, Suite 200, Lanham, Maryland 20706
www.rowman.com

86-90 Paul Street, London EC2A 4NE



British Library Cataloguing in Publication Information Available

**Library of Congress Cataloging-in-Publication Data Available**

Library of Congress Control Number: 2024944020

ISBN 978-1-66696-271-0 (cloth)
ISBN 978-1-66696-272-7 (electronic)

# Contents

# Foreword

Sara Rizvi Jafree

I am very happy and honored to write a foreword for this edited volume by Dr. Saman Nazir, titled *Contextuality of Healthcare Choices in Pakistan*. There is no doubt that healthcare decision-making is one of the key issues in Pakistan preventing adequate uptake. Not surprisingly, improvements in the supply of healthcare or interventions to improve the quality of health services will remain ineffective unless issues of uptake and choice to pursue healthcare are not tackled first or then simultaneously. This book does not just address issues of cultural barriers to health-seeking, which are historic and commonly known, but delves into the complexity of preferences for alternative healthcare and lack of awareness for adequate or complete health-seeking. An example of the latter is that both literate and illiterate women in Pakistan have an awareness about the benefits of breastfeeding, but they lack awareness of adequate nutrition for their child, resulting in alarming rates of stunting and wasting.

As the world is being impacted by social change, environmental degradation, and technological advances, the well-being of nations is highly dependent on how efficient the healthcare system and policymakers are. Whether it is infectious diseases, non-communicable diseases, or multimorbidity, continuous interventions are needed, especially in developing regions, to support population health uptake and informed decision-making. Remote locations of Pakistan, provincial diversity, and high rates of illiteracy, partial literacy, or language barriers contribute to questions about which interventions for improved health choices are best, regionally appropriate, culturally sensitive, and sustainable.

This book has nine chapters and is divided into three thematic areas: (i) contextuality of healthcare choices; (ii) power dynamics and the health of the marginalized; and (iii) emerging challenges and healthcare responses.

The strengths of this book lie in the theoretical background and empirical evidence gathered through primary data to present arguments for how social and environmental factors can be changed to improve decision-making for better health choices. The book considers various aspects, such as healthcare provider challenges, inhabitants of different regions and cultures, how their environment affects choices for health-seeking, and the quality of interaction between providers and patients, which affects choice to return for treatment. Efforts have been made to give particular attention to marginalized and stigmatized population groups of the country, including the transgender community and those seeking mental healthcare.

This resource is recommended not just for researchers, students, and academicians interested in teaching a course related to health, policy-makers, and healthcare professionals, but also for the wider public and readers in global health who would gain insight into the sociocultural realities framing the choice for health-seeking in Pakistan. I believe this is a timely and much-needed collection of chapters, made coherent by an experienced editor, who has valuable experience working and researching in the field and has now successfully presented evidence to propel Pakistan's health agenda toward investment for improved uptake and informed decision-making for health.

Sara Rizvi Jafree, PhD,
Associate Professor and Chair,
Department of Sociology, Forman Christian College (A Chartered University)
Editor, *Forman Journal of Social Sciences*

# Acknowledgments

I want to extend my sincere gratitude to Emma Ebert, the associate acquisitions editor of this book, for her unwavering support and efficient facilitation throughout its development. Collaborating with her has been a rewarding experience.

I am thankful to the two brilliant scholars I have the privilege of having as friends. Dr. Mariam Moshin's constant encouragement to edit this book has been invaluable. I am grateful to Dr. Sundus Saleemi for her thorough reading of my work and for providing valuable feedback. I cannot express enough gratitude for their support.

Lastly, I am forever thankful to my wonderful family for their unwavering support in all aspects of my academic and personal endeavors. To my husband, Furqan, and my two incredible daughters, Umme Hani and Fatiha, your presence fills me with gratitude every day. Thank you all for being part of my journey.

# Introduction

Saman Nazir

Healthcare choices are socially produced, shaped, and structured, as decisions related to health are made within intricate societal interconnections and dependencies (Collyer et al., 2015). Being healthy has many meanings; in absolute terms, it may be just the absence of disease. Nevertheless, for millions, health is a privilege; for many, a status commodity; for a few, a lifestyle; and for some, it serves as an expression of the status quo or sustained stratification. Health and healthcare choices may not necessarily stem from the individuality paradigm. Healthcare choices may seem agentic but are mainly informed by communal, social, and institutional contextualities and structures. Seeing healthcare choice only as an agentic and rational decision is problematic, as rightly put by Nordgren (2010, p. 122), "in the discourses of choice, we do not see any suffering or vulnerability."

Here, healthcare choice is not used as a notion in economic neoliberalism, which centers on individual rationality and portrays patients primarily as consumers. Although mainly produced in the global north, we can find scholarship on healthcare choices that contest the notion of choice in a pure neoliberal sense. For instance, Annemarie Mol (2008) criticizes viewing patients solely as consumers, emphasizing that genuine care arises from collaborative efforts among patients, healthcare professionals, and technologies. Similarly, Collyer et al. (2015) work on healthcare choices provides theoretical insights into this social dimension of choice. They discuss how social structures influence choices and why viewing patients as "rational actors"—individuals strategically seeking the best outcomes—demands scrutiny. They scrutinize three critical assumptions of rational choice theory on human behavior. Firstly, it assumes that patients/consumers can independently switch healthcare facilities if dissatisfied. Secondly, individuals maintain decision-making consistency even in uncertainty. Lastly, there is an underlying assumption that individuals inherently value an abundance of choices, suggesting an inexhaustible human capacity and inclination toward expanded options (Collyer et al., 2015). Importantly, detaching healthcare choices from their contextuality contributes to a limited understanding of the healthcare system. Improving the healthcare system requires understanding how individuals make choices in varied social, cultural, economic, and geographical contexts.

This book focuses on the contextuality of healthcare choices in Pakistan. The Pakistani healthcare system presents a complex structure with a good mix of public and private healthcare providers, partly regulated and mainly allopathic. However, a considerable portion of the population also uses and believes in alternative medicines and methods to cure various diseases, ranging from seasonal flu and diarrhea to cardiovascular and mental health issues. More importantly, the healthcare system constitutes just one facet within the broader spectrum of healthcare. While it plays a pivotal role in the treatment of diseases, disease prevention transpires beyond the confines of this system. For instance, stunting in the population is alarmingly prevalent, yet it often goes unnoticed by the public. Decisions impacting health unfold in daily choices, spanning dietary practices, nutritional considerations, living arrangements, and engagement in physical activity, to name a few. Creating health-supportive environments, including sanitation, hygiene, and access to clean water, significantly influences overall health outcomes. Moreover, research and dissemination of state-of-the-art research on healthcare or human health significantly influence the health practices of a population. Hardly any studies examine the everyday health choices made by individuals in Pakistan, a topic of great relevance in the present scenario. Most of the available literature focuses on maternal and child health, which is crucial in its own right, given the severely poor state of maternal and neonatal health. Nevertheless, it is equally important to comprehensively understand the healthcare choices the population makes when they experience all kinds of sickness and the contexts in which these choices are made.

In Pakistan, the current population health profile indicates a depressing picture. The burden of both communicable and non-communicable diseases (NCDs) is escalating. NCDs contribute to 58 percent of all deaths, whereas 35 percent of deaths are linked to communicable, maternal, perinatal, and nutritional conditions (World Health Organization, 2018, p. 157). Cardiovascular diseases cause 29 percent of deaths, while 32 percent of adults in the country live inactive lifestyles, with more than half of the population relying primarily on polluting fuels and technologies in households (World Health Organization, 2018). Given the current economic situation, Universal Health Care is a distant reality. In the fiscal year 2019–2020, only 39.8 percent of Pakistan's overall health spending came from the general government. In 2019–2020, Pakistan's annual per capita Current Health Expenditures (CHE) were US$

40.7, compared to US$ 48.1 in 2017–2018. The percentage of out-of-pocket (OOP) health expenditures in relation to CHE is 35 percent, indicating a substantial dependence on household OOP spending for financing the health system (Pakistan Bureau of Statistics, 2022, p. xvi).

The purpose is not to bombard readers with grim health statistics but to point out how unhealthy the situation of health in the country is. In this situation, not only concentrating on the availability and accessibility of healthcare but, more importantly, understanding how people make health choices in different social contexts is extremely important. The people's choices about their health and bodies, though these choices are context-dependent, collectively define the health status of the population in a country.

The primary aim of this book is to comprehend healthcare decision-making by dissecting it through various sociological and critical perspectives. The main question that the book explores is how social "contextuality" shapes healthcare choices in Pakistan, considering the multifaceted challenges arising from rapid urbanization, globalization, evolving lifestyles, and parallel or alternative healthcare options, among others. More than having a healthcare system in place is required. It is crucial to understand people's approach to health, the obstacles they encounter, and the strategies they employ. Additionally, the book covers a wide range of topics, including the parallel informal healthcare system and its use, marginalized communities, and power dynamics, which are often overlooked in current literature. Through its inclusive approach, the book provides valuable insights into various essential issues that have not been studied before or are understudied.

Conceptually, the book can be divided into three themes. Each theme has three chapters. The first three chapters explore the contextuality of health and healthcare choices. The discussion revolves around how people make decisions about their health based on where they live and their social environment. It highlights the significant influence of geography and social context on health-related choices. The first study is informed by Bourdieu's concepts of Habitus, Field, and Space, which contribute to contemporary research on healthcare choices in Pakistan. The study explores how people in different parts of Islamabad opt for different types of healthcare and how living in different geographical areas and different social contexts impacts their overall health-related decisions. The second study explores the situation regarding non-degree allopathic practitioners (NDAPs) in the Twin Cities (Rawalpindi and Islamabad) and District Swabi. The authors examine the NDAPS licensing procedures and the preferences of patients regarding NDAP utilization. It specifically brings attention to disparities between officially reported healthcare establishments and the actual on-the-ground situations, revealing persistent challenges in oversight. The third study explores the surprising situation of not exclusively breastfeeding, even in a culture that supports it, seeking to uncover the reasons behind this choice. The study explores women's experiences regarding breastfeeding choices in various social, economic, and cultural situations.

The following three chapters can be conceptualized under the themes of power dynamics and the health of the marginalized. They discuss power imbalances in patient-doctor interactions, mental health—a pressing but unacknowledged and unaddressed issue in Pakistan, and finally, the health of transgender people, a discriminated and marginalized community in Pakistan. The first chapter under this theme explores the imbalances in power, where patients with limited health knowledge face authoritative doctors. Drawing from Michel Foucault's theory on power dynamics underscores how this imbalance contributes to widespread negligence and malpractice. The second chapter offers a clinical perspective on mental health challenges in Pakistani society, showing how cultural norms, community values, and economic disparities contribute to the stigmatization and neglect of mental health. The chapter also looks at the influence of gender dynamics, societal expectations, and family structures on mental health experiences. The last chapter under this section looks at the prevalence of HIV/AIDS at-risk behaviors in the transgender community. Through personal stories and a framework of transactional relationships, the research uncovers complex dynamics, highlighting economic arrangements that both empower and constrain marginalized populations. This emphasizes the necessity for inclusive policies and interventions within the broader power dynamics of Pakistani society.

The last three chapters can be conceptualized under the theme of Emerging Challenges and Healthcare Response. The first chapter looks at the systematic dynamics of the recently introduced social health insurance model, the Sehat Sahulat Program (SSP), in the country. The research objective is to analyze provider accreditation within the SSP and explore provider experiences, including challenges faced. The second chapter under this theme provides a comprehensive overview of Hepatitis B and C infections in Sindh, Pakistan. In Pakistan, almost 12 million people are suffering from hepatitis B or C. The chapter examines the historical context, transmission modes, and socioeconomic implications of these infections, particularly within Sindh. The chapter highlights unique factors contributing to their high prevalence, including issues in healthcare infrastructure, cultural practices, and demographics. The last chapter looks into the escalating NCD burden in Pakistan, examining its repercussions on health outcomes and economic and social challenges, and proposing strategies for prevention and improvement.

Overall, this book explores how various interconnected factors influence healthcare choices in Pakistan. It challenges the simplistic idea that these choices are solely individual and logical, highlighting the impact of communal, social, and institutional factors on personal decisions. While covering contextuality, power dynamics, marginalized communities, and emerging challenges in healthcare, the book provides valuable insights into overlooked aspects of healthcare decision-making. Through sociological and critical perspectives, it carefully analyzes how social context influences health decisions, especially in the face of challenges like the double burden of diseases, rapid urbanization, globalization, and alternative healthcare options. The book argues for a comprehensive approach beyond the mere availability of healthcare, considering the nuanced fabric of people's health choices and their broader societal implications.

## REFERENCES

Collyer, F. M., Willis, K. F., Franklin, M., Harley, K., & Short, S. D. (2015). Healthcare Choice: Bourdieu's Capital, Habitus and Field. *Current Sociology, 63*(5): 685–699.

Mol, A. (2008). *The Logic of Care: Health and the Problem of Patient Choice.* London: Routledge.

Nordgren, L. (2010). Mostly Empty Words—What the Discourse of "Choice" in Health Care Does. *Journal of Health Organization and Management, 24*(2): 109–126.

Pakistan Bureau of Statistics. (2022). National Health Accounts Pakistan 2019–2020. Retrieved from https://www.pbs.gov.pk/sites/default/files/national_accounts/national_health_accounts/NHA-Pakistan_2019-20.pdf.

World Health Organization. (2018). Noncommunicable Diseases Country Profiles 2018. Retrieved from https://www.who.int/publications/i/item/9789241514620.

# *Section I*

# CONTEXTUALITY OF HEALTHCARE CHOICES

## *Chapter 1*

# Reflecting with Bourdieu

## *Understanding Healthcare Choices in Pakistan*

Saman Nazir and Abdullah Emran

Understanding health-related choices is critical for recognizing structural shortcomings, targeting health-promoting policy interventions, and mapping out people-centered institutional improvements. In Pakistan, understanding how healthcare choices are made within varied social contexts is timely as the burden of both communicable and non-communicable diseases (NCDs) is escalating (World Health Organization, 2018). The rise in NCDs worldwide is multifaceted and based on key factors, including globalization, the expansion of supermarkets, rapid urbanization, and an increase in inactive lifestyles (Wagner & Brath, 2012). However, healthcare response to morbidity may vary even within a society, considering the socio-cultural fabric of a community living in a particular place/ space plays a vital role in how people do health.

There is an abundance of literature available on the determinate of healthcare utilization and access to healthcare in Pakistan, especially in the context of maternal and neonatal health (Iqbal et al., 2017; Mumtaz et al., 2014; Zakar et al., 2017). However, the evidence regarding how people approach health on a daily basis and make choices when experiencing sickness is widely lacking. Studies show a considerable time delay before people consider seeking formal healthcare (Khan et al., 2015; Mirza et al., 2009). For instance, a study on community management of intellectual disabilities in a rural area found that the time delay between identification and seeking treatment for children who suffer from developmental issues ranged from 2.92 to 4.17 years (Mirza et al., 2009). The implications of delaying treatment and health choices people make until they seek treatment or not seek treatment altogether are astronomical on health outcomes, healthcare systems' capacity, and, more importantly, well-being at individual and familial levels.

Along with formal public and private allopathic healthcare that dominate healthcare systems in Pakistan, informal providers practicing allopathy, homeopathy, and eastern medicine are considered to make up a significant portion of the overall healthcare market. Literature from Pakistan and other countries show several reasons that shape healthcare choices, including but not limited to the type of provider (public vs. private), the prestige of a health facility (quality of services and symbolical prestige), geography, income and education levels of population, availability of tangible and intangible capital availed to people, socio-cultural norms and acceptability, belief system about a specific disease/condition, and social fabric of a community (Jafree, 2020; Naydenova et al., 2017; Mumtaz et al., 2013; Willis & Collyer 2018). For example, Naydenova et al. (2017) found that despite having limited means, slum dwellers in Mumbai prefer to see private providers for most health conditions apart from pregnancy. People judge the quality of healthcare services based on the status or reputation of the areas where the service is located (Lewis et al., 2018). The place can make it easier or harder to make wise healthcare decisions. People differ in their abilities to mobilize resources and overcome the (perceived) limitations of place (Lewis et al., 2018).

In the study, we aim to understand the healthcare choices of people living in Islamabad in different geographical locations. We also look at how they try to maintain their health on a daily basis. The study will help understand varied or similar health-related choices of people living in the same city but in different social domains, communities, and geographical locations. Through the understating of healthcare choices, the study findings will contribute to indicating structural shortcomings affecting these choices, which are necessary for mapping out people-centered healthcare system improvements.

## THEORETICAL ORIENTATION

This study draws on contemporary work exploring healthcare choices, building on Bourdieu's concepts of Habitus, Field, and Space (Collyer et al., 2015; Lewis et al., 2018). Collyer et al. (2015) explain that Bourdieu's concepts can help theorize healthcare choices. They explain how frequently people make decisions and build strategies when interacting with many social domains, acting unintentionally according to their habitus. Similarly, Lewis, Willis, and Collyer (2018) use Bourdieu's concept of space to explore healthcare choices and navigation. They propose that Bourdieu's work can be used to understand connections between geographic location, social circumstances, and healthcare choices. Geography not only reveals status differences between neighborhoods but also the fundamental power imbalances that exist between locals and other actors. The structure of healthcare choices can be explained by weaving bourdieusian concepts together in interconnected and dynamic ways (Collyer et al., 2015).

Bourdieu explains habitus as an organizing action, with a meaning close to that of words such as structure; it also designates a way of being, a habitual state (especially of the body) and, in particular, a predisposition, tendency, propensity or inclination ( Bourdieu, 1984, p. 562).

Habitus is a system of dispositions that explains how people behave in socially acceptable ways without having their thoughts, attitudes, and behaviors entirely dictated by the social structure. Bourdieu characterized habitus as the outcomes of social conditioning linked to specific conditions, resulting in a structured collection of goods and properties. These elements are interconnected by a shared stylistic affinity that aligns with various class positions. A primary purpose of the habitus concept is to explain the cohesive style that connects the actions and possessions of an individual or a group of individuals (Bourdieu, 1996, p. 15). People's decisions are informed by their habitus. Health related decisions and choices seem like the manifestation of agency; however, these decisions are also socially structured (Collyer et al., 2015).

Field can refer to a social space (e.g., a healthcare field) and a configuration or network of relationships with a particular power dynamic. Collyer et al. (2015) delineated the healthcare field as a battleground of differing viewpoints. This encompasses the medical perspective emphasizing health as the absence of illness, the capitalist orientation treating health as a marketable commodity, the challenges faced by the capitalist state in reconciling medical definitions of health with addressing societal health disparities, and other perspectives within the field, such as patient rights, public health, or alternative medicine. Understanding the specific field is essential to grasp the underlying structures guiding these decisions (Collyer et al., 2015).

Collyer et al. (2015) explain why choices about health need to be understood, the socially constructed nature of decision-making. Economic liberalism's theoretical foundation rests on the premise that individuals operate as independent and rational agents, consistently making decisions regardless of their social context or prevailing uncertainties. However, it's crucial to differentiate between patients and consumers, as individuals in vulnerable states may find it challenging to make informed choices (Collyer et al., 2015).

Bourdieu discusses the parallels between social and physical space. While physical space is marked by the external relationships among its components, social space is shaped by the distinct positions that define it, forming a structure of positioned social roles. Individuals and objects, once appropriated and transformed into properties by these individuals, occupy specific positions within this social space. These positions can be distinguished by their relative placement to others, whether above, below, or amid them, as well as the distances that set them apart (Bourdieu, 1996, p. 12).

Bourdieu stresses that social space is an invisible network of connections that has a propensity to directly or indirectly translate into physical space in the form of a definite distributional arrangement of agents and characteristics, for example, the contrast between downtown and suburbs. Bourdieu contended that spatial distances mirror social distances. Agents within this space are positioned such that closer proximity indicates more remarkable similarity in these two dimensions, while greater distance signifies less shared characteristics (Bourdieu, 1996, p. 13, 14).

Research shows that a geographical area's status or reputation is frequently used to form judgments about the quality of its healthcare services; place perceptions and judgments about healthcare services are related. Geographical factors affect how people decide what constitutes acceptable treatment and how they approach healthcare decisions. Although participants' capacities to mobilize resources and overcome (perceived) obstacles vary, the place might help or impede one's ability to make (good) healthcare decisions (Lewis et al., 2018).

## METHODOLOGY

In this study, we explore in-depth how people manage their health and make health-related choices when they experience sickness. We used semi-structured, in-depth interviews to acquire data from people currently living in Islamabad. We developed an interview guide to explore the people's lived experiences regarding their health. Answers to all of the questions in the interview guide were sought in every interview. However, it is important to mention that additional questions were asked to the participants for clarification purposes or to assist them in articulating their thoughts meaningfully.

We have collected data from three different residential areas in Islamabad that represent people from different income groups. The first area is Nurpur Shahan, a rural locality in Islamabad. Most of the interviewed participants live in this community and have houses built of mixed construction (pucca and kutcha) with five or fewer marla-covered areas and without a proper sewage system. We consider this low-income rural community based on the residential and area characteristics.

The second area where we collected the data is the G-6 and G-9 sectors of Islamabad. We collected the data from participants living in houses of five marlas or less. This urban area has main markets, hospitals, and schools. We consider participants for these residential areas to be middle-income groups in our sample. The third area from where we collected the data was the F8 and F7 sectors. These sectors are considered to be the posh residential areas of the city. Thus, we consider the participants in these sectors to be from a high-income category.

We collected data in two ways, that is, face-to-face and online. All face-to-face interviews were conducted in various settings, including participants' homes, mosques (in residential areas), and shops (located in that area), all at the respondent's discretion. All the interviews in Nurpur Shahan were conducted face-to-face. Only a few people declined to give us an interview. Almost half of the interviews in both the G and F sectors were done online. The main reason for conducting the interview online was the high rejection rate to face-to-face interviews when contacted at people's residences. People mentioned security issues as the main reason for declining the interview, followed by a lack of time for the interview at the moment. For the online interviews, social media networking sites such as Facebook were immensely helpful in getting the word out about this research. A short description of the study was posted on the Facebook groups. Each participant who showed interest in participating in the study was contacted through Facebook Messenger to set up an interview.

Interviews were started with basic demographic questions to document the participant's age, education, work status, marital status, and number of children. Participants were asked follow-up questions to get them to talk about their experiences with healthcare choices. Before the interview, each respondent was asked to read and sign the consent form, in which the purpose, risks, and benefits of the study were explicitly defined (no obvious risk has been perceived, and there are no financial benefits for participation in this study). We read the consent form in Urdu for all the respondents who could not read it themselves. For online interviews, a consent form was sent to the participant electronically and received back before the interview began.

All the interviews were audio-recorded with prior permission from the respondents. The entire audio recording was deleted after transcription. No real names are being used in the study to protect the privacy of respondents. All interviews were transcribed verbatim. Except for three participants, all other participants allowed us to audio record the interview. On average, each interview took twenty-five to thirty minutes. After each interview, each participant was asked if there was anything else they wanted to say that we had missed, and they were also given the option to ask further questions. Interviews took place from February 2022 to April 2022.

## SAMPLE CHARACTERISTICS

We conducted forty-three in-depth interviews in total. The age of participants ranged between thirty and forty-nine years. Most female participants from low-income residential areas have no formal education or basic elementary

**Table 1.1 Sample Characteristics**

| *Sample* | | *Nurpur Shahan* | | *G Sector* | | *F Sector* | |
|---|---|---|---|---|---|---|---|
| | | *Men* | *Women* | *Men* | *Women* | *Men* | *Women* |
| Average Age | | 47.87 | 39.33 | 36.09 | 35 | 49 | 43.4 |
| Working Status | Working | 6 | 2 | 8 | 2 | 4 | 3 |
| | Not Working | 2 | 7 | 3 | 2 | 2 | 2 |
| Marital Status | Married | 7 | 7 | 8 | 2 | 5 | 4 |
| | Never Married | 1 | 1 | 3 | 2 | 1 | 0 |
| | Widowed/ Divorced | 0 | 1 | 0 | 0 | 0 | 1 |
| Average No of Children | | 3.42 | 4.22 | 2.5 | 3.5 | 3.2 | 2.25 |
| Average Number of Participants | | 8 | 9 | 11 | 4 | 6 | 5 |

*Source*: Author—based on sample data.

education. Except for two participants, both men and women from the middle- and high-income residential areas have high school, college degrees, or professional degrees. Most men we interviewed in all the localities are working, compared to female participants, who are not mostly working in the labor market. Only two out of nine women from Nurpur Shahan are working. Half of the women in our sample from the middle- and upper-income residential areas are working in the labor market. Most of our interviewees are married and have children. Only five men and two women in our sample have never married. We have seventeen participants from Nurpur Shahan, fifteen from the G sector, and eleven from the F sector (table 1.1).

## ANALYSIS

After collecting data from the participants, we mined the data for emergent themes. We started mining the data by reading and coding each interview line by line. We coded the data to look for common themes in the interviews that recurred and patterns in people's experiences with healthcare choices. After completing the initial coding, we focused on the codes that made the most analytic sense for categorizing data incisively. We completed the last phase of coding, known as axial coding, to identify major categories, subcategories, and concepts that could be clustered together. At this stage, we renamed, narrowed, or combined some coding categories and finalized our themes. We came up with seven themes in total, discussed in detail in the results section.

## DELAY AND SELF-TREATMENT

Most participants in our study mentioned that their first response to any sickness is self-treatment at home. They only seek formal allopathic care if they perceive the issue as a "serious" health threat. Participants self-treat seasonal flu, fever, and cough with home remedies using herbs and over-the-counter medications such as paracetamol. Most participants mentioned that they seek formal health care if they do not get better at home. However, that is a common pattern across residential groups; participants delayed seeing a doctor until the health issue worsened.

> We try home remedies first, only when the disease is painful, or it gets serious, then we see a doctor. (A participant from the middle-income residential area)

Almost all the participants seek healthcare (of different types) when they perceive sickness as untreatable at home.

> First, we try not to go to these cruel doctors. We try home remedies and use medicine like Panadol. If we find any relief, well and good. If not, then we have to go to the hospital. Wherever we need to go to the hospital, the first thing that comes to mind is that they (doctors) are going to charge us insanely for treatment. (A participant from the low-income residential area)

Participants' engagement with healthcare is a product of the overall health culture prevailing in the community. For example, most of the participants in Nurpur Shahan (a low-income residential community) and a few participants from the middle-income residential area visit private Non-Degree Allopathic Practitioners (NDAPs) for acute illness episodes. Participants from the area mentioned that they know they are not doctors, but they have some experience in formal allopathic medicine. For most of the respondents from the area, these NDAPs are as good as doctors with formal medical degrees. Participants mentioned these NDAPs give them an "injection" on their demand that effectively cures different kinds of sickness, including indigestion, fever, diarrhea, and body pain.

> I do know if he is a doctor or not. His clinic is nearby, and he listens to us. We get better every time we see him. He gave us medicine. If a person in my family gets very sick, he gives us a drip (IV). It works for us. (A participant from the low-income residential area while talking about NDAP)

Another participant mentioned

> We use medicine for problems like fever; if it does not work, then we go to the public hospital, and if we still feel sick, then we go to the private XYZ clinic. They use 3 or 4 injections, and the patient feels fine. (A participant from the middle-income income residential area)

A participant from the high-income residential area, who is a doctor (but not doing practice), mentioned how NDAPs work in the city.

> It is a first-hand experience; many people have offered me to get permission for starting a clinic, and they say a compounder (paramedic) will see everything. You will not have to do anything. It told them this was not right. It is happening in Islamabad. We supposedly have regulation here. Despite being a big city, where most people are educated, this still happens here. (A participant from the high-income residential area).

Interestingly, most of the participants in low-income residential areas prefer to see private healthcare providers and only visit public health facilities when they perceive a treatment to be costly. Participants from the G sector mostly see nearby public health facilities. In comparison, the participants from the F sector have designated specialist physicians in private health care.

## MAINTAINING HEALTH

The participants in our study maintain their health by different means. Most of the participants from Nurpur Shahan do not believe in taking supplements and find a healthy diet a prerequisite for good health. A few participants from the locality mentioned taking supplements, but the doctor prescribes that. The use of supplements without prescription is very common among the participants from the G and F sectors. Many participants mentioned that they have relatives abroad, and when they visit Pakistan, they bring vitamin supplements as gifts for them. They also perceive imported vitamins as of superior quality.

> My aunt lives in England. Whenever she visits Pakistan, she brings us Vitamin supplements. We use that; we do not believe in the quality of locally made supplements. (A participant from the middle-income residential area).

A participant from the F sector explained how her husband is obsessed with having supplements to maintain his health.

> My husband is obsessed with the idea of maintaining health. He takes supplements for everything (laugh) . . . You name it, he takes supplements for that. (A participant from the high-income residential area)

## DISSATISFACTION WITH HEALTHCARE

Most respondents from all three localities express their dissatisfaction with the current allopathic health care system. Participants reported several types of grievances, including mistreatment by the hospital staff and doctors, medical negligence, costly treatments, overcharging, crowded OPDs, and malpractice, to name a few.

> I do not trust the system . . . the medicines are of low quality. Secondly, private hospitals are just here to make money out of people's miseries. (A participant from the middle-income residential area)

A respondent mentioned why he could not trust the healthcare system.

> We take our children to the doctors less often, but if the elders have to go, then we go to XYZ (a private hospital). They are good, and I think it has become a business. They know when to conduct surgery and make an extra bill. My uncle works there, and he tells us about these problems. We don't have 100% satisfaction because the doctor only recommends a specific company's medicine, which they profit from. This a huge issue. (A participant from the high-income residential area).

A few respondents, based on their experiences, use analogies like butchers and thieves for healthcare partitioners. A few respondents, mostly from middle-income residential areas, mentioned that public hospitals are good and inexpensive. However, they added that most tertiary care hospitals are crowded and have very unhygienic environments.

> You just cannot use a toilet in a public facility. There (toilets) are so smelly and dirty that you feel like you will die with disgust. (A participant from the middle-income residential area).

## HOMEOPATHY—A PARALLEL TREATMENT

It is noteworthy that homeopathy is a very popular alternative and parallel treatment among participants from all three localities. The trust and positive perception of homeopathy as an effective treatment for many diseases as compared to allopathy prevail among participants. The positive belief in homeopathic treatment is more prevalent than we expected among participants.

A few participants mentioned that homeopathic treatment takes a long time to cure a disease compared to allopathic medicine, but homeopathy has no side effects on the body, which is a big plus for them. Participants reported that many diseases do not have any cure in allopathy, and for that reason, they opt for homeopathic treatment. Many participants use both allopathic and homeopathic medicine for a specific disease.

> I have recently used homeopathic medicine because I have thyroid. There is no cure for it in allopathy, and the solution is to remove it. I have been taking their medicine for the last 8 to 9 months. And it feels better with the homeopathic treatment. I am not sure what will happen next, whether they will have a solution, but I am feeling better. (A participant from the high-income residential area)

Participants seek homeopathic treatment for kidney stones, sciatica, stomach issues, unexplained headaches, arthritis, skin diseases, and stroke.

> My mother had a stroke two and half years ago she used homeopathic medicine . . . she is fine now. (A participant from the low-income residential area)

## RELIGIOUS HEALING

Almost half of the respondents from the Nurpur Shahan, exclusively or in parallel with medicinal treatment, seek religious healing as an option to cure diseases. For that, most of the participants see a pious religious figure in the community who blows (called "dam") some holy verses on a patient to cure a certain disease. A participant mentioned opting for "dam" for various diseases, including infertility, sepsis, unexplained headaches, hepatitis, kidney stones, heart diseases, and rabies.

> Some time ago, my wife had 12-mm stones in her kidney. Even after taking medicine, she did not get any relief, but a Pashtun man gave her six liters of water (he blew on it). And after drinking it, the stones fell down. When we re-tested it, only sand was left, and the stones were gone. (A participant from the low-income residential area)

For a study participant, seeking religious healing and delaying treatment cost the life of his son.

> Now, we do not delay treatment my 2.5-year-old son died. A stray dog bit him; when it happened, I went to a shrine hoping to find a cure for him. After two months, there were germs on the wound; people would tell me at the shrine to take my son home; I cried helplessly there that night, he died. (A participant from the low-income residential area)

Most of the participants from the G and F sectors have not shown a strong inclination toward such kind of treatment. However, a few of the participants mentioned they do believe in getting damm in times of mental distress. Damm usually is a process when verses from the Quran are recited, and the person who recites blows them over water (that would be drunk later by the person who needs damm) or recites a specific verse or prayer and then blows directly onto the person who needs damm.

> If children in our home get sick from the evil sight, we take them for the damm. (A participant from the middle-income residential area)

Another participant mentioned

> Whenever someone in our family gets sick because of evil eye or has red spots on the skin, we go for damm. (A participant from the middle-income residential area)

It is noteworthy that most participants from middle and high-income residential areas distance themselves from seeking religious healing for apparently physical diseases but strongly believe in religious healing regarding mental health.

> Everyone these days is depressed in one way or another. I recite some verses from the Quran to give me peace whenever I get depressed. It calms me. It helps. (A participant from the high-income residential area)

Another participant from the high-income residential area said

> I have some issues in the past that still bother me . . . I got divorced and was in a bad relationship. It happened a long time ago, but I still feel depressed about it. It's not that I am not thankful . . . I have a precious son. I think, at times like these, I seek Allah's help; that's all we can do. He is the protector, and he is the only one that can take us out of despair.

In our sample, only one participant mentioned that they sought therapy for an issue related to mental health.

## SEEKING HEALTH INFORMATION

The respondents from the three localities seek health information from different sources. A majority of participants from NurpurShahan mentioned that they either ask their relatives, friends, neighbors, or healthcare partitioners about what to do while having any health issue. Only two respondents from the locality mentioned that they look on the internet for a cure for a certain disease.

Most of the participants from the G sector mentioned that they go to doctors for advice related to their health. They occasionally explored symptoms related to a health issue on the internet, but the practice is not common. The prevalence of googling health issues is very common among the participants of the F sector.

> Without Google, life is incomplete. For small medicine, we google its formula before buying it. We definitely research and discuss this very often in the family. Both the research and discussion happen here. (A participant from the high-income residential area)

It is noteworthy that most of the participants have a doctor or doctors in their immediate family, extended family, or in their friends' circle. They mention consulting them first for any health trouble they have.

> I don't go anywhere. In our family, there are many doctors. My aunt is a doctor, my two uncles are doctors, and my three cousins are fresh doctors. We don't get into much trouble. Things get settled with one or another's help Alhamdulillah. (A participant from the high-income residential area).

Another participant from the high-income residential area said,

> We have a doctor in our family, he is my uncle. . . . And one of my cousins is also a doctor. Normally, we discuss minor issues with them and, in fact, major issues as well, but if it's an issue that we have to visit a doctor for, then yes, we go see a doctor.

Participants from this sector also mentioned that they opt for a second opinion from another doctor if they are not satisfied with or have doubts about the diagnosis of the doctor whom they contacted first.

## NAVIGATING ALLOPATHIC HEALTHCARE

Almost all the respondents from all three localities, at some point in their lives, interact with the formal allopathic health care system. The participants from the Nurpur Shahan and G sectors mostly see the public health facilities. However, they report that most public health facilities are less costly but crowded and time-consuming.

> We go to government hospitals and private hospitals as well . . . usually we prefer to go to a private hospital. Government hospitals are very crowded . . . long lines, they make you wait for too long. (A participant from the middle-income residential area)

It is noteworthy that residents of the Nurpur Shahan prefer to see a private partitioner than see a doctor in a public hospital. Participants only prefer to go to public hospitals if there are many lab investigations involved; therefore, they find them far less costly than the private sector. Most of the participants from the F sector have designated specialist partners for their health issues. Almost all of the participants seek private care.

## DISCUSSION AND CONCLUSIONS

The study draws on Bourdieu's concept of Habitus, Field, and Space to understand the healthcare choices in Pakistan. The study locale is the three different communities in Islamabad, roughly representing participants living in low, middle, and high-income residential areas. We aimed to look at how participants living in different geographic locations/spaces in one city with different social positions make healthcare choices. In this case, the healthcare field is the formal and informal healthcare systems, irrespective of their legality status of operating in the city.

We have found that delays in seeking formal care are common across residential areas. However, it is important to understand that the participants from the high-income residential areas have the means to manage the sickness if they are not seeking any formal care. For instance, the majority in the high-income residential areas mentioned that somebody in their social network is a doctor, and in case of any health issue, they consult them first. It implies that participants living in high-income residential areas consult qualified doctors through their social networking, so in this case, delay in seeking formal care may not result in bad health outcomes. However, delays in seeking formal care by low-income residential areas, who do not have medically qualified social networking, may cause adverse health outcomes. Studies from Pakistan show worrisome evidence that people delay treatment and try other means to treat diseases. Khan et al. (2015) found that about 40.7 percent of breast cancer patients who delayed seeking allopathic health care first wasted time using alternative medicines. A considerable majority of women with breast cancer in North Pakistan are enduring presentation delays due to their misunderstandings about the disease.

Our study findings show that people from low-income and high-income residential areas prefer to visit private health practitioners. Private formal healthcare in Pakistan is socially perceived as better than public healthcare. The preference to see a private health partitioner in low-income residential areas may be due to the fact that people aspire to things that people of higher social status do. The distance to tertiary care hospitals is also a factor for not seeking public healthcare; travel and time add to the cost. It is noteworthy that participants from low-income residential areas may not necessarily be consulting qualified private medical partitioners. The practitioners who do not own a medical degree but practice allopathic or mixed medicine are mostly concentrated in low-income and rural communities.

Participants from the rural residential area of our study often see NDAPs for acute illness episodes. Studies from other countries show that the trust in NDAPs by rural residents is due to the reason that they are community insiders. They know the culture, language, financial constraints, and psychology of the people in the community. May, Roth, and Panda (2014) argue that local NDAPs are usually the first contact points for patients. Authors argued that that is because NDAPs are not only geographically, financially, and culturally accessible but are familiar with patients' belief systems. Studies from Pakistan show the mistreatment of patients by NDAPs /quacks (Aziz et al.,

2019; Asif, 2019; Mustafa et al., 2021). In many cases, NDAPs employ inadequate infection prevention and control practices by using recycled syringes and intravenous drip sets. The HIV outbreak in Sindh in 2019 is one such example that could explain the worrisome effects of NDAPs on population health in the country.

The participants from the high-income residential hardly see doctors in a public facility. Most of the participants see private formal allopathic doctors/specialists for treatment. Despite having public tertiary care hospitals located nearby, the preference for private health facilities and doctors is not surprising. Private healthcare is considered time-effective and offers quality treatment. For instance, Irfan and Ijaz (2011) measured patients' perceptions of the service quality of public and private hospitals using the following dimensions: empathy, tangibles, assurance, timeliness, and assurance. Except for the assurance dimension, the majority of respondents who use services from private hospitals believe that patients are treated more effectively at private hospitals than in public hospitals. Moreover, people seeking treatment from private high-cost hospitals construct their healthcare preferences as a symbol of wealth and status (Mumtaz et al., 2013). This symbolic association of seeing private partitioners with social status may somewhat explain why participants from low-income residential areas prefer private health consultation.

We found that high usage of unprescribed supplements is common in middle and high-income residential areas. This is due to the accessibility and affordability of available information about health maintenance and modern lifestyle to the participants of the high-income residential area. The participants' use of the internet and the affordability of smartphones/electronic devices play an important role in acquiring information about the supplements for different requirements. It is worth mentioning that supplements, especially multivitamins, are expensive in Pakistan. Monthly, if buying out of pocket, can add substantial costs to the household budget that participants from the low-income residential area could not afford.

Most of the participants showed dissatisfaction with formal allopathic healthcare in Pakistan. The main reason is that participants feel lost and helpless if they experience medical malpractice. The healthcare system is fragmented and not properly regulated. Most of the participants need to learn where to file a complaint. Nazir (2021) argues that there is a lack of a patient-centric approach in medical practices in Pakistan. Patients feel unheard and not appropriately understood due to a lack of attention and empathy by the medical staff/doctors. On the other hand, public hospitals are overburdened with patients, and the chances of errors increase with most of the systems still not being digital.

Religious healing to treat mental health illnesses is common among participants in all residential areas. The lack of mental health facilities and the stigma associated with mental health treatment makes people rely substantially on religious healing. The participants from the high-income residential area distance themselves from visiting shamans or using amulets for mental health being; however, they do rely on religion in some ways (reciting verses or parting) to cope with mental health issues. On the other hand, participants from low-income residential areas solely rely on all means except psychiatry or psychology for their mental health issues.

Different studies discussed the causes of limited consumption of mental health services in Pakistan, such as stigma, traditional healing practices, knowledge deficit, poor access to treatment, mistrust, illiteracy, and shortage of psychiatrists (Bibi et al., 2019; Qadir et al., 2013). For example, a study reported that before seeking mental health services, the majority (86 percent) of patients with severe symptoms of major mental illness consulted traditional healers (Shah et al., 2019). Mental illnesses have also been misattributed to factors such as the possession of ghosts or other supernatural powers resulting from "black magic," "evil eye," or participation in "poor deeds" in a previous life (Khalifa et al., 2011). As (Gadit, 2007) discussed, shamans enjoy welcoming large numbers of people who approach them with less fear of stigma, low cost, and simple accessibility for their mental health issues. However, malpractice and adverse outcomes have been recorded in some shamanic practices, including adverse drug reactions described above, delays in getting adequate medical attention in cases of organic pathologies, and even death during rituals (Gadit, 2007).

In summary, the delay in treatment for participants living in different spaces in the same city would not result in the same adverse health outcomes. Health in high-income residential areas is done through social networking, where informal consultation with qualified practitioners is one call away. On the other hand, the participants living in low-income residential areas delay seeking care; when they do, they probably consult a non-degree allopathic practitioner. We found that participants from the high-income resident areas prefer to see private practitioners. The perception that private healthcare is superior to public healthcare is grounded in the fact that health is taken as a status commodity. The perception benefits NDAPs by having their clinical concentration under minimum regulation in rural areas, being community insiders, and enjoying the trust of patients. The dissatisfaction with allopathic formal care is profound and common among participants in almost all residential areas. Homeopathy as an alternative medicine is trusted widely. The utilization of mental healthcare is almost non-existent and unthinkable for the participants of low- and middle-income residential areas. Relying on religious healing for mental health issues is the most prevalent care method that uncontestably is holding our study participants' worlds together.

## REFERENCES

Abdullah, M., & Zakar, P. D. R. (2020). Health literacy in South Asia: Clarifying the connections between health literacy and wellbeing in Pakistan. *South Asian Studies, 34*(2), 575–589.

Ansari, I. (2015). Mental health Pakistan: Optimizing brains. *International Journal of Emergency Mental Health, 17*(1), 228.

Asif, A. F. (2019). Appraisal of national response to chronic hepatitis in Pakistan. *Journal of Islamabad Medical & Dental College, 8*(1), 3–7.

Aziz, M. M., Jiang, M., Masood, I., Chang, J., Zhu, S., Raza, M. A., . . . & Fang, Y. (2019). Patients' anticipation for the pharmacies of rural communities: A qualitative study from Pakistan. *International Journal of Environmental Research and Public Health, 16*(1), 143.

Bibi, A., Blackwell, S. E., & Margraf, J. (2019). Mental health, suicidal ideation, and experience of bullying among university students in Pakistan. *Journal of Health Psychology, 26*(8), 1185–1196.

Bourdieu, P. (1977). *Outline of a Theory of Practice.* Cambridge: Cambridge University Press.

Bourdieu, P. (1984). Translated by Richard Nice. *Distinction.* Harvard University Press: Cambridge, MA.

Bourdieu, P. (1996). Physical space, social space and habitus. *Vilhelm Aubert Memorial Lecture, Report, 10*, 87–101.

Collyer, F. M., Willis, K. F., Franklin, M., Harley, K., & Short, S. D. (2015). Healthcare choice: Bourdieu's capital, habitus and field. *Current Sociology, 63*(5), 685–699.

Gadit, A. M. (2006). Mental health in Pakistan: Where do we stand? *Journal of Pakistan Medical Association. Editorial, 56,* 198–199.

Gadit, A. A. M. (2007). Psychiatry in Pakistan: 1947–2006: A new balance sheet. *Journal of Pakistan Medical Association, 57*(9), 453–463.

Haynes, R., Lovett, A., & Sünnenberg, G. (2003). Potential accessibility, travel time, and consumer choice: Geographical variations in general medical practice registrations in Eastern England. *Environment and Planning A, 35*(10), 1733–1750.

Iqbal, S., Maqsood, S., Zakar, R., Zakar, M. Z., & Fischer, F. (2017). Continuum of care in maternal, newborn and child health in Pakistan: Analysis of trends and determinants from 2006 to 2012. *BMC Health Services Research, 17*(1), 1–15.

Irfan, S. M., & Ijaz, A. (2011). Comparison of service quality between private and public hospitals: Empirical evidences from Pakistan. *Journal of Quality and Technology Management, 7*(1), 1–22.

Jafree, S. R. (Ed.). (2020). *The Sociology of South Asian Women's Health. Cham: Springer.*

Khalid, F., & Abbasi, A. N. (2018): Challenges faced by Pakistani healthcare system: Clinician's perspective. https://ecommons.aku.edu/cgi/viewcontent.cgi?article=1065&context=pakistan_fhs_mc_radiat_oncol.

Khalifa, N., Hardie, T., Latif, S., Jamil, I., & Walker, D. M. (2011). Beliefs about Jinn, black magic and the evil eye among Muslims: Age, gender and first language influences. *International Journal of Culture and Mental Health, 4*(1), 68–77.

Khalily, M. T. (2011). Mental health problems in Pakistani society as a consequence of violence and trauma: A case for better integration of care. *International Journal of Integrated Care, 11,* e128.

Khan, M. A., Hanif, S., Iqbal, S., Shahzad, M. F., Shafique, S., & Khan, M. T. (2015). Presentation delay in breast cancer patients and its association with sociodemographic factors in North Pakistan. *Chinese Journal of Cancer Research, 27*(3), 288.

Lewis, S., Willis, K., & Collyer, F. (2018). Navigating and making choices about healthcare: The role of place. *Health & Place, 52,* 215–220.

May, C., Roth, K., & Panda, P. (2014). Non-degree allopathic practitioners as first contact points for acute illness episodes: Insights from a qualitative study in rural northern India. *BMC Health Services Research, 14*(1), 1–11.

Mirza, I., Tareen, A., Davidson, L. L., & Rahman, A. (2009). Community management of intellectual disabilities in Pakistan: A mixed methods study. *Journal of Intellectual Disability Research, 53*(6), 559–570.

Mumtaz, Z., Levay, A., Bhatti, A., & Salway, S. (2013). Signalling, status and inequities in maternal healthcare use in Punjab, Pakistan. *Social Science & Medicine, 94*, 98–105.

Mumtaz, Z., Salway, S., Bhatti, A., Shanner, L., Zaman, S., Laing, L., & Ellison, G. T. (2014). Improving maternal health in Pakistan: toward a deeper understanding of the social determinants of poor women's access to maternal health services. *American Journal of Public Health, 104*(S1), S17–S24.

Mustufa, M. A., Khan, R., Hussain, S., & Qidwai, M. A. (2021). Regulation of quackery amid unprecedented HIV outbreak in Sindh, Pakistan. *JPMA. The Journal of the Pakistan Medical Association, 71*(8), S22–S25.

Naydenova, E., Raghu, A., Ernst, J., Sahariah, S. A., Gandhi, M., & Murphy, G. (2017). Healthcare choices in Mumbai slums: A cross-sectional study. *Wellcome Open Research, 2,* 115.

Nazir, A. (2021). Understanding the power knowledge relationship in the health care practices in Pakistan: A case study from the health care facility in Islamabad. *Thesis, MPhil Development Studies.* PIDE.

Qadir, F., Khalid, A., Haqqani, S., & Medhin, G. (2013). The association of marital relationship and perceived social support with mental health of women in Pakistan. *BMC Public Health, 13*(1), 1–13.

Sabzwari, S. R. (2017). Health literacy in Pakistan: Exploring new ways of addressing an old challenge. *Journal of Pakistan Medical Association, 67*(12), 1901.

Shah, I., Khalily, M. T., Ahmad, I., & Hallahan, B. (2019). Impact of conventional beliefs and social stigma on attitude toward access to mental health services in Pakistan. *Community Mental Health Journal, 55*(3), 527–533.

Wagner, K. H., & Brath, H. (2012). A global view on the development of non communicable diseases. *Preventive Medicine, 54,* S38–S41.

World Health Organization. (2021). *Non-communicable Diseases Country Profiles* 2018. https://apps.who.int/iris/handle/10665/274512.

World Health Organization. (2023). https://www.emro.who.int/pak/pakistan-news/who-pakistan-celebrates-world-mental-health-day.html.

Zakar, R., Zakar, M. Z., Aqil, N., Chaudhry, A., & Nasrullah, M. (2017). Determinants of maternal health care services utilization in Pakistan: Evidence from Pakistan demographic and health survey, 2012–13. *Journal of Obstetrics and Gynaecology, 37*(3), 330–337.

*Chapter 2*

# Situation Analysis of Non-Degree Allopathic Practitioners (NDAPs) in Pakistan

Asad Saleem and Saman Nazir

According to the Pakistan Medical and Dental Council, an estimated 600,000 quacks are operating in Pakistan, predominantly in Sindh and Khyber Pakhtunkhwa (SHCC, 2016). The Punjab Health Commission Act 2010 defines a *quack* as an individual who offers health services without being registered with the Medical and Dental Council, Council of Tibb, Council for Homeopathy, or Nursing Council (Punjab Healthcare Commission, 2010). Additionally, registered physicians, surgeons, or dentists may be deemed quacks if they do not adhere to the established Code of Ethics (Punjab Healthcare Commission, 2015).

This chapter analyzes the prevailing situation concerning non-degree allopathic practitioners (NDAPs) in the Swabi District and Twin Cities (Islamabad and Rawalpindi) while focusing on NDAPs only and not all quacks. NDAPs lack the requisite qualifications; NDAPs practice allopathic medicine without formal medical degrees, often operating within allopathic medical systems, and can mislead patients by creating a false impression of legitimacy. It is also essential to mention that the practice of non-degree allopathic practitioners falls under the category of quacks. NDAPs do not necessarily have medical education degrees but might have some experience working in an allopathic medical system in some capacity (Iqbal, 2009). In contrast, qualified allopathic practitioners have formal medical education from accredited institutes and use modern allopathic medicine for treatment to help patients with a variety of diseases or medical conditions. Allopathic medicine is often known as mainstream, conventional, Western, or orthodox medicine (Brennan, 2021). A formal allopathic practitioner is licensed to make diagnoses and treat diseases.

In regulatory acts, there is no differentiation between NDAPs and quacks; the criteria that apply to quacks also apply to NDAPs. Khyber Pakhtun Khwa Health Care Commission Anti-Quackery Regulations, 2021, classifies quacks into four categories:

1. Duly qualified but not validly registered with Pakistan Medical & Dental Council/PMC, Council for Tibb and Homeopathy, and Nursing Council; or
2. Neither qualified nor registered with the relevant council; or
3. Duly qualified and validly registered but providing services beyond the provisions of his/her registration; or
4. Neither duly qualified nor validly registered but practicing under the name of a qualified and validly registered medical practitioner.

South Asia has a shortage of a qualified labor force to provide healthcare services. This shortage is made worse by an uneven distribution of healthcare professionals by geographic region (rural vs urban), skill mix (nurses/midwives against specialists), level of health institution (primary versus tertiary), gender, and scope of services (basic versus advanced) (Chol, 2006). Consequently, informal providers, primarily unqualified allopathic practitioners (UAP), dominate healthcare provision for low-income households in countries like India, Pakistan, and Bangladesh (Wahed et al., 2010). Facilities remain underutilized despite basic healthcare units in rural areas. Patients from low-income backgrounds often prefer private NDAPs over public institutions due to perceived accessibility and familiarity.

Recently, there have been many anti-quackery crackdowns across the country. Between June and July 2022, the Khyber Pakhtunkhwa Health Care Commission (KPHCC) closed at least 310 healthcare establishments after inspecting numerous facilities (KPHCC, 2023). These closures stemmed from concerns such as unqualified staff, unsanitary conditions, and the utilization of outdated medical equipment. Additionally, the KPHCC issued show-cause letters to 317 institutions operating without the requisite documentation. Similarly, in 2022, the Punjab Healthcare Commission (PHC) intensified its crackdown on quackery, closing down 267 outlets operated by quacks in twenty-nine districts over three weeks. In a series of 2,234 raids on various treatment centers across different cities, enforcement teams of the PHC revealed that 587 quacks had ceased their operations voluntarily (PHC, 2022).

As of the updated data from the Punjab Health Commission (PHC, 2024), the commission has taken significant actions in the ongoing crackdown on quackery: Quackery outlets sealed: 48,921.

1. Outlets found legitimate: 4,157
2. Outlets marked for surveillance: 28,326

3. Quacks who abandoned their business: 28,418
4. Other actions: 1,133

In Islamabad, district authorities sealed three clinics on the outskirts of the city. A joint team from the Islamabad Capital Territory Administration and District Health Office conducted the operation in Sihala, revealing that individuals with no recognized medical education or qualifications operated the clinics. The quacks responsible for prescribing medicines and administering injections were arrested and placed in judicial custody (Tribune News, 2018). The crackdowns across provinces and the federal capital reflect the ongoing efforts to eliminate quackery, protect public health, and ensure the quality and legitimacy of healthcare services (PHC, 2022) but also how prevalent this problem is across regions.

In this study, we explore the operations of NDAPs, licensing processes, and patients' preferences for NDAP utilization. Specifically, the research highlights discrepancies between reported healthcare establishments and the actual ground realities, illuminating ongoing challenges in oversight. A primary concern arises regarding patient safety, given that unregistered healthcare establishments often operate outside established regulatory boundaries. We carried out this study in Islamabad, Rawalpindi (Twin Cities), and District Swabi. These study locales are chosen mainly for the following reasons. First, there is a perception that NDAPs exist mostly in remote areas and less in developed districts, while in the capital and big cities like Rawalpindi, the prevalence of NDAPs must be low. This underlies the assumption that in the capital and big urban centers, the health regulatory system must be efficient, which makes the operation of NDAPs difficult. Twin Cities have decent formal public and private healthcare facilities in terms of availability and accessibility to the population and quality of healthcare services. In contrast to Twin Cities, which are big urban centers in Pakistan, District Swabi has a mix of urban and rural geographical units. It has one big city, which is the Swabi district center, where the overall district administration is located. Swabi has four tehsils, which are further categorized by 27 neighborhood councils, 56 union councils, and 133 village councils. There is a significant gap in health outcomes between urban and rural areas. Healthcare facilities are scarce in rural areas, creating a challenge for the local population, whereas urban areas enjoy the advantage of having readily accessible health services. Consequently, residents from rural areas often seek medical assistance from unqualified practitioners in their local communities or travel to distant hospitals in district cities. Thus, the data from these study locals will provide a wider overview related to our study objectives. The second reason is that one of the researchers is from the city of Swabi, and the other one is from Islamabad, giving researchers an advantage in collecting the data from NDAPs from these locales.

In our initial research, we found that in Maini, a village council in District Swabi, out of eleven NDAPs, only three are registered with the Khyber Pakhtunkhwa Health Care Commission (KPHCC). The remaining establishments either use counterfeit licenses or operate under licenses belonging to other practitioners. Similar irregularities exist in other regions of Swabi district and various localities within the Twin Cities, including Burma Town and Saddar in Rawalpindi, as well as Bani Gala and Bhara Kahao in Islamabad. The estimated numbers of NDAPs are approximately 15,000 and 5,000 in the Twin Cities and District Swabi, respectively.

Our research reveals the critical significance of addressing the spread of NDAPs in Pakistan. The unregulated presence of non-degree allopathic practitioners poses substantial threats to public health and patient safety. The implications are twofold: firstly, the direct harm caused by substandard medical care puts the well-being of patients at risk, and secondly, the erosion of trust in the healthcare system undermines efforts to promote evidence-based medical practices. For a developing country like Pakistan, the indirect costs of permitting NDAPs, ranging from misdiagnoses to improper treatments, can be immense.

## LITERATURE REVIEW

In Pakistan, the issue of unqualified practitioners, commonly known as quacks, is a cause for serious concern. The Pakistan Medical and Dental Council reports over 600,000 such practitioners nationwide, with one-third concentrated in the Sindh region. Shockingly, around 200,000 individuals are actively practicing in the province (SHCC, 2016). This alarming situation was highlighted by a study conducted by Altaf, Iqbal, and Shah (2019), which revealed three HIV outbreaks in the rural town of Larkana, Sindh. The outbreaks were linked to untrained healthcare providers in the Rato Dero area, who were found to improperly reuse injection equipment such as syringes, needles, and drip sets, significantly contributing to the spread of HIV. Mustafa, Khan, Hussain, and Qidwai's (2021) study in Sindh province uncovered a concerning situation among healthcare providers, where out of 4315 practitioners, 3022 (70 percent) were unlicensed doctors engaging in prescribing medicines, injections, and intravenous (IV) drips. This group of unlicensed practitioners encompassed individuals lacking proper training, unlicensed personnel, lady health visitors, homeopaths, medical establishments dispensing injections and IV drips, and laboratories prescribing medicines using a doctor's name.

The situation in other provinces is also concerning. Recently, the Punjab Healthcare Commission (PHC) took decisive action against quackery in the province (Hussain, 2023). PHC's enforcement teams sealed 1,013 quackery outlets following raids on 4,623 treatment centers. Notably, Lahore witnessed the highest number of closures (88 centers), with other significant closures in Rawalpindi, Faisalabad, Jhang, Kasur, Sahiwal, Gujranwala, and Sialkot.

Millions of people in Pakistan fall prey to quacks and face disastrous health outcomes. The rise in HIV cases in Pakistan is a grave concern attributed to the practices of untrained and uncertified quack doctors, particularly fake dentists, as highlighted by the Pakistan Medical Association (PMA) (Xinhua, 2019). These quacks contribute to the virus's spread by using non-sterilized instruments despite the availability of free antiretroviral drugs in government hospitals. Unfortunately, the mortality rate among HIV-positive patients is on the rise.

Contrary to historical perceptions of low HIV prevalence, the United Nations reports a rapid expansion of the disease in Pakistan, with approximately 20,000 new cases in 2017 alone. Wahid's (2019) study highlights the escalating HIV epidemic in Kot Imrana. A distressingly high mortality rate characterizes the situation. Interviews with patients revealed a shocking revelation: a quack who had used the same syringe on multiple individuals succumbed to AIDS in 2018. This unfortunate incident resulted in hundreds of patients contracting HIV, underscoring the urgent need for measures to address such public health risks.

Similarly, Kahaani et al. (2018) record a severe issue with chronic hepatitis, ranking Pakistan among the top globally. About 150,000 new cases of hepatitis B and C are diagnosed in the country each year in Pakistan (Waheed, 2017). Asif (2019) described the situation of non-degree allopathic practitioner clinics, where the widespread reuse of syringes and inadequate sterilization significantly contribute to the spread of hepatitis infections in the Pakistani population. The study underscores the role of quacks, who often administer unnecessary intravenous steroids and antibiotics, in spreading infectious diseases and promoting antibiotic resistance through substandard treatment methods.

Research shows different reasons for the high prevalence of quackery in Pakistan. Momina and Zakar (2021) assert that a lack of political and administrative will is Pakistan's most substantial hurdle in controlling quackery (Momina & Zakar, 2021). Additionally, challenges such as inappropriate staff selection, untrained personnel, insufficient legislation, and the deep-seated roots of quackery in society further undermine the effectiveness of the Anti-Quackery Cell. Aziz, Masood, and Jiang (2019) argue that pharmacy owners actively promote quackery. Adopting a demeanor akin to medical professionals, these owners position themselves as pseudo-doctors, advocating for patients to seek their guidance on medication. This conduct mirrors the practices of non-degree allopathic practitioners.

Consequently, patients express dissatisfaction with the behavior of pharmacy owners, leading them to perceive these owners as contributors to the promotion of quackery, particularly in rural villages. Niazi (2018) concludes in his research that effectively addressing quackery proves challenging due to its strong ties to Pakistan's socioeconomic and cultural context. Nevertheless, the study suggests that the path forward involves implementing robust legislation, fostering professional development among healthcare staff, and securing unwavering political and administrative commitment.

Studies from the South Asian region show considerable utilization of quacks by population. In Bangladesh, there is a demand for delivery-related care provided by UAPs among slum women during home births (Wahed et al., 2010). The study reveals that a significant proportion of women with lower educational levels, especially those experiencing their first pregnancy, seek care from UAPs, indicating a potential risk due to practices deviating from WHO recommendations.

In Andhra Pradesh (AP) and Orissa, India, people from rural communities prefer seeking initial curative healthcare from non-degreed allopathic practitioners (Vikram & Pradeep, 2016). In rural India, the role of Non-Degree Allopathic Practitioners (NDAPs) in practice is a first-level access point for primary curative care, filling a gap left by the public healthcare system (Gautham et al., 2011). Similarly, Raza et al. (2015) study reveals that most respondents seek some form of healthcare, with prevalent reliance on private services. Among these services, a noteworthy portion is provided by non-degree allopathic providers (NDAP), also known as rural medical practitioners, and the primary motivation for choosing these unqualified providers is their nearness. They found that the direct cost of care does not significantly influence the selection of healthcare providers. They suggest that there is a pivotal role of proximity in health decisions; potential solutions include initiatives like mobile medical tours to villages and insurance schemes that encompass coverage of transportation expenses and reimbursement for forgone earnings (Raza et al., 2015).

Different factors that influence people's decisions for the utilization of quacks have been discussed in the literature. For instance, Zubair and Ali (2017) found that an individual's income directly influences their lifestyle, access to a better environment, and availability of biomedical facilities. They argue that individuals in low-income groups often resort to quacks for biomedical services due to limited alternatives. Another study explores the connection between poverty and health in Pakistan, emphasizing that the privatization of healthcare has driven low-income individuals toward alternative healing methods, including the reliance on quacks (Hafeez, 2014).

Ullhaq (2016) reveals the multifaceted nature of quackery, identifying key factors that significantly contribute to its prevalence: insufficient education, legal shortcomings, quacks' limited understanding, and issues within the healthcare system.

Similarly, Zubair and Ali (2017) identify three primary causes of quackery. The foremost factor is the inadequate number of registered medical practitioners relative to the population's needs, leading to quacks becoming a perceived necessity in society. The second significant factor is the absence of a professional attitude and behavior among registered medical practitioners, coupled with a lack of attention to psychological treatment for patient satisfaction. The third notable factor is the constant availability of quacks at a low cost. Consequently, the study concludes that many people view quacks as indispensable to society.

## ANALYSIS OF THE KHYBER PAKHTUNKHWA HEALTH CARE COMMISSION'S ANTI-QUACKERY POLICY AND HEALTH ACTIVITIES REPORTS

The Khyber Pakhtunkhwa Health Care Commission (KP-HCC), established under the Khyber Pakhtunkhwa Health Care Commission Act of 2015, is pivotal in promoting healthcare quality and eradicating quackery in the province (Khyber Pakhtunkhwa Law Department, 2015). This analysis examines the critical aspects of the commission's initiatives, focusing on its anti-quackery policy, annual health activities report, and quarterly fact sheets.

The KP-HCC, in adherence to Section 6 (2) of the Act, has established a specialized anti-quackery cell. This cell operates within a comprehensive framework encompassing multiple strategies for combating quackery, such as registering and licensing qualified healthcare professionals, public awareness campaigns, complaint management, fines, and sealing non-compliant establishments. The commission has proactively developed MSDS for various Health Care Establishments (HCEs) to ensure a uniform, high-quality healthcare system. This includes eleven reference manuals covering different categories of HCEs and setting benchmarks for service quality and patient expectations.

To enhance the competency of healthcare personnel, the KP-HCC has conducted 16 training sessions, reaching 110 hospitals and healthcare establishments. A total of 303 staff members were trained, including healthcare managers, clinicians, pharmacists, nurses, biomedical engineers, and pathologists. In collaboration with the Project Management Implementation Unit, the commission signed an MoU for revamping Secondary Care Hospitals. During the past year, provisional licenses were awarded to 110 healthcare establishments, and an impressive 6,860 new HCEs were registered, emphasizing the commission's commitment to expanding and regulating healthcare services (KPHCC, 2023).

The commission's multi-pronged approach to eradicating quackery involves stringent measures such as the registration and licensing of qualified professionals, anti-quackery campaigns, complaint management, fines, sealing establishments, and public awareness initiatives. These efforts are essential in safeguarding public health and ensuring the legitimacy of healthcare providers. A strategic initiative to develop a comprehensive database and GIS mapping of all HCEs in the province is underway, with support from the World Bank. This innovative approach enhances regulatory oversight and facilitates informed decision-making.

The KP-HCC has implemented an effective mechanism for managing complaints, with 1,642 complaints received and 1,470 resolved in the last year, underscoring the commission's commitment to addressing public concerns. The commission has submitted amendments to the Act and Licensing Rules to align with contemporary healthcare standards. Moreover, efforts toward digitization, including online systems for complaint management, quackery reporting, and registration, aim to enhance efficiency and transparency. The commission's proactive engagement in awareness campaigns through diverse channels, including media, social platforms, door-to-door initiatives, and televised awareness shows, highlights its dedication to educating citizens about their rights and regulatory frameworks. Active participation in federal-level committees and consultative dialogues showcases the commission's commitment to contributing to policy discourse, sharing best practices, and ensuring uniformity in healthcare policies and standards.

The report mentions that the commission has conducted inspections, issued Show Cause Notices, and sealed healthcare establishments that do not meet the standards. They have also awarded provisional licenses and full licenses to compliant HCEs. The report does not provide the exact number of non-degree Allopathic practitioners excluded or penalized. The progress in eradicating non-degree Allopathic practitioners will depend on several factors, including the commission's continued efforts, the effectiveness of awareness campaigns, and the willingness of the public to report quackery. If the commission maintains its rigorous inspections and public awareness initiatives, significant progress can be expected in the coming years. However, the complete eradication of quacks may not be possible or may take time, as it involves a continuous effort to ensure compliance with standards and regulations. The commission can achieve substantial progress by strengthening its enforcement mechanisms and expanding its reach to remote areas where quackery is prevalent. Additionally, collaboration with other healthcare authorities and regulatory bodies can further enhance the effectiveness of these efforts.

## ANALYSIS OF ANTI-QUACKERY INITIATIVES OF THE ISLAMABAD HEALTH REGULATORY AUTHORITIES' PROGRESS IN 2022–2023

The analysis of the Islamabad Healthcare Regulatory Authority's (IHRA) performance in 2022 and 2023 highlights a proactive and rigorous approach for monitoring and regulating healthcare establishments within the Islamabad Capital Territory (IHRA, 2023). Throughout 2022, IHRA conducted thorough inspections covering various healthcare facilities, including hospitals, clinics, diagnostic labs, and rehabilitation centers. The authority consistently addressed malpractices by sealing establishments, suspending services, and serving notices for minor non-compliance. The diversity of issues identified during inspections, such as unqualified staff, unhygienic conditions, and the use of expired reagents and kits, underscored IHRA's commitment to upholding high standards in healthcare delivery. Recommendations for registration and revocation of suspension indicated a balanced approach, encouraging compliance while facilitating improvements.

In 2023, IHRA continued its vigilant regulatory activities, focusing on diverse healthcare establishments. The authority took decisive actions by sealing establishments, suspending services, and serving notices for non-compliance. Similar to the previous year, the issues addressed varied, including malpractices related to unqualified staff, expired materials, and unhygienic conditions. Recommendations for registration and revocation of suspensions highlighted IHRA's commitment to guiding establishments toward compliance and improvement.

The overall summary of the two years indicates a comprehensive and consistent approach by IHRA. The inspections covered a wide range of healthcare facilities, reflecting the authority's dedication to ensuring the quality and safety of healthcare services. IHRA's response to identified malpractices, recommendations for improvement, and regular issuance of notices for minor non-compliances collectively showcase a commitment to maintaining a high standard of healthcare within the Islamabad Capital Territory. The closure and sealing actions against non-compliant establishments further emphasize IHRA's role in enforcing adherence to regulations and standards, contributing to enhancing the healthcare landscape in the region.

## RESEARCH METHODOLOGY

Using a qualitative research design, our study aimed to investigate the roles and practices of non-degree allopathic practitioners (NDAPs) in Pakistan. We have employed an ethnographic approach to collect data from Islamabad,

Rawalpindi (the Twin Cities), and District Swabi (one rural and one urban area from the four tehsils) by frequently visiting NDAP clinics in both areas. The field visits for the study were carried out from August 2022 to December 2023. We observed the interactions and practices of NDAPs without revealing our research intentions, maintaining our anonymity as either patients or casual visitors. Importantly, we ensured that our observations did not pose any risk to the NDAPs involved.

Additionally, we engaged in informal conversations with patients, exploring their reasons for choosing specific clinics, visit frequencies, and health concerns. It's crucial to note that patients were informed about our research objectives, emphasizing the importance of their insights in understanding NDAPs' functioning and patients' preferences to get treated by those operating in their area. Drawing from our observations and patient interactions, we developed a structured interview guide. Our research comprised fifteen in-depth interviews with key officials from health regulatory bodies, including the Islamabad Health Care Commission (IHCC) and the Khyber-Pakhtunkhwa Health Care Commission. Additionally, we interviewed twenty patients across diverse regions, such as the Twin Cities, Peshawar, and Swabi District. To validate our findings, we cross-referenced interview data with observational notes from various healthcare establishments, addressing discrepancies between official reports and on-site observations. We transcribed the interviews and applied an open-coding method to derive meaningful insights from the collected data. Through several reiterative rounds of coding, we identified six key thematic areas covering licensing cycle challenges and individual perspectives to opt not to consult qualified medical professionals and regulatory authorities' official viewpoints on underlying reasons for the existence of non-degree allopathic practitioners.

## CHALLENGES IN LICENSING CYCLES AND THE EXISTENCE OF NDAP

In Swabi, Khyber Pakhtunkhwa, research on NDAPs shows significant challenges in licensing cycles. Discrepancies between reported and actual healthcare establishments, challenges in oversight, and a persistent threat to patient safety from unregistered healthcare establishments demand a comprehensive and adaptive regulatory approach. Psycho-social factors such as language and cultural comfort, easy access to NDAP, and an absence of perceived doctor-patient domination contribute to the continued prevalence of non-registered healthcare establishments. Stakeholder perspectives, including patient concerns and doctors' insights, underscore the existing challenges in the healthcare system.

The situation in the Twin Cities further highlights the healthcare challenges, reflecting a pattern observed nationwide. Urban areas with high population density necessitate an increased demand for healthcare services. This demand, in turn, has led to a higher prevalence of non-degree allopathic practitioners in the Twin Cities. NDAPs are particularly prominent in the suburban areas surrounding the Twin Cities, such as Tramri, Bara Kaho, Chaklala Scheme, and Burma Town. The regulatory authority, IHRA, which operates at the federal level, enforces regulations rigorously. However, a significant challenge arises due to the complex network of both qualified and unqualified healthcare professionals in the Twin Cities. A key issue in this context is the difficulty in identifying and tracing NDAPs effectively. A collaborative network within the medical community exacerbates this challenge. In interviews, study participants expose a concerning practice where qualified doctors facilitate the licensing process for NDAPs by obtaining licenses in their names, leading to a covert support system. In return, qualified doctors who facilitate NDAPs getting their licenses receive financial compensation from NDAPs monthly.

The interdependence among qualified and unqualified practitioners in the Twin Cities creates a formidable obstacle for regulatory bodies like the IHRA. Participants' revelation underscores the collusion between healthcare professionals, making it challenging for inspection teams to uncover malpractices. The need for comprehensive reforms to address these systemic issues is evident, emphasizing the imperative for a thorough review of licensing procedures and regulatory oversight in urban healthcare settings.

The NDAP clinics are established by individuals who have medical training as assistants to qualified doctors in the past, or they may have some diplomas and face financial challenges. These practitioners often rent or set up clinics, sometimes using the name of a qualified doctor, and provide financial support to maintain the appearance of legitimacy.

> In the suburbs of twin cities, many assistants or technicians, locals of the area, have opened clinics and work as quacks (non-degree allopathic practitioners). They either rent or own these places and may register under the name of another qualified doctor to whom they give monthly payments. Some individuals with experience in healthcare open clinics with illegal documents to sustain their livelihood. (A health officer from Islamabad)

## LIMITED ACCESS TO HEALTHCARE AND SHORTAGE OF QUALIFIED HEALTHCARE PROFESSIONALS

Limited access to healthcare and a shortage of qualified healthcare professionals are interrelated factors. The limited availability of formal healthcare services in specific areas creates opportunities for NDAPs. In times of need, people seek immediate medical attention from any available source, even if the practitioners lack formal qualifications. Our field study revealed insufficient formal healthcare services in remote and underserved areas of district Swabi. In villages without nearby hospitals or clinics, non-degree practitioners often address the community's urgent healthcare needs.

A few villages in Swabi have populations exceeding ten thousand, but they do not even have a Basic Health Unit (BHU) or a dispensary. This scarcity has given rise to non-degree practitioners who benefit from the chance to offer accessible and affordable healthcare. Regions with low numbers of qualified doctors per capita reinforce the dependence on non-degree practitioners in such areas. In remote villages with limited medical facilities, the absence of qualified healthcare professionals leads people to turn to non-degree practitioners for assistance.

The study participants mentioned that they had faced difficulties in reaching government-operated Basic Health Units (BHUs). When asked why they choose NDAPs over local BHUs, many patients mention that they avoid visiting BHUs altogether. Most patients believe that the BHU system lacks efficiency. Some patients who have previously visited BHUs mentioned that doctors were often unavailable, and paramedical staff prescribed their medicines. Additionally, staff at BHUs make patients wait for hours to see a doctor, as doctors often come to the BHU later than the official times. Patients who have visited BHUs earlier mentioned that the testing process is not well managed. It is reported that only those who have very low incomes go to BHUs. As a result, many patients prefer private doctors, feeling that BHUs are not as dependable or efficient.

> Even though our population exceeded 17 thousand, we do not have a government hospital in our village. Our people get treatment from private doctors located in the village. When they get ill, we take our patients to the tehsil headquarters hospital in Topi, or the District headquarters hospital (Bacha Khan Hospital Swabi). (A community member from District Swabi, Tehsil Topi, Village Gani Chhatra)

Beside Gani Chhatra village, we visited a densely populated village named Gandaf in Tehsil Topi, District Swabi. In the 2017 census, the population of the area was reported as 39,103, but local residents assert that it has surpassed 45,000. The village has just one poorly maintained Basic Health Unit (BHU) with no regular medical staff and inadequate infrastructure for these forty thousand people.

## NDAPS BREAKING LANGUAGE BARRIERS AND HAVE COMMUNITY TRUST

In our study, a large number of participants (patients) voiced concerns about receiving medical care from doctors who couldn't speak their language. The ability to communicate in a patient's native language significantly influences their choice to consult with NDAP, particularly in the Twin Cities. A considerable portion of Twin's Cities' locals communicate primarily in Potohari and another native language. When doctors in hospitals cannot converse in their language, it leads to communication challenges. However, NDAPs practicing in rural Islamabad can speak the local languages, making patients feel more at ease consulting with them. Most of the NDAPs are from the same community where they are operating. Thus, an element of trust from the patients in NDAPs as a community insiders also exists. This sentiment is supported by comments from one of the patients interviewed during our study. A patient at the NDAP clinic said,

> Most of the time, we need to visit a foreign doctor (a doctor who is not from their local area) for treatment; they do not understand our native language. Consulting our village doctor (NDAP) seems better as we can communicate effectively about our symptoms. (A patient from Islamabad, Potohar Region)

## FINANCIAL BARRIERS AND AFFORDABILITY

In Swabi, Khyber Pakhtunkhwa, research on NDAP shows that financial constraints often lead patients to seek treatment from NDAPs as they offer lower costs. The substantial costs linked with consultations, tests, and treatments from licensed doctors make NDAPs a more viable option for economically disadvantaged patients. Many NDAPs offer services at minimal fees; in certain instances, patients can defer payment until later. This affordability factor resonates with many participants in our study. Additionally, NDAPs are typically situated within local communities, eliminating the need for patients to undertake long journeys to access healthcare facilities. As noted by one study participant, this proximity proves beneficial.

> To get treatment from good doctors, first, we have to get their number (appointment), then we need to pay huge fees for their consultation, which is not less than five hundred rupees. Then, they ask for various medical tests, which cost thousands. Therefore, we come to the village doctor for treatment, who us in a very less amount. (A participant from District Swabi, Tehsil Razar, Village Yar Hussain)

## TRUST IN TRADITIONAL MEDICINE

Most of the NDAPs used a mix of allopathic and traditional medicine to treat patients. They often treat the patients according to their preferences for the type of medicine. Some of the participants in our study showed concern over the use of allopathic medicine as they think allopathic medicines have many side effects. Patients choose NDAPs due to trust in traditional healing methods, such as those provided by Hakeem (eastern medicine practitioners) or Pansari (herbalists). The belief in natural herbs and the perceived safety of these treatments contribute to the preference for non-degree allopathic practitioners. Many of the patients responded with common related words, as given below.

> We are cured by Hakeem and Pansari medicine, so we get treatment from them (NDAPs). They have medicines made from natural herbs, which, if not capable of curing the patient's disease, cannot harm the patient either. (A participant from District Swabi: Tehsil Lahore, Village Manki)

## UNEMPLOYMENT IN FORMAL HEALTHCARE SECTOR

Interviews with health experts indicate that the high unemployment rates among young health professionals significantly contribute to the rise of NDAPs. Financial challenges for individuals from low- to middle-income families in Pakistan sometimes push those with medical training to turn to unauthorized medical practices for income. Often, these individuals have backgrounds as medical assistants, technicians, or nurses. They might open clinics without the necessary permissions when they cannot find work in their trained roles. These technicians, nurses, or paramedics often label themselves as doctors when setting up their clinics (NDAPs clinics).

> The majority of middle-class people in Pakistan suffer from a financial crisis. Suppose a person qualifies as a nurse or assistant or another minor field in the medical field and does not have a job opportunity, so they resort to illegal works (non-degree allopathic practices) when faced with limited opportunities for employment in their field. (A health officer from Peshawar)

## CONCLUSION

This chapter investigates the prevalence of non-degree allopathic practitioners (NDAPs) in Swabi District, Khyber Pakhtunkhwa, and in the urban areas of Islamabad and Rawalpindi. Various factors, such as economic constraints, language barriers, trust in traditional medicine, limited healthcare access, and a shortage of a qualified professionals, contribute to the emergence of NDAPs. From an official standpoint, economic factors, including the steep cost of medical education and high unemployment rates, drive individuals to practice allopathic medicine without proper qualifications. Many of these NDAPs possess some form of medical training, such as diplomas or background experience in related fields. Recognizing the demand for allopathic healthcare, they establish their clinics. However, the challenge lies in effectively identifying and regulating these practitioners. Some qualified doctors facilitate the licensing process for NDAPs by obtaining licenses under their names, forming a clandestine support system. In exchange, these facilitating doctors receive monthly financial compensation from NDAPs. This collusion between licensed and unlicensed practitioners presents a significant challenge for regulatory bodies like the IHRA, hindering their ability to detect malpractices. Consequently, there is a pressing need for comprehensive reforms, including reevaluating licensing procedures and regulatory oversight in urban healthcare settings.

The absence of stringent regulatory measures allows NDAPs to operate. Economic motivations prompt some individuals to establish clinics without proper qualifications, offering cheaper services. Despite regulatory efforts to raise awareness about the risks of consulting NDAPs, these campaigns progress slowly. Extending these awareness initiatives beyond rural areas to urban settings is essential, as awareness about the risks of seeking medical help from NDAPs is also inadequate. Strengthening these campaigns will empower patients to make informed healthcare choices, reducing reliance on NDAPs.

Patients often consult NDAPs due to factors like language barriers, community trust in NDAPs, faith in traditional medicine, and financial constraints. Limited awareness about the qualifications required for healthcare professionals among rural patients, many of whom have low literacy levels, further exacerbates this issue. Future research should explore mechanisms to regulate NDAPs while ensuring patient safety. Researchers from a few South Asian countries, such as India, have explored the role of NDAPs in the healthcare system (Raza et al., 2015) and suggest that there might be a possibility of integrating NDAPs into formal healthcare systems with appropriate safeguards, acknowledging that eliminating NDAPs is challenging due to the trust and accessibility they offer to communities (May et al., 2014). Policy initiatives need to focus on comprehensive regulatory reforms. This involves ensuring that NDAPs and qualified health professionals do not jointly exploit licensing processes. Additionally, there is a need for enhanced awareness campaigns and initiatives aimed at increasing access to qualified healthcare professionals. Training of health professionals should align with specific community values. Exploring potential integration strategies for NDAPs within formal healthcare systems, where possible, is crucial to ensure patient safety and informed choices.

## REFERENCES

Alam, M. M. (2018). Rawalpindi-Islamabad citizens for action against quacks! Retrieved from https://newspakistan.tv/rawalpindi-islamabad-citizens-for-action-against-quacks/.

Altaf, A., Iqbal, S., & Shah, S. A. (2019). A third major human immunodeficiency viruses (HIV) outbreak in Larkana, Pakistan: Caused by unsafe injection practices. *Journal of the Pakistan Medical Association*, *69*, 1068–1069.

Asif, A. F. (2019). Appraisal of national response to chronic hepatitis in Pakistan. *Journal of Islamabad Medical & Dental College, 8*(1), 3–7.

Aziz, M. M., Masood, I., & Jiang, M. (2019). Patients' anticipation for the pharmacies of rural communities: A qualitative study from Pakistan. *International Journal of Environmental Research and Public Health, 16*(1), 143.

Brennan, D. (2021). *WebMD Editorial Contributors*. Retrieved July 22, 2022, from WebMD: https://www.webmd.com/a-to-z-guides/what-is-allopathic-doctor.

Chot, P. T. (2006). Human resources for Primary Health Care in the South-East Asia region: Categories and job descriptions. In *Regional Health Forum,* 10(1), 65.

Gautham, M., Binnendijk, E., Koren, R., & Dror, D. M. (2011). "First we go to the small doctor": First contact for curative health care sought by rural communities in Andhra Pradesh & Orissa, India. *The Indian Journal of Medical Research, 134*(5), 627.

Hafeez, M. (2014). Poverty and poor health in Pakistan: Exploring the effects of privatizing. *Harvard International Review*. Retrieved from http://hir.harvard.edu/article/?a=5768.

Hussain, F. (2023). *PHC's Crackdown on Quacks: 1,013 Businesses Sealed.* Lahore: Pakistan Observer. Retrieved from https://pakobserver.net/phcs-crackdown-on-quacks-1013-businesses-sealed/.

IHRA. (2023). Press Release. *Islamabad Healthcare Regulatory Authority (Government Of Pakistan).*

Iqbal, M., Hanifi, S. M. A., & Wahed, T. (2009). Characteristics of village doctors. *Health for the Rural Masses: Insights from Chakaria*. Dhaka, Bangladesh: ICDDR, B, 39–53.

Kahaani, Z. A., Mahmud, S., Kouyoumjian, S. P., & Abu-Raddad, L. J. (2018). The epidemiology of hepatitis C virus in Pakistan: Systematic review and meta-analyses. *Royal Society Open Science, 5*(4), 180257. Retrieved from https://royalsocietypublishing.org/doi/abs/10.1098/rsos.180257.

Khyber Pakhtunkhwa Law Department. (2015). Health Care Commission Act, 2015. https://kpcode.kp.gov.pk/homepage/lawDetails/835.

KPHCC. (2023). Annual Report 2022–23 Khyber Pakhtunkhwa Health Care Commission. Retrieved from https://hcc.kp.gov.pk/wp-content/uploads/2023/11/Annual-Report-.pdf.

May, C., Roth, K., & Panda, P. (2014). Non-degree allopathic practitioners as first contact points for acute illness episodes: Insights from a qualitative study in rural northern India. *BMC Health Services Research, 14*(1), 1–11.

Momina, A., & Zakar, M. (2021). Implementation of the anti-quackery mandate Punjab healthcare commission: Challenges and limitations. *Pakistan Journal of Medical and Health Sciences, 15*(9), 2150–2153.

Mustafa, M. A., Khan, R., Hussain, S., & Qidwai, M. A. (2021). Regulation of quackery amid unprecedented HIV outbreak in Sindh, Pakistan. *JPMA The Journal of the Pakistan Medical Association, 71*(8), S22–S25.

Niazi, S. A. (2018). A Sargodha village under the shadow of HIV/AIDS. *DAWN*. Sargodha, Punjab. Retrieved Dec 5, 2023, from https://www.dawn.com/news/1390440.

Pakistan Healthcare Commission. (2010). *The Punjab Healthcare Commission Act 2010 Act XVI of 2010*. Retrieved from https://os.phc.org.pk/downloads/PHC_Final_Act.pdf.

PAKISTAN. Retrieved from https://newspakistan.tv/rawalpindi-islamabad-citizens- for-action-against-quacks/.

PHC. (2022). *Punjab Healthcare Commission*. Retrieved from https://os.phc.org.pk/newsFrm.aspx.

PHC. (2024). *Punjab Healthcare Commission (Government Of Pakistan)*. Retrieved from https://os.phc.org.pk/quackList.aspx.

Punjab Healthcare Commission. (2015). *Anti-Quackery Strategy 2015*. Retrieved from https://phkh.nhsrc.pk/sites/default/files/2019-06/Punjab%20Healthcare%20Commission%20Anti%20Quackery%20Strategy%202015.pdf.

Raza, W. A., Poel, E. V., Panda, P., Dror, D., & Bedi, A. (2015). Healthcare seeking behaviour among self- help group households in Rural Bihar and Uttar Pradesh, India. *BMC Health Services Research, 16*(1), 1–13.

Retrieved January 4, 2024, from https://ihra.gov.pk/press-release/.

SHCC. (2016). *Sind Health Care commission*. Retrieved Dec 5, 2023, from SHCC Anti-quackery: https://shcc.org.pk/introduction-to-anti-quackery/.

Tribune News. (2017). PHC seals 118 clinics of quacks in three days. *The Express Tribune*. Retrieved from https://tribune.com.pk/story/1462637/phc-seals-118-clinics-quacks-three-days.

Tribune News. (2018). Illegal operations: Clinics run by quacks sealed. *The Express Tribune*. Retrieved from https://tribune.com.pk/story/1804459/illegal-operations-clinics-run-quacks-sealed.

Ullhaq, I. (2016). Medical malpractice in Pakistan: "Quackery must stop, full stop". *The Professional Medical Journal, 23*, 1–3.

Vikram, R., & Pradeep, P. (2016). Private non-degree practitioners and spatial access to out-patient care in rural India. *GeoJournal, 81*(2), 267–280.

Wahed, T., Moran, A. C., & Iqbal, M. (2010). The perspectives of clients and unqualified allopathic practitioners on the management of delivery care in urban slums,

Dhaka, Bangladesh—a mixed method study. *BMC Pregnancy and Childbirth, 10*(1), 1–9.

Waheed, M. (2017). *Prevention and Control of Hepatitis.* Retrieved Dec 6, 2023, from World Health Organization Eastern Mediterranean Region: https://www.emro.who.int/pak/programmes/prevention-a-control-of-hepatitis.html.

Wahid, B. (2019). An update on the severe outbreak of HIV in Kot Imrana, Pakistan. *The Lancet Infectious Diseases, 19*(3), 241.

Xinhua. (2019). *Pakistani Doctors Blame Quacks for Alarming Rise in HIV Cases.* Xinhua News. http://www.xinhuanet.com/english/2019-06/12/c_138137776.htm

Zubair, M., & Ali, A. (2017, July). Quackery is the need of society. *Age, 16*(30), 119.

*Chapter 3*

# Exploring the Choice of Non-Exclusive Breastfeeding in Pakistan

Saman Nazir

Breastfeeding, which extends maternal protection for neonates from the prenatal environment to the postnatal world, is well-documented as a vital and cost-effective measure against infections, malnutrition, and developmental delays (World Health Organization, 2003). The World Health Organization (WHO) recommends exclusive breastfeeding for the first six months of life, as it can significantly save infants' lives and reduce the burden of disease in developing countries (World Health Organization, 2009). Moreover, women who breastfeed experience greater protection against breast and ovarian cancer and type II diabetes (Victora et al., 2016). The Pakistan Demographic and Health Survey 2017–2018 reveals that only 48 percent of children aged 0–5 months are exclusively breastfed (National Institute of Population Studies [NIPS] [Pakistan] & ICF International, 2019).

The health status of neonates in Pakistan paints a grim picture: the percentage of stunted and underweight children under age five is as high as 38 and 23 percent, respectively (National Institute of Population Studies [NIPS] [Pakistan] & ICF International 2019, p. 211). Despite the seemingly favorable conditions for exclusive breastfeeding in Pakistan, where only 25 percent of women are involved in formal or informal labor markets, and Islam advocates breastfeeding for up to two years, a considerable proportion of infants are not exclusively breastfed even during the first six months of their lives. Moreover, formula milk, as an alternative to breastfeeding, presents a financial challenge for many lower-middle-income families due to its high cost, often exceeding their budgetary constraints.

Pakistan is also one of 118 countries that endorsed the "International Code of Marketing of Breastmilk Substitutes" in 1981, aiming to promote and sustain breastfeeding practices to enhance the health of neonates and infants in the country (World Health Organization, 1981). However, due to inadequate response in adhering to the law, the National Assembly of Pakistan endorsed a national breastfeeding law in 2002 (Salasibew et al., 2008). Following the devolution of the Ministry of Health in 2009, the provinces of Pakistan have enacted the Protection and Promotion of Breastfeeding and Child Nutrition Act since 2012 (National Institute of Population Studies [NIPS] [Pakistan] & ICF International, 2019). In the early 1990s, the World Health Organization (WHO) and UNICEF established baby-friendly hospitals in Pakistan to encourage mothers to breastfeed immediately after birth (Kearney & Thieren, 2018). Despite these initiatives, statistics reveal that only 20 percent of neonates are reported to have breastfed within one hour of birth (National Institute of Population Studies [Pakistan] & ICF International, 2019). Even with these apparently favorable conditions, particularly for exclusive breastfeeding, it remains puzzling why there are still such low rates of exclusive breastfeeding in Pakistan.

The Pakistan Demographic and Health Survey (PDHS) reports on the reasons cited by women for not breastfeeding or discontinuing breastfeeding. Among last-born living children who are breastfed, the main reasons for discontinuation are primarily related to the mother's health concerns (42 percent) or the occurrence of the next pregnancy (22 percent). Moreover, several studies on traditional feeding beliefs and practices provide valuable insights into understanding the barriers to achieving the desired rate of exclusive breastfeeding (Fikree et al., 2005; Khadduri et al., 2008; Premani et al., 2011). These studies reveal practices such as pre-lacteals, delays in the first feed, and supplemental feeds. Infants are also often given substances like honey, Ghutti, and water, which are considered laxative remedies to reduce colic (Fikree et al., 2005). Barriers to initiating breastfeeding include limited access to information about the initiation of breastfeeding, a lack of decision-making power in health matters, and the influence of older women's beliefs in infant feeding practices (Sharma & Byrne, 2016).

Many current studies on breastfeeding primarily use data from demographic and health surveys or rely on quantitative survey-based information. Most questionnaires are pre-designed, offering limited options when inquiring about reasons for non-exclusive or cessation of breastfeeding. The reasons why women choose non-exclusive breastfeeding need an in-depth exploration. This study aims to investigate, through women's experiences, the factors influencing their decision to either exclusively breastfeed, not breastfeed at all, or choose a different approach. I conducted interviews with both women who did not exclusively breastfeed their babies and those who did, aiming to uncover the reasons behind their choices.

## METHODOLOGY

I developed an interview guide to explore women's experiences with non/exclusive breastfeeding. I interviewed thirty women living in different urban and rural areas in Pakistan. Eight in-person interviews were conducted in Islamabad, while twenty-two were conducted online. I posted on social media to invite women to participate in the study. Those who volunteered were then sent a consent form outlining the study's purpose, risks, and benefits. I interviewed women who have children aged three or younger, while focusing on their latest breastfeeding experiences. However, I also included discussions on their past breastfeeding experiences when they referred to them. All interviews were audio-recorded with prior permission from the respondents. The entire audio recording was deleted after transcription. To protect the data, I removed all possible identifiers. No real names were used to ensure respondent privacy. All interviews were transcribed verbatim, each lasting an average of twenty-five minutes.

After each interview, participants were allowed to share any additional thoughts or ask further questions. I remained reflexive during the interviews, sharing some of my own experiences as a mother of two children who were exclusively breastfed for six months. This deliberate act aimed to foster openness, as Hermanowicz argued that respondents are more likely to talk openly when they detect openness on the interviewer's part (Hermanowicz, 2002).

After collecting the data, I examined it to identify recurring themes. I started by carefully reviewing and categorizing each interview line by line, aiming to discover common patterns in the participants' experiences. Following the initial coding, I focused on the codes that best facilitated the precise data categorization. This process revealed ten overarching themes, each encompassing various sub-themes. In the study sample, thirty female participants represent diverse demographic and socioeconomic backgrounds. Among them, sixteen held a master's degree or higher, and twenty resided in urban areas. Eight women in our sample work in the formal or informal labor market. The data indicated a general cultural inclination toward encouraging breastfeeding in Pakistan; however, findings revealed that there is a prevalent discouragement of exclusive breastfeeding. The ten key themes that are exerted from the data are discussed in detail below.

## CONTEXTUALITY OF CHOICE BEHIND NON-EXCLUSIVE BREASTFEEDING

### What Options Do Working Women Have?

Some women in the study chose not to breastfeed and relied on bottle-feeding for their children. Among them, five were employed full-time in the labor market, and none had access to daycare facilities at their workplace. Due to the demands of their work, these women opted for bottle-feeding and did not consider pumping and storing milk, perceiving it as an additional burden. A participant indicated that she breastfed her infant briefly following delivery, recognizing that she would eventually need to give formula milk to the baby when returning to work after maternity leave.

> Even at that time, my baby was on a mixed feed. Knowing that I needed to return to work after 45 days, I made sure that my baby fully accepted the bottle. Breastfeeding while working a 9–5 job seemed impossible to me. It's not that I am unaware of the benefits of breastfeeding, but I felt I had no other option.

Three participants in our study were employed as house helpers in the informal labor market. The children of these women were on mixed feeding, receiving breastfeeding at night and whenever time allowed during the day. While at work, these mothers utilized bottle-feeding for their children. Notably, the use of bottles extended beyond milk; these women commonly fed their babies water, green tea, and honey water, indicating a variety of non-milk substances introduced to infants under six months of age.

## Who Will Do the Household Chores?

In our sample, most stay-at-home mothers did not opt for exclusive breastfeeding, and some chose not to breastfeed altogether. One prevalent reason cited by these mothers was the burden of household responsibilities. They expressed concerns that choosing to breastfeed exclusively would add to their already considerable workload. Four stay-at-home mothers decided not to breastfeed their babies altogether. Among them, three specifically mentioned the existing high level of responsibilities at home as a deterrent. These women also mentioned privacy issues when breastfeeding their babies.

It is crucial to highlight that most participants in this study who chose not to breastfeed were living in a joint family system, a common living arrangement in Pakistan where two or more generations live together. In joint family setups, women are often responsible for caring for multiple members of the husband's family, contributing to their decision-making process regarding breastfeeding practices. One participant mentioned

> I really wanted to breastfeed my baby, but you know how it is with a ton of stuff to do at home. I live in this big family, and my in-laws were like, 'You should breastfeed your baby,' but, at the same time, no one helps with the house chores. Juggling everything became a real struggle, like seriously hard.

## Have No Energy to Breastfeed

Some participants shared their experience that they did not consider breastfeeding because they felt they lacked the necessary energy. They attributed this lack of energy to the exhaustion of both childbearing and child-rearing, making them physically weary and finding breastfeeding a particularly energy-intensive task.

> I have house help, but I still feel tired with no energy whatsoever. That is why I didn't consider breastfeeding at all.

Another participant mentioned,

> You need a support system. I feel lucky that my husband supports me in this. My sister doesn't even consider breastfeeding. She says I do not have enough energy for this. She lives alone (nuclear family system). Many people are not well-informed about how nutritious breast milk is.

## Not Enough Milk, Not Enough Nutrition

One primary reason mentioned by women for not exclusively breastfeeding is the belief that their breast milk might not be sufficient to meet their babies' nutritional needs. This perception significantly influences their choice to engage in mixed feeding or refrain from breastfeeding altogether. Furthermore, it is noteworthy that individuals whose opinions hold significance for these participants, such as mothers-in-law, their own mothers, and other experienced women with children, often advise them to opt for a combination of bottle and breast milk, asserting that breast milk alone might not adequately fulfill the baby's requirements or is not nutritious enough for babies.

> At first, my baby was on mixed feeding. Afterward, I switched entirely to formula. Surprisingly, my in-laws didn't force me to breastfeed at all. They believe diet matters a lot and think that just breastfeeding might not make babies grow well because it's not super nutritious. My mother-in-law even told my sister-in-law, who was breastfeeding her baby, that my kids, getting formula, are stronger than hers, and she suggested giving formula milk to her baby as well.

Another participant mentioned,

> I sensed that my child was consistently hungry, and breastfeeding alone was not meeting his needs. I had to make a switch. Additionally, with the prospect of returning to work in a few months, I transitioned to formula milk exclusively.

## C-Section and Breastfeeding

One of the primary reasons cited by women for not exclusively breastfeeding or not breastfeeding at all is that they had C-sections. Notably, mothers find it challenging to breastfeed after a C-section. Doctors may introduce formula milk to feed the baby during this period. Even after recovering from the surgery, many women in our sample faced difficulties in transitioning their babies to exclusive breastfeeding. A participant who had a C-section mentioned,

> I was in pain after surgery, and I couldn't breastfeed my baby. He began feeding from a bottle. When I recovered, I attempted to breastfeed him, but he couldn't latch. So, we decided just to give him formula milk. Initially, he was on formula, but it was expensive. After two months, we shifted him to fresh milk (cow or buffalo).

Another participant referred to her sister's experience after a C-section.

> My sister just had a baby through a C-section. She could not breastfeed initially, and the baby was hungry and dehydrated. My mother and her mother-in-law gave the baby some green tea with a spoon. It was not a large amount. We did not inform the doctor and gave the green tea secretly because the doctors were against it.

It is noteworthy that only one woman in our sample exclusively breastfed after undergoing a C-section.

> For the first feeding, they (hospital staff) told me to feed without any instructions. I was clueless, and no family members were allowed in the recovery room. My mother-in-law could have helped me, but they didn't care. My baby struggled to latch on. Then, they handed me three formula milk and said, 'You can use any formula.' When I got home, I started breastfeeding my baby. I was determined to breastfeed him. I did feel pressure to switch to mixed feeding, but I didn't give up on breastfeeding. I wanted to give the best to my baby.

## Exclusive Breastfeeding: A Lonely Journey

Women participants in our sample who decided to exclusively breastfeed their babies described exclusive breastfeeding as a lonely journey, particularly those who are relatively young and experiencing motherhood for the first time. Most of these women are from affluent or decent-earning backgrounds, possess a college degree or higher, and reside in nuclear family units. These women express the challenges they face, noting that society at large is not very supportive of exclusive breastfeeding. They emphasize the need to let go of various aspects of their lives if they decide to breastfeed their child exclusively.

> I've wanted to give up so many times, but I haven't. Breastfeeding is painful.

Another participant said

> You feel so alone on this journey. You have to let go of so many things you love to exclusively breastfeed your baby. Doubts creep in often, wondering if the baby is being fed properly. Breastfeeding is exhausting and tough. Yet, I believe it's worth it as long as it's the best for your baby.

## Mix-Feeding Is Socially Encouraged

It is worth highlighting that mixed feeding is socially encouraged in contemporary Pakistani urban society. This encouragement extends beyond close relatives, emanating from a broader social circle comprising friends, peers, extended relatives, colleagues, and community members. Breastfeeding in various public places such as markets, functions, offices, taxis, malls, and parks is often perceived as burdensome for mothers. In contrast, opting for bottle-feeding in these settings is seen as a way to bring convenience to mothers' lives.

> I cannot go out. What is wrong with Pakistani people peeping into cars? I'm a shy person. I went to a wedding and asked if they had a separate room where I could feed my baby, but people here did not grasp the concept of privacy. I'm a private person, and everyone keeps knocking. They don't understand. Older women say, "we used to breastfeed everywhere, so you can do that too." But I cannot. My cousins and everyone I know tell me to put my baby on mixed feeding; that way, it will be easier for me to attend events.

Another young mother mentioned

> There are no places in malls or restaurants to breastfeed your baby. I almost gave up on my social life because of this issue.

## Cannot Afford Formula Milk

Many participants from rural areas highlight the economic factor, emphasizing that many people cannot afford formula milk. The unaffordability of formula milk compels them to rely on breastfeeding. Additionally, it is noteworthy that a more open and breastfeeding-friendly culture exists in less urban or rural areas, where people actively encourage and support breastfeeding practices.

It is also important to mention that exclusive breastfeeding typically lasts for around four months, after which children are gradually introduced to semi-solid foods. This practice aligns with local customs and nutritional practices within these communities. A participant explains how people cannot afford formula milk or cow's milk for their infants.

> People encourage breastfeeding here (Dara Ismael Khan). This is not a wealthy urban area. People cannot afford formula milk or cow's or goat's milk for their infants.

Another woman mentioned,

> Here (in Khohat), women breastfeed their babies. Formula milk is too expensive; I do not know how people can afford it.

## Hospitals without Lactation Specialists

There is a mixed response from mothers who delivered at hospitals regarding the encouragement of breastfeeding immediately after birth. Some participants noted that hospital staff typically advise mothers to breastfeed after delivery but often fail to provide adequate support. On the other hand, other participants mentioned positive experiences, stating that nurses actively assist mothers during the initial breastfeeding sessions. It is important to note that, according to a participant, Pakistani hospitals lack lactation specialists, leaving young mothers to navigate breastfeeding challenges on their own. This highlights a potential gap in specialized support for breastfeeding within hospital settings.

> There are no lactation consultants in hospitals in Pakistan. My sister only breastfed for three months. Her gynecologist said her baby was crying because he was just hungry; there was no specialist. There is a difference between gynecologists and lactation consultants. The doctors don't provide much guidance. Nobody advises women on how to handle it.

## Learning from Social Media

First-time mothers in the study sample expressed that they acquired knowledge about breastfeeding through the internet and social media support groups. These mothers actively sought information for the well-being of their babies, engaging in learning about various stages of childbearing and rearing through online platforms and support groups. A positive impact of social media support groups on encouraging exclusive breastfeeding was evident.

Two participants, who extensively rely on social media for information on exclusive breastfeeding and beyond, emphasized their profound resonance with other young mothers. They highlighted the mutual support and shared experiences within these online communities, illustrating the collaborative nature of their journeys in child-rearing and feeding.

> I learned from Instagram and social media that breastfeeding is good. My husband is very involved. I have joined many breastfeeding support groups on Facebook. I post about any issues related to breastfeeding there, and I get advice from other women who share similar experiences. It makes me feel I am not alone, and it's a great help.

## DISCUSSION AND WAY FORWARD

Breastfeeding is usually encouraged in Pakistan, but that is not the case when it comes to exclusively breastfeeding. Study participants working in the labor market find it difficult to manage breastfeeding responsibilities and work. Unsurprisingly, working women opt for mix-feeding or not breastfeeding at all, as we find in the literature (Netshandama, 2002; Sabin et al., 2017; Spitzmueller et al., 2016). However, most female participants working in formal employment mentioned that they do not have daycare facilities. For working women in the formal sector, their babies are often taken care of at home by family members such as a mother or mother-in-law. Not having a childcare facility at work is an essential factor that could contribute to giving up on exclusive breastfeeding. It is also important to mention that not many women in Pakistan consider pumping and storing breast milk for their babies. Another critical factor that is missing from the promotional campaigns about breastfeeding in Pakistan is the proper educational content about how to pump and store breast milk and how to make it consumable for babies, which can contribute positively to exclusive breastfeeding practices.

Women who work in informal sectors struggle with financially supporting their families with almost no work rights and breastfeeding their babies. Literature shows that women from the poorest quintile are less likely to breastfeed their babies (Nazir, 2019). No formal institutional policies for breastfeeding could work for women working in the informal economy. Therefore, it is imperative to implement population-specific programs aimed at these women to enhance the overall health status of children.

Women who are not working in the labor market also struggle to manage housework and breastfeeding. Most of the women mentioned opted for non-exclusive breastfeeding because they felt burdened, as they were expected to do all the house chores and take care of any family members in joint family setups. Women living in joint-family households have expressed privacy concerns when it comes to exclusively breastfeeding their babies. This is particularly challenging, as they may not always have the necessary privacy, especially in the presence of male family members (Premani et al., 2011). While it may seem that these women choose to let go of the feeding needs of their babies mainly to manage the workload at home or due to privacy issues, this highlights how the fabric of Pakistani society is unsupportive to women by not sparing them from household responsibilities, not even for six months, which would impact both women's and children's health. Breastfeeding advocacy campaigns should also encourage support for mothers from their families and create an enabling environment for exclusive breastfeeding.

There were participants in this study who perceived that breast milk was not enough for a baby and that exclusive breastfeeding may lead to malnutrition. Therefore, they do not opt for exclusive breastfeeding. This is one of the biggest misconceptions that women perceive, and it is also enforced by close relatives whose opinions matter to these women. In literature, such factors lead to breastfeeding cessation or switching to mix-feeding practices (Morrison et al., 2019; Zakar et al., 2018). There is a need to address these misconceptions about exclusive breastfeeding. Consultation with parents after the baby is born in hospitals, explaining how much milk is enough for the baby and how baby growth should be measured, along with the benefits of exclusive breastfeeding, can be considered at the institutional level. Since not all women give birth at hospitals, the same information to break such myths should be available through different communication methods such as radio, social media, and TV.

Women who undergo a C-section often face difficulties in continuing breastfeeding. Immediately after a C-section, which is a major surgery, many women find it challenging to initiate breastfeeding. Doctors commonly prescribe formula milk when mothers are unable to breastfeed right after a C-section. Unfortunately, transitioning back to exclusive breastfeeding in most cases does not happen. The literature indicates that women who have C-sections are less likely to breastfeed even after being discharged from the hospital (Nazir, 2019). The unnecessarily high rates of C-sections in Pakistan have a negative impact on breastfeeding practices. Furthermore, mothers often report a lack of support during hospital deliveries, with a shortage of experts and minimal guidance provided.

Notably, none of the participants in our study mentioned ceasing breastfeeding due to the occurrence of the subsequent pregnancy. This is cited as one of the two main reasons for breastfeeding discontinuation in PDHS. It might be because participants in this study were asked about exclusive breastfeeding, which is recommended for only six months, compared to non-exclusive breastfeeding, which often extends up to two years in the country.

The median birth interval in Pakistan is 28.2 months, with 37 percent of births occurring within 24 months of the preceding birth (National Institute of Population Studies [NIPS] & ICF International, 2019). These factors may explain why the occurrence of a subsequent pregnancy did not emerge as a primary reason in interviews with participants. However, it is essential to mention that PDHS reports the main cause of discontinuation of breastfeeding as women's health issues. The PDHS survey does not provide information about which health issues women experience that lead them to discontinue breastfeeding. In this study, we find that women who have C-sections often cannot breastfeed due to post-surgery pain, or women who reported feeling no energy or exhaustion capture a glimpse of what women refer to as health issues. Strategies to reduce medically unnecessary C-sections in the country and targeted nutritional programs for women with infants would indirectly but positively impact breastfeeding choices.

Exclusive breastfeeding is not socially encouraged. Exclusive breastfeeding is considered a burden for mothers at social events. This is extra pressure on women, even those who choose to breastfeed their children exclusively. Relatives, friends, and colleagues suggest it is wise to give the baby both breast and formula/cow milk so the mother will feel comfortable if she has to attend an event or go outside the home. It takes to the larger issue that most places in Pakistan are not breastfeeding-friendly. For example, in shopping malls, airports, terminals, and restaurants, there are hardly any rooms where a mother can privately feed her baby. The responsibility for people's discomfort with breastfeeding in public places should not be placed on women, but it does come into the conversation that women feel shy breastfeeding their babies in public spaces. There should be some level of facilitation at public places for mothers to breastfeed their babies in private. It is noteworthy that I have observed women breastfeeding in restrooms or fitting rooms of malls and offices. Restricting the promotion of campaigns and policy strategies targeting exclusive breastfeeding solely to hospitals, homes, or workplaces overlooks the crucial aspect of creating a breastfeeding-friendly environment in public spaces.

There is also a need to take everyone on board rather than only targeting women in breastfeeding campaigns. Women participants in our study who decided to breastfeed their children exclusively felt exhausted and referred to it as a lonely journey. It is evident that people encourage non-exclusive breastfeeding, so everyone should be the target audience in awareness campaigns on exclusive breastfeeding. Additionally, young women find social media a valuable resource for obtaining support during their breastfeeding journeys. Many rely on social media support groups for guidance. This proves particularly advantageous and can be deemed effective in advocating for exclusive breastfeeding in Pakistan.

## REFERENCES

Fikree, F. F., Ali, T. S., Durocher, J. M., & Rahbar, M. H. (2005). Newborn care practices in low socioeconomic settlements of Karachi, Pakistan. *Social Science & Medicine*, *60*(5), 911–921.

Hermanowicz, J. C. (2002). The great interview: 25 strategies for studying people in bed. *Qualitative Sociology*, *25*, 479–499.

Kearney, A., & Thieren, M. (2018). Feeding babies. Retrieved from https://www.unicef.org/pakistan/media_10019.html.

Khadduri, R., Marsh, D. R., Rasmussen, B., Bari, A., Nazir, R., & Darmstadt, G. L. (2008). Household knowledge and practices of newborn and maternal health in Haripur district, Pakistan. *Journal of Perinatology*, *28*(3), 182–187.

Morrison, A. H., Gentry, R., & Anderson, J. (2019). Mothers' reasons for early breastfeeding cessation. *MCN: The American Journal of Maternal/Child Nursing*, *44*(6), 325–330.

National Institute of Population Studies (NIPS) [Pakistan] and ICF. (2019). *Pakistan Demographic and Health Survey 2017–18*. Islamabad, Pakistan, and Rockville, Maryland, USA: NIPS and ICF.

Nazir, S. (2019). *Cesarean Section Delivery and Exclusive Breastfeeding in Pakistan: Emerging Challenges* (Doctoral dissertation, University of North Texas).

Netshandama, V. O. (2002). Breastfeeding practices of working women. *Curationis*, *25*(1), 21–27.

Premani, S. Z., Kurji, Z., & Mithani, Y. (2011). *To Explore the Experiences of Women on Reasons in Initiating and Maintaining Breastfeeding in Urban Area of Karachi.* Pakistan: An Exploratory Study. *ISRN pediatrics.* https://doi.org/10.5402/2011/514323.

Sabin, A., Manzur, F., & Adil, S. (2017). Exclusive breastfeeding practices in working women of Pakistan: A cross sectional study. *Pakistan Journal of Medical Sciences*, *33*(5), 1148.

Salasibew, M., Kiani, A., Faragher, B., & Garner, P. (2008). Awareness and reported violations of the WHO International Code and Pakistan's national breastfeeding legislation; A descriptive cross-sectional survey. *International Breastfeeding Journal*, *3*(24), 1–7.

Sharma, I. K., & Byrne, A. (2016). Early initiation of breastfeeding: A systematic literature review of factors and barriers in South Asia. *International Breastfeeding Journal*, *11*(17), 1–12.

Spitzmueller, C., Wang, Z., Zhang, J., Thomas, C. L., Fisher, G. G., Matthews, R. A., & Strathearn, L. (2016). Got milk? Workplace factors related to breastfeeding among working mothers. *Journal of Organizational Behavior*, *37*(5), 692–718.

Victora, G. C. et al. (2016). Breastfeeding in the 21st century: epidemiology, mechanisms, and lifelong effect. *The Lancet, 387*, 475–490.

World Health Organization. (1981). International code of marketing of breast-milk substitutes. Retrieved from https://www.who.int/nutrition/publications/infantfeeding/9241541601/en/.

World Health Organization. (2003). Community-based strategies for breastfeeding promotion and support in developing countries. Retrieved from https://www.who.int/maternal_child_adolescent/documents/9241591218/en/.

World Health Organization. (2009). Infant and young child feeding: model chapter for textbooks for medical students and allied health professionals. Retrieved from http://apps.who.int/iris/bitstream/handle/10665/44117/9789241597494_eng.pdf;jsessionid=D8F6B665B09E11BD7B55D5F6FFCFC1F4?sequence=1.

Zakar, R., Zakar, M. Z., Zaheer, L., & Fischer, F. (2018). Exploring parental perceptions and knowledge regarding breastfeeding practices in Rajanpur, Punjab Province, Pakistan. *International Breastfeeding Journal*, *13*(1), 1–12.

*Section II*

# POWER DYNAMICS AND THE HEALTH OF THE MARGINALIZED

## Chapter 4

# Reframing Doctor–Patient Interactions in Pakistani Healthcare

## *A Foucauldian Analysis of Power–Knowledge Relationship*

Ayesha Nazir and Saman Nazir

In Pakistan, healthcare regulatory measures are a significant policy concern, specifically in addressing structural loopholes related to assessing professionals' qualifications, practices, and performance while protecting patients' rights. Focusing on human resources solely, Kazim (2007) highlights that the Pakistan Medical Commission (PMC), formerly known as the Pakistan Medical and Dental Council (PM&DC), emphasizes beneficence, confidentiality, and non-maleficence in its code of ethics. However, it excludes patient autonomy by using ambiguous language that can result in several interpretations, and there is no legal binding to it. This contributes to a lack of accountability among doctors, who enjoy elevated societal status and wield significant authority in medical decision-making. In case of medical malpractice, medical professionals can face criminal charges, though courts in Pakistan are often hesitant to apply the Pakistan Penal Code in such situations. Instead, they prefer to address these cases through civil liability proceedings (Waraich, 2018). As Waraich (2018, p. 85) noted, incorporating medical services within the consumer law capacity is unfair and abominable. There is also a discrepancy in compensation.

Peerson (1995) has examined the power-knowledge relationship articulated by Michel Foucault. According to this perspective, the state, physicians, surgeons, and families aim to preserve the body's political anatomy for their interests and control over an individual in society. This is because an increase in knowledge leads to an increase in power. Foucault considers medical encounters a supreme example of surveillance as the doctors investigate and the patients comply (Lupton, 2003, p.26). However, he argues that the dominance of medical practitioners benefits both doctors and patients, as any challenge from the patient disrupts the entire medical encounter. The medical encounter is only successful if the doctor is deemed "good," that is, someone who diagnoses a patient quickly, does not spend a long time with the patient, handles difficult situations such as fatalities and awkward treatments, and assumes authority in advising patients on appropriate treatment and procedures (Lupton, 2003, p.127). This is because the base of their medical training is the positivist scientific method; that is, the focus is on the accumulation of facts rather than consideration of human communication or the epistemology of medicine. They are also expected to possess strong moral and value judgments based on gender, social class, ethnicity, age, physical attractiveness, and type of illness (Lupton, 2003, p.124). Therefore, doctors do not consider patients' concerns when making a medical decision; they have a child-parent relationship (Lupton, 2003, p.127). Patients tend to accept the doctors' fault, do not question their negligence or malpractice, and comply dutifully with their medical decisions and outcomes.

In the last two decades, healthcare systems worldwide have moved toward a patient-centered approach. This chapter will attempt to assess the current situation of Pakistan's healthcare system in terms of doctor-patient interactions. We will evaluate the level of awareness among patients regarding their medical rights, doctors' medical dominance, and other issues that prevail during a medical encounter. We will analyze the importance and implementation of the PMC code of ethics and draw attention to the reasons behind the increasing negligence cases in Pakistan. Furthermore, we explore the issues above through the lens of the Foucauldian model and propose solutions for their improvement.

## AN OVERVIEW OF THE HEALTHCARE SYSTEM AND CODE OF ETHICS

Pakistan's allopathic healthcare system operates within a mixed delivery framework that includes both public and private providers (Khan, 2019). The public sector consists of government-funded hospitals and clinics, while the private sector, driven by profit-oriented motives, plays a substantial role in healthcare delivery. A formal referral system exists within the public healthcare system to ensure a structured patient care pathway. However, this system faces challenges such as high patient volumes, resource constraints, and increasing service demands (Khan, 2019). Regulatory bodies overseeing healthcare practices have struggled with efficiency, resulting in inadequate monitoring and enforcement of standards. These challenges contribute to variations in healthcare quality and accessibility, posing significant obstacles to the overall effectiveness of Pakistan's healthcare system (Ali et al., 2021).

Concerns in the literature highlight challenges related to human resources. The healthcare workforce experiences strain due to high patient load, leading to burnout and compromised service delivery (Muhammad et al., 2023). Inadequate training programs, limited professional development opportunities, and the migration of skilled healthcare workers abroad further strain the human resources within the healthcare sector. In response to these challenges, doctors often operate private clinics alongside their public roles, driven by the absence of incentives to enhance their performance (Kurji et al., 2016, p. 603).

Patient literacy is a significant challenge in Pakistan's healthcare landscape, with limited health literacy among the population impacting their comprehension of medical information, adherence to treatment plans, and ability to make informed healthcare decisions. Socioeconomic disparities, cultural factors, and language barriers hinder effective communication between healthcare providers and patients. The power dynamic in doctor-patient interactions leaves patients in a passive position, particularly those who are less educated or from disadvantaged backgrounds. This imbalance contributes to inequities, resulting in patients from marginalized backgrounds receiving poorer care and having limited choices (Lupton, 2003).

The Pakistan Medical Commission's code of ethics highlights the ethical principles and standards that regulate the responsibilities and morality of doctors/physicians. It is derived from the World Medical Association (WMA) and Islamic bioethical laws. According to PMC, the WMA ethics code focuses on individual rights, whereas Islamic bioethics focuses on the liabilities and obligations of doctors and patients: preserve life or seek treatment (World Medical Association, n.d.). Therefore, PMC has incorporated both when forming its code of ethics. It was first proposed by the PMC Ordinance in 1962 and was approved in 1968. After that, the Council revised it twice, in 1974 and 2001. The code of ethics was projected to become a document that would educate the public on professional ethics so that *everyone knows their rights*. If any medical professional is questioned, they will be judged according to this code. The PMC code of ethics declares:

> I solemnly pledge myself to consecrate my life to the service of humanity… the health of my patient will be my first consideration; I will respect the secrets which are confided in me, even after the patient has died; . . . I will not permit considerations of age, disease or disability, creed, ethnic origin, gender, nationality, political affiliation, race, sexual orientation, or social standing to intervene between my duty and my patient; I will protect human life in all stages and under all circumstances, doing my utmost to rescue it from death, malady, pain

> and anxiety. To be, all the way, an instrument of Allah's mercy, extending medical care to near and far, virtuous and sinner and friend and enemy.
>
> (Pakistan Medical and Dental Council, 2018, p.22)

In Pakistan, where the majority of the population is Muslim, and a higher value is placed on Islamic guidance in health and mortality matters, it is noteworthy that Islamic jurists were not involved in formulating the PMC code of ethics (Kazim, 2007). Islamic bioethical concepts are not fully incorporated or are left ambiguous. Such as the "end-of-life care" concept, where Islamic bioethics supports the autonomy of the patient and the family, but the PMC code has a paternalistic approach to it where doctors are the primary decision-makers and can refuse further treatment if they deem it to be futile.

The language of the code of ethics is ambiguous, such as the section regarding ethics being taught to medical students; PMC has stated its expectations regarding it and proposed that ethics courses should be taught at medical schools. They have mentioned that a course of ethics code is to be included in the curriculum. However, they have not made it mandatory and have left it at the discretion of the administration and academic professionals to find ways to include it as they see fit.

The lack of research in Pakistan regarding bioethical issues and ethical codes further proves how it is ignored or neglected. The lack of implementation of the code of ethics has led to increasing malpractices in clinical and research medicine. Research shows that doctors have low awareness of ethical concepts such as confidentiality, non-maleficence, informed consent, respect for privacy, and desirable attitudes in healthcare professionals (Farooq et al., 2018). It is essential to mention that while the PMC's revised curriculum includes an ethics course, it remains optional, leading to a significant gap between theoretical ethical principles and their application in medical practice (Kazim, 2007). Despite medical institutions adopting patient-centered curricula, student doctors still lack sufficient empathy, proposing early exposure to patients during training (Ahmad et al., 2015). Akbani et al. (2020) emphasized understanding patients' preferred attributes for building trust and enhancing the healthcare quality delivered by future doctors in Pakistan.

## THEORETICAL ORIENTATION

This research integrates Michel Foucault's foundational concept of the power-knowledge relationship with contemporary studies based on Foucauldian theories. The objective is to scrutinize the overarching influence of medical professionals over patients in Pakistan. Rather than viewing power as an innate characteristic of a dominant class, it is conceptualized here as a strategic tool. As Lupton (1995, p.159) posits, power is often transferred from those possessing knowledge to those lacking it.

Patients are encouraged to place unwavering trust in their doctors' expertise, refraining from challenging their judgments, especially given the uncertainties tied to illnesses and treatments. Such sentiments resonate with the reverence accorded to clergy members, who, despite their authoritative roles, are perceived as benevolent and caring (Lupton, 1995, p.159). Foucault's scholarship suggests that the dominance exerted by medical practitioners in patient interactions aligns with both parties' mutual expectations and is not inherently oppressive (Lupton, 2003, p.121); nonetheless, Foucault advocates for a critical evaluation of this authority. While benefiting from doctors' expertise, patients should remain empowered to seek clarifications or additional insights.

Foucault posits that doctors should act decisively, streamline interactions with patients, and embrace a paternalistic stance in diagnosis and treatment (Lupton, 2003, p.127). Nevertheless, procedures are communicated transparently to patients to mitigate potential malpractice claims. This approach echoes the principle of informed consent, emphasizing that individuals should make informed decisions about their care and understand the associated risks and benefits (Foucault, 2002, p.31). Furthermore, competent physicians must possess robust moral judgments, given that the biomedical model is shaped by both medical and value-based assessments influenced by variables such as gender, ethnicity, age, and illness type (Lupton, 2003, p.134).

A nuanced understanding of the power-knowledge dynamic within Pakistan's healthcare system is imperative. This necessitates an exploration of the steadfast trust patients vest in their doctors and how institutional bodies, like the Pakistan Medical Council, validate doctors' authority through medical dominance. Given the prevalent illiteracy rates, doctors rarely encounter resistance and can evade accountability due to the healthcare system's vulnerabilities. According to Foucault, the prevailing cultural ethos reinforces doctors' authority, rendering patient skepticism futile (Lupton, 2003, p. 121).

In the context of Pakistan's healthcare landscape, there's a growing patient resistance attributed to escalating medical negligence cases and systemic inadequacies. This skepticism stems from perceived discrepancies between doctors' capabilities and patient expectations. Medical students often acquire communication skills in simulated settings, leading to potential diagnostic shortcomings when confronted with real-world patient scenarios (Marshall &

Bleakley, 2008, cited in Bleakly & Bligh, 2009, p. 378). This accentuates the need for patient-centric medical encounters.

Emerging theories on the power-knowledge relationship suggest mutual agency between patients and doctors. While physicians wield decision-making authority, patients frequently contest medical practices influenced by societal factors. For instance, Bleakley and Bligh (2009) propose reevaluating doctor-patient dynamics in the context of technological advancements, incorporating Foucauldian perspectives for future frameworks. Despite advocating for balanced power dynamics, merely enhancing communication skills in medical curricula might not bridge the knowledge gap, risking a disconnect between simulated and real clinical experiences (Bleakley et al., 2009, p. 382).

Postmodern theorists such as Deleuze and Guattari introduced the "body-without-organs" concept. While medical discourses may attempt to delineate the body, potential patient resistance persists (Lupton, 2003, p.123). When applied to Pakistan's healthcare context, challenges remain due to widespread illiteracy and limited doctor availability. Therefore, physicians must take responsibility, using their expertise to build stronger doctor-patient relationships, reduce medical oversights, and strengthen the healthcare system.

## DATA AND METHODS

We use a qualitative research strategy and an inductive approach to study the power-knowledge relationships in doctor–patient interactions in Pakistan. It is important to mention that we collected the data in 2020, during the Covid-19 pandemic. We were not able to conduct interviews in person. To collect the data, we designed a structured questionnaire with open-ended questions. It helped develop knowledge and understanding of the changing opinions of doctors and patients by asking about the challenges they have faced in medical encounters and trying to find the reasons behind these challenges. Their responses helped explain the current situation of doctor-patient interactions and provided suggestions for improvement. To better understand the challenges faced by doctors and patients, two separate questionnaires were created via Google Forms. The forms/questionnaires are fully recorded solely by the authors to ensure the accuracy of each form in coding, that is, thematic analysis.

Data collection units include patients residing in Islamabad and Rawalpindi and doctors working at Islamabad and Rawalpindi hospitals. Non-probability purposive sampling was conducted via online social platforms. The total sample population is thirty-eight participants (twenty-nine patients and nine doctors). The identity of the participants/respondents has been kept confidential. A consent form was added at the beginning of the questionnaires, which explained the background of the research study and its purpose, and asked their permission to save, store, transcribe, and use their form outputs solely for academic and research purposes. Only those questionnaires that meet the criteria are included. The respondents reside in Islamabad or Rawalpindi and visit or work at the hospitals in these cities only. The respondents gave consent for their answers/forms to be used in this research.

After the data collection, the thematic analysis approach by Braun and Clarke (2006) was adopted to systematically identify, organize, and offer insights into patterns of themes. The analysis included reviewing the answers, identifying codes, defining themes, and generating findings. The analysis was data-driven to avoid any analyst-oriented biases. All the answers were read repeatedly and coded manually. The repeated themes were organized in a table to determine the feedback of most participants. A table was created for our understanding to organize the information that included all the major themes and sub-themes; for example, compassion is a central theme, and the sub-themes were codes such as understanding, empathy, and kindness. Our results and analysis section indicates Patient with P and Doctor with D, wherever directly quoting them.

## RESULTS AND ANALYSIS

The nine key themes we extracted from the data are compassion, attentiveness, competency, medical jargon, unexplained diagnosis, second opinion, medical encounter, medical malpractice, and medical curriculum.

### Compassion

Our study participants discussed the qualities that patients and doctors think a professional physician should possess for an effective medical encounter. Doctors should understand the patient's situation and be non-judgmental, empathetic, polite, humble, kind, and friendly so that the patient feels comfortable explaining his/her symptoms.

> P09: Some doctors don't take me seriously or say negative things about what led the symptoms to happen instead of being non-judgmental.

> P21: (A doctor should be) attentive, friendly, ask questions to determine the reason.

Some patients felt that the doctors were not considerate enough and would prescribe expensive medicines and tests that were very difficult to find in the market.

P13: He (doctor) should not start prescribing all the medicines he knows of, and before prescribing he (doctor) should also inquire about the budget of the patient. Everyone cannot afford high-end imported medicines.

P26: (A good doctor should) pay attention to details, no attitude, provide proper guidance and most importantly prescribe generic medicine.

Most doctors believe that to be a "good doctor," one must be compassionate, empathetic, humble, and kind when dealing with patients.

D06: A good doctor should be humble and sincere.

D09: Doctors should be empathetic and caring.

## Attentiveness

Attentiveness in this analysis explains one of the main qualities of a doctor. An attentive doctor who is a *good listener* and *gives time and energy* to his/her patient will most likely have an effective medical encounter. If the patients feel heard and listened to, they will be more willing to explain their symptoms in detail, resulting in a better diagnosis. Very few doctors mentioned attentiveness as an essential characteristic of being a "good" doctor. Many patients feel that the doctors do not give them appropriate time and *diagnose mid-sentence*.

P01: A doctor should be willing to give time and energy. His should have the ability to put aside all externalities.

P04: Doctors should be good listeners, do a detailed check-up of patients rather than being in a hurry to accommodate as many patients as possible.

Conversely, most doctors commented that the patients do not convey their symptoms properly, and they have to ask specific questions to help the patient report their symptoms more clearly.

D04: They change history when a senior comes.

D09: Patients are always vague in the description of their symptoms.

D06: I need to ask some specific questions to get to the right diagnosis.

The issue of attentiveness can also be linked to the limited consultation time. Patients wait in long queues, and when they finally meet the doctor, they are not given proper time as the doctors are in a hurry to move on to the next patient.

> P04: There are long queues at the main reception. The sitting area is over-crowded. There is a lack of guidance and help from the staff. The doctors are not open to discussing every tiny aspect of the problem.

> P10: Doctors often disregard the patients' concerns and give a diagnosis after only a cursory examination.

However, doctors pointed out the deficiencies in the hospital management, which might have caused these issues, such as tough schedules and inadequate resources.

> D02: Doctors have long duty hours and a tough schedule.

> D07: Patient load is too much; we cannot give proper time to individual patients.

## Competency

This theme discusses a doctor's capability as the interviewees' preferred attribute. The medical profession is a challenging career path, and doctors undergo rigorous education and training before becoming doctors. Patients want their doctors to have a firm grasp of knowledge. They should be competent enough to diagnose efficiently and be professional.

> P06: Doctors should be specialized in his/her area of concern and could diagnose the problem properly.

Doctors have also stressed this characteristic a lot. According to them, doctors must be efficient in diagnosing diseases and be smart and professional when dealing with patients or their relatives. When asked about the characteristics of a "good doctor," they replied that a good doctor should be

> D03: Honest, careful, professional, competent and kind.

> D04: Smart and have good documentation.

## Medical Jargon

Language barrier is one of the pressing issues in doctors' and patients' interaction. Sometimes, patients do not understand the diagnosis that the doctors are trying to explain due to medical jargon. It is difficult for the patients to explain their symptoms to the doctors, which might lead to a wrong diagnosis.

> P04: One of the challenges in explaining symptoms to the doctor is lack of understanding of proper medical terms. They (doctors) should take time to understand patient problems and then identify the disease and provide an appropriate solution.

> P13: Sometimes, you are not aware of the correct medical term to describe the symptoms, and doctors start their assumptions way too early.

Doctors find a lack of knowledge/language barrier as a considerable challenges when it comes to dealing with patients.

> D08: Illiterate patients are difficult to counsel.

> D09: A patient's poor understanding/description of their issue causes problems for the doctors.

## Unexplained Diagnosis

Many patients in our sample complained that the doctors did not explain the diagnosis. Doctors should be able to explain the diagnosis well and discuss the options with the patients before prescribing medicines and tests. Otherwise, patients are very confused and unsure regarding the diagnosis made, making them more inquisitive.

> P20: Doctors listen but do not comment on symptoms/issues that I tell them, making the issues sound very insignificant. They just prescribe medicine and tell me to come for a follow-up. Even if they do explain, they have a very "isn't it obvious" attitude. I would prefer someone who explains the possibilities of the symptoms I am having and what can be done about it rather than just giving me medicines.

> P22: My encounters with the doctors are not very informative. They (doctors) give us options and procedures that they will carry out, but we do not know the reason of what is actually happening unless specific question is asked.

All the doctors are of the opinion that it is helpful to explain the diagnosis to the patients. The diagnoses are mostly explained to the patients and their guardians. If the patient is stubborn, doctors tend to exercise patience and explain the consequences of the disease and the treatment to them and their relatives/attendants.

D03: It is very difficult to explain, but I try by giving reasoning and logic behind every point.

D07: I try talking with his/her attendant and make them understand the patient's issues.

Doctors try to be empathetic and supportive if the patients require palliative care. They do so,

D04: . . . by giving supportive care, listening to him/her with more care.

D06: . . . by explaining the exact demands of their disease.

## Second Opinion

This theme analyzes how a bad medical encounter usually leads to patients opting for a second opinion or visiting another doctor. Patients usually opt for a second opinion because either they are *unsatisfied* by the first diagnosis, or the treatment did not go as well as they had hoped.

P01: Mostly for anything and everything, doctors suggest surgery right away. I go to other doctors to make sure, if that is the case. For example, recently, for a stomachache, I was asked to get admitted to a hospital for an appendectomy.

P10: Some doctors are money-making machines. Once, my mom was severely constipated, and we took her to the doctor. The doctor first administered an IV drip, then a few injections, then an ultrasound, and at the end of the day, he called me to his room to tell me that she has some sort of cancer. I was just heartbroken, crying alone in the corridor. Then my brother he took her to another doctor, and he said she was completely fine. I wanted to sue him (the doctor) for his wrong diagnosis.

Patients think that the doctors are *insincere*; hence, they look for multiple opinions, especially if the diagnosis is too severe.

P08: Not all doctors are sincere to the patient, so there is a need to get multiple opinions in order to make a better decision.

P10: Yes, (I visit more than one doctor) because usually two different doctors provide two different opinions: one extreme and one mild.

## Medical Encounter

This theme elaborates on the good and bad medical encounters, which ultimately show the strength of doctor-patient interactions. In the results, patients are divided between good and bad encounters. Those with bad encounters repeated the issue of inattentiveness and less consultation time. However, there were other causes as well, such as wrong diagnosis:

> P01: I have had doctors commenting on my appearance. Mostly, doctors are apparently chasing a train, and are in such a hurry that they do not listen. Many just blame it on genetics. Many are rude as they've had a long day.

Social discrimination is also one of the reasons for a bad medical encounter.

> P01: I wear an "Ali" necklace. My doctor told me how all Shias are Kafir and exaggerate everything, just like I was exaggerating my symptoms.

> P20: Usually, when we took our terminally ill mother to the hospital in an emergency, we would be in informal clothes, and the doctors were rude, thinking we wouldn't be able to understand their diagnosis given our appearances. They would yell that they can't do anything other than giving palliative medicines.

> P25: She (the doctor) performed the surgery in a random room instead of an OT. Maybe because the patient was a civilian.

The majority of the doctors agreed that the doctor-patient relationship in Pakistan needs improvement.

> D02: It is not as good as it should be. There are several barriers.

> D07: Most patients don't respect doctors and usually demand to get a specific test or medication, and if you don't do it, they get angry.

Some doctors were of the view that they were blamed for everything, even if it is out of their control.

> D03: Patients sometimes assume that everything is in the doctor's hands, so they blame him or her for every failure. The hospital management does not take any responsibility if something goes wrong. Doctors suffer at the end of every dispute.

## Medical Malpractice

We asked whether patients had ever experienced medical malpractice and what they had done about it. We found that many patients have experienced medical malpractice; however, none of them has ever filed a lawsuit:

> P01: A tiny part of a surgical tool was left inside my dad's abdomen when they opened him up for an appendectomy. My doctor ignored my symptoms of diabetes for the longest period of time.

> P09: My mother recently had some issues with her liver/gallbladder. She told the doctor that she was unable to take very high doses of medications because of her ulcer. However, the doctor ignored her concern, and she fell severely ill. When we went to another doctor for a second opinion, she told us that the first doctor had overmedicated my mother.

> P17: My dentist did not listen properly and started treating the wrong tooth.

> P20: My mother was diagnosed with TB by the doctor without conducting proper tests. She had breast cancer. The TB medicine made her lung condition worse.

A patient mentioned a traumatic experience that happened in her family,

> P13: My sister-in-law's baby died due to a heavy dose of an injection. She was hospitalized for three months just for the protection of the baby. The doctor did not inform my brother or my sister-in-law about the baby's death and kept prescribing more injections. After one week, my sister-in-law started having labor pains in her eighth month; the doctor told them that the baby had died a week ago.

Most of the patients agreed that a *lawsuit* should be filed in case of medical malpractice, but few believe that it is a hassle in Pakistan and not worth the time or effort.

> P20: You need a strong background for it. I don't think you will win the case otherwise.

Most of the doctors also agreed that medical malpractice occurs quite often. The major reasons are tough schedules, weak systems and policies, and lack of knowledge.

> D04: Negligence in the medical field often occurs because of long duty hours of doctors when they are already sleep-deprived and often when there are fewer doctors during duty hours. It can be minimized by decreasing the doctor-patient ratio.

> D07: Malpractice happens all the time because there is no proper check on doctors.

> D08: Malpractice means not treating patients rationally. Yes, it happens in the hospitals due to lack of knowledge.

### Medical Curriculum

This theme analyzes whether the doctors are familiar with the PMC code of ethics and satisfied with the medical curriculum. Most doctors were familiar with the PMC code of ethics and did not propose any changes to it. However, a few did not know about the code. When asked about the medical curriculum and their experience as a student, half of the sample population of doctors termed the medical curriculum "Good" as compared to the other half that commented it was "Excellent."

> D02: It was hectic yet learning. There should be more practical exposure of medical students with patients, so they are sufficiently trained for practical work in house job.

> D04: It is satisfactory but must be updated yearly.

A few doctors proposed introducing a *modular system* to make it easier for the students.

> D07: The curriculum is okay, but the annual examination method needs to change. There should be a quarterly modular system.

## DISCUSSION

Our analysis shows that the concept of doctor-patient interaction in Pakistan needs significant improvement. If we look through the lens of both doctors and patients, the duties and rights of both parties are unfulfilled. Most patients are unaware of their rights and duties. The hospital procedures could be more straightforward regarding the appointment and payment procedures. Patients have to wait in long queues for their turn, indicating that doctors have tight schedules, as Qidwai et al. (2003) confirmed. They found that the average waiting time for patients was 30 minutes compared to the expected 12.69 minutes. Patients have also complained about the uncooperative and rude hospital staff who are unwilling to help in either understanding the hospital procedures or in guiding on the availability of doctors.

It is worth mentioning that although this chapter is only concerned with the doctor-patient relationship, doctors mostly hold the hospital management responsible for most of the issues mentioned by the patients. The doctors mentioned that management provides inadequate resources and allows demanding schedules. Work politics are involved, which causes a stressful environment and hinders an adequate diagnosis.

Defining the attributes of a "good doctor," patients believe that someone compassionate, attentive, considerate, and professional explains the symptoms and diagnosis before prescribing tests and medicines. This is because they should be more involved in caring for and avoiding future recurrences. They will be fully aware of the risks and benefits involved in the treatment and the consequences if they choose to ignore it. However, patients find it challenging to have a proper conversation with doctors regarding their symptoms due to the absence of these qualities, which aligns with existing research on the current healthcare system. The priority in the healthcare system has shifted from doctors making all the decisions to keeping patients in the loop about what and why something is happening, that is, the diagnosis and treatment (Akbani et al., 2020). However, doctors lack empathy and are not considerate enough. They prescribe tests and medicines that are often expensive or unavailable.

In the last two decades, the healthcare system has become more patient-centered. Doctors must explain the diagnosis to the patients in simple terms and preferably in their language to avoid confusion, as they are often nervous or embarrassed to ask obvious questions (Rimmer, 2014). Akbani et al. (2020) have also noted in their research that patients prefer doctors who can communicate in their language. This eliminates the communication gap and helps the patients explain their symptoms more clearly. Often, patients' agony or discomfort is not taken seriously and is judged based on their values; therefore, patients are also reluctant to convey their medical history.

On the other hand, doctors believe that they usually explain the diagnosis to the patients and their attendants because having them onboard for the treatment is necessary. However, it is difficult to make them understand the diagnosis given the patient's lack of knowledge, also concluded by Rimmer (2014). A lot of patience and good communication is required. They need time, so the issue lies with long working hours and tight schedules.

Doctors have less consultation time; therefore, doctor-patient interactions are rushed. Research shows that patients prefer doctors who take the time to listen to their concerns (Akbani et al., 2020). According to Michael Foucault's theory, this is a satisfactory medical encounter as a "good" doctor has a paternalistic approach and gets things done quickly and efficiently, that is, in a limited time. However, doctors have to explain the diagnosis to the patients. Patients should have complete trust in the ability of the doctors and should ask questions for a better understanding of the diagnosis. However, they should not try to take control of the medical encounter because it would render it futile (Lupton, 2003, p. 121). However, this "resistance" or questioning can only occur if the patients are well-versed in medical knowledge or have higher social status.

Many patients have complained that doctors start diagnosing mid-sentence rather than listening to them. Doctors *do not* explain the diagnosis as they lack patience or tolerance, which leaves the patients confused and very dependent on the decisions of the doctors as they have more power and knowledge. Even if they do explain, doctors are either hesitant or have an "isn't-it-obvious" attitude which further widens the barrier in doctor-patient interactions. Much like what Qidwai et al. (2003) proposed in their research, patients would prefer an explanation of the diagnosis rather than just being prescribed medicines and treatments. Doctors must be aware of the absence and presence in consultation (Bleakley & Bligh, 2009).

Effective communication creates a "meaningful and trustworthy relationship" (Akbani et al., 2020, p.812). In line with Naseer et al. (2012), trust in doctors and word of mouth are highly and positively associated between doctors and patients. Many patients have had bad encounters with doctors, and due to this, there is a rise in "resistance"—a term used by postmodern theorists Deleuze and Guattari. Day by day, patients are becoming more aware and confident regarding their expectations from the healthcare system, especially in urban areas such as Islamabad and Rawalpindi; therefore, an effective doctor-patient relationship is needed to deliver modern medicines (Ahmad et al., 2015, p.2).

Patients have started visiting multiple doctors before following the initial prescription and often opt for the mildest treatment out of all the opinions. This is also because the first treatment reacted badly or worsened the conditions of the patients or their relatives. Patients receive wrong injections or heavy dosages, as also recognized by Khowaja et al. (2008), and the basis is again a lack of knowledge, poor communication skills, and long working hours, which contribute to a stressful environment. Most of the patients claimed that they did not face any social discrimination from the doctors, given their social status, caste, and so on. However, those who did experience a very rude medical encounter. This has further made them question the competency and sincerity of the doctors.

Most participants in our study encountered numerous incidences where the doctors made major mistakes in diagnosing symptoms, jeopardizing their health or the health of their relatives. Patients believe that a lawsuit must be filed against medical malpractice; however, they are unaware of the procedure for filing a lawsuit. Others believe that it is not beneficial to do so in Pakistan, given the weak judicial system (Gadit, 2012, p.406). Even after all the incidents mentioned by the patients, none of them filed a complaint or a lawsuit against their respective doctors. This can be linked to the power-knowledge relationship because, as stated earlier, doctors are not held liable in criminal courts, as the courts are reluctant to charge them with criminal liability under the Pakistan Penal Code. It is unfair to charge criminal cases equivalent to consumer laws, and the compensation is unequal as well (Waraich, 2018, p.92).

Analysis shows that doctors are also of the view that medical malpractice occurs because of weak systems, overburdened doctors, and a *lack of accountability* and knowledge. Few doctors in this research even stated that they are unaware of the code of ethics for medical professionals. This further highlights making the course of ethics mandatory in medical schools and colleges. Ahmad et al. (2015, p. 7) also concluded that the current medical education curriculum is not fulfilling its aim. Students should be exposed to more patient-centered care from the beginning of their medical education. Effective communication skills training programs in tertiary care hospitals should focus on cultural and lingual diversity (Adnan et al., 2020, p. 56). There is a lack of communication-based training, which affects the interpersonal and social communication between doctors and patients (Adnan et al., 2020).

## CONCLUSION AND RECOMMENDATION

During the last two decades, the healthcare system in Pakistan has experienced significant transformations, moving toward a more patient-centric paradigm. Despite this shift, findings from this research indicate that a significant proportion of patients feel unheard and inadequately understood. This sentiment stems from a perceived lack of attentiveness and empathy during medical interactions, fostering skepticism about prognoses and eroding trust in healthcare providers. Paradoxically, patient resistance presents challenges for physicians, giving rise to a detrimental cycle in which patient inquiries generate a perception of professional challenge.

A genuine commitment to a patient-centered approach is imperative to break this cycle. Physicians must adapt to evolving times by actively involving patients in discussions surrounding diagnoses and treatment plans. Establishing a more comfortable environment involves articulating symptoms, proposing diagnoses, and explaining treatment options to patients. A crucial facet of reform involves revising medical curricula. The Pakistan Medical Commission (PMC) should mandate an ethics course for all medical students, ensuring awareness of professional responsibilities, rights, and the consequences of ethical violations. Practical exposure should commence early in medical education, allowing students' supervised interaction with patients and attendants, and providing firsthand experience in effective medical encounters.

While acknowledging patients' occasional challenges, it remains incumbent upon doctors, in adherence to PMC's ethical guidelines, to approach their profession with empathy and kindness. Implementing the code of ethics demands revising language and adopting a definitive and authoritative tone with specified consequences for non-compliance. Strict punitive measures should be taken against errant doctors to uphold accountability, transcending mere warnings in disciplinary hearings.

A shift from civil to criminal liability in legal proceedings in cases of extreme negligence can be considered to address medical malpractice. This change aims to underscore the gravity of accountability issues within the medical profession. The complexity of the complaint procedure at PMC warrants a more accessible and widely advertised process, ensuring public awareness of the steps involved. Moreover, health commissions can start campaigns to inform the public about patients' and doctors' rights and responsibilities, explaining how to file complaints. While the initial influx of emotionally charged and unrelated queries may be anticipated, in the long term, such initiatives benefit the healthcare system by fostering a new structure for monitoring medical services.

## REFERENCES

Adnan, M., Latif, F., & Abid, S. (2020). Communication barriers in Pakistan: Interpretative Phenomenological Analysis. *Paradigms*, *14*(1), 53–57.

Ahmad, W., Krupat, E., Asma, Y., Attique, R., Mahmood, U., & Waqas, A. (2015). Attitudes of medical students in Lahore, Pakistan toward the doctor–patient relationship. *PeerJ*, *3*, e1050.

Akbani, S. K., Bibi, F., Jabeen, S., Nayyer, F., Shoaib, S. K., & Gul, Z. (2020). Patients' preferences for attributes among health care providers in Karachi, Pakistan: A cross-sectional study. *Global Scientific Journals*, *8*(1), 810–835.

Ali, A., Ahmad, F., Danish, S. H., Zahid, N., Israr, N., & Farooq, S. (2021). Healthcare system of Pakistan: Strengths and weaknesses. *Advances in Research*, *22*(2), 45–49.

Bleakley, A., & Bligh, J. (2009). Who can resist Foucault?. *Journal of Medicine and Philosophy*, *34*(4), 368–383.

Braun, V., & Clarke, V. (2006). Using thematic analysis in psychology. *Qualitative Research in Psychology*, *3*(2), 77–101.

Farooq, W., Jafarey, A., & Arshad, A. (2018). Awareness of medical ethics principles and their applications among healthcare professionals in Pakistan. *Pakistan Journal of Medicine and Dentistry*, *7*(4), 8.

Foucault, M. (2002). *The Birth of the Clinic*.London: Routledge.

Gadit, A. A. (2012). Medical errors: Who is to be blamed?. *JPMA. The Journal of the Pakistan Medical Association*, *62*(4), 406–407.

Kazim, F. (2007). Critical analysis of the Pakistan Medical Dental [specific title or description of the work]. *Semantic Scholar*. Retrieved from https://www.semanticscholar.org/paper/Critical-analysis-of-the-Pakistan-Medical-Dental-Kazim/40216fbe0bd9b2d26490a5ce219cbb41aa0384ab.

Khan, S. A. (2019). Situation analysis of health care system of Pakistan: Post 18 amendments. *Health Care Current Reviews*, *7*(3), 244.

Khowaja, K., Nizar, R., Merchant, R. J., Dias, J., Bustamante-Gavino, I., & Malik, A. (2008). A systematic approach of tracking and reporting medication errors at a tertiary care university hospital, Karachi, Pakistan. *Therapeutics and Clinical Risk Management*, *4*(4), 673–679.

Khurji, Z., Premani, Z. S., & Mithani, Y. (2016). Analysis of the health care system of pakistan: Lessons learnt and way forward. *Journal of Ayub Medical College Abbottabad*, *28*(3), 601–604.

Lupton, D. (1995). Perspectives on power, communication and the medical encounter: Implications for nursing theory and practice. *Nursing Inquiry*, *2*(3), 157–163.

Lupton, D. (2003). Power relations and the medical encounter [E-book]. In D. Lupton, *Medicine as Culture: Illness, Disease and the Body* (Third ed., pp. 105–136). Thousand Oaks: SAGE Publications Ltd.

Muhammad, Q., Eiman, H., Fazal, F., Ibrahim, M., & Gondal, M. F. (2023). Healthcare in Pakistan: Navigating challenges and building a brighter future. *Cureus*, *15*(6).

Naseer, M., Zahidie, A., & Shaikh, B. (2012). Determinants of patient's satisfaction with health care system in Pakistan: A critical review. *Pakistan Journal of Public Health*, *2*(2), 56–61.

Pakistan Medical and Dental Council. (2018). PMDC Code of Ethics 2018. Retrieved from https://www.pmc.gov.pk/Documents/law/PMDC%20Code%20of%20Ethics%202018.pdf.

Peerson, A. (1995). Foucault and modern medicine. *Nursing Inquiry*, *2*(2), 106–114.

Qidwai, W., Dhanani, R. H., & Khan, F. M. (2003). Implications for the practice of a patient expectation and satisfaction survey, at a teaching hospital in Karachi, Pakistan. *Journal of Pakistan Medical Association*, *53*, 122.

Rimmer, A. (2014). Doctors must avoid jargon when talking to patients, royal college says. *BMJ*, g4131.

Waraich, R. S. (2018). Healthcare system and medical malpractice law in Pakistan. *Policy Perspectives*, *15*(3), 85–98.

World Medical Association. (n.d.). *WMA International Code of Medical Ethics*. World Medical Association. https://www.wma.net/policies-post/wma-international-code-of-medical-ethics/.

*Chapter 5*

# Understanding Mental Health Barriers in Pakistani Society

Halima S. Qureshi

The landscape of mental health in Pakistani society is intricate, shaped by a myriad of factors deeply rooted in cultural values, societal norms, and socioeconomic realities. In this chapter, we embark on a journey to unravel the complexities of mental health barriers in Pakistan, delving into the intersections of communal values, cultural norms, and socioeconomic disparities. By examining the issue through a cultural and clinical lens, we aim to shed light on the multifaceted challenges hindering mental health well-being and access to adequate support.

As we explore mental health challenges in Pakistani society, we begin by acknowledging the pivotal role played by the cultural context. A study by Choudhry, Khan, and Munawar (2021) sheds light on the impact of collectivist values on mental health stigma, emphasizing the imperative need for culturally tailored interventions. Despite constituting a global health burden and a significant contributor to morbidity worldwide, including in Pakistan, mental health disorders remain a neglected concern within our nation. Over the years, we have witnessed substantial advancements in treating physical health conditions in Pakistan. However, mental health issues continue to receive limited attention and priority. Notably, Pakistan is currently the sixth most populous country, with a population of 241.49 million and an annual growth rate of 2.5 percent (PBS, 2023). This demographic scale underscores the urgency of addressing mental health concerns as an integral component of overall public health initiatives. Within this framework, we navigate through the intricate interplay of communal values, cultural norms, and socioeconomic disparities that collectively shape the complex landscape of mental health barriers in Pakistan.

## INTERSECTION OF COMMUNAL VALUES, CULTURAL NORMS, AND SOCIOECONOMIC DISPARITIES

Our journey into the mental health dynamics of the Pakistani community extends across various regions, offering insights into the cultural fabric that shapes their understanding of mental illness and health problems. Studies, such as the work on "highly expressed emotions," have uncovered distinctive cultural manifestations within the Pakistani community, whether they reside within the country or abroad (Ikram et al., 2011; Bhugra & McKenzie, 2003). This exploration underscores a continuity of values and attitudes, reflecting the enduring influence of communal values and cultural norms within the Pakistani community. As we navigate these cultural intricacies, it becomes increasingly evident that the communal values intertwined with cultural norms play a pivotal role in shaping perceptions of mental health, a theme we introduced in the earlier sections of our exploration.

## COMMUNAL VALUES: ADDRESSING THE SILENCE SURROUNDING MENTAL HEALTH

In the rich tapestry of Pakistani culture, mental health often exists in the periphery, a crucial yet understated narrative. Despite the prevalent challenges posed by psychiatric disorders, seeking help for mental health concerns remains disproportionately low. This paradox can be traced back to the communal values that shape the Pakistani mindset, where a pronounced stigma dissuades open discussions about mental well-being (Ali et al., 2017).

Communal values, deeply embedded in the societal fabric, are pivotal in shaping the perception and discourse surrounding mental health. The reluctance to openly address mental health concerns reflects a broader cultural norm, where these discussions often take place in more private settings. Ali, Lalani, and Charania's (2015) exploration of community mental health initiatives in Pakistan sheds light on the intricate relationship between communal values and mental health awareness. It underscores the necessity for culturally sensitive approaches to diminish the stigma surrounding mental health, fostering an environment where seeking support is considered a natural aspect of overall well-being.

In the realm of addressing mental health challenges in Pakistan, the preference of practitioners chosen by the populace becomes a notable consideration. Several studies, including one conducted by Mirza, Mujtaba, Chaudhry, and Jenkins in 2006, discovered that individuals often opt for General Practitioners and Hakims to seek assistance for their mental health issues. This insight emerges from their investigation into primary mental health care in rural Punjab, shedding light on both the providers' perspectives and users' perceptions of the effectiveness of treatments (Mirza et al., 2006). The diverse choices of practitioners reflect the intricate landscape of mental health care-seeking behaviors in this context.

The challenge lies not only in understanding the impact of communal values on mental health but also in discerning how these values influence societal attitudes toward individuals dealing with mental health issues. By constructing a narrative that seamlessly integrates communal values with mental health awareness, we begin to uncover the layers of stigma, creating a foundation for transformative change.

## CULTURAL NORMS: UNTANGLING MENTAL HEALTH FROM SUPERNATURAL THREADS

Cultural norms in Pakistan, diverse and intricate, significantly contribute to the complex tapestry of societal attitudes toward mental health. Within this context, delays in mental health treatment often result from false beliefs and supernatural associations linked to mental health problems (Khan & Sanober, 2016; Munawar et al., 2020). The common misconception that mental illness is connected to supernatural phenomena and demonic possessions reflects the profound impact of cultural norms on the understanding of mental health.

In our exploration, studies by Munawar et al. (2020) and Khan and Sanober (2016) guide our understanding of how cultural norms shape mental health literacy and perceptions. These studies underscore the need for interventions that correct misbeliefs and enhance awareness within communities. The challenge lies not just in demystifying mental health but in navigating a cultural landscape where supernatural explanations often take precedence over evidence-based understanding. Our insights highlight the importance of bridging the gap between cultural norms and evidence-based mental health education. By fostering a more informed perspective within the community, we aim to dismantle the barriers rooted in cultural norms and empower individuals to seek mental health support without the burden of supernatural stigma.

## SOCIOECONOMIC DISPARITIES: NAVIGATING THE UNEVEN TERRAIN OF MENTAL HEALTH CARE

The challenges of mental healthcare in Pakistan extend beyond cultural factors to include significant socioeconomic disparities. A shortage of specialized mental health units, a limited number of psychiatric professionals, and low awareness of available therapies contribute to delayed treatment (Javed et al., 2020; Ali et al., 2017). With only two to three psychiatrists per million people, the current ratio reflects a severe shortage of mental health providers (Javed et al., 2020). Javed et al. (2020) provide valuable insights into mental healthcare in Pakistan, emphasizing the need for increased investment in training programs and expanding mental health infrastructure. The Asian Development Bank's (ADB) report on poverty in Pakistan (ADB, 2021) further underscores the socioeconomic challenges that impede access to mental health services, highlighting the necessity for comprehensive reforms to address these disparities.

The uneven terrain of mental health care in Pakistan reflects a broader socioeconomic struggle, where vulnerable populations bear the brunt of limited resources and inadequate infrastructure. The scarcity of psychiatric professionals and treatment facilities exacerbates the already challenging landscape, leaving many without access to crucial mental health support. In crafting solutions, we explore the intersectionality of communal values, cultural norms, and socioeconomic factors. By providing a holistic understanding of mental health challenges in Pakistan, we aim to pave the way for transformative initiatives that dismantle stigma, demystify cultural perceptions, and address the socioeconomic disparities plaguing mental healthcare. In doing so, we envision a future where mental health is embraced with open arms, and seeking support is viewed as a courageous step toward holistic well-being.

In conclusion, our exploration of mental health barriers in Pakistani society unveils a complex interplay of communal values, cultural norms, and socioeconomic disparities. Communal values, deeply embedded in the societal fabric, shape perceptions and contribute to a pronounced stigma around mental health. Despite the challenges posed by psychiatric disorders, seeking help remains disproportionately low due to these communal values. Cultural norms, intricate and diverse, significantly contribute to societal attitudes toward mental health. False beliefs tied to supernatural phenomena create delays in mental health treatment. Bridging the gap between cultural norms and evidence-based mental health education is crucial for dismantling barriers and empowering individuals to seek support without the burden of supernatural stigma.

Socioeconomic disparities present significant challenges in mental healthcare. A shortage of specialized mental health units, psychiatric professionals, and low awareness of available therapies contribute to delayed treatment. The severe shortage of mental health providers exacerbates the already challenging landscape, leaving vulnerable populations without access to crucial mental health support. Our exploration paves the way for transformative initiatives that address stigma, demystify cultural perceptions, and rectify socioeconomic disparities. By providing a holistic understanding of mental health challenges in Pakistan, we strive for a future where mental health is embraced and seeking support is viewed as a courageous step toward holistic well-being.

## What People Say?

In Pakistan, cultural stigma weaves a complex narrative around mental health. Individuals seeking mental health services often grapple with the weight of societal expectations, leading to silence and isolation. A young woman, reflecting on her journey, shares,

> In our culture, mental health is seen as a weakness. When I sought help for anxiety, I felt judged and misunderstood.

Apart from this young woman, a lot of other people shared their experiences regarding the cultural resistance they faced:

> Growing up, mental health was never discussed openly in our family. Seeking therapy was considered a betrayal to our strong family image. When I finally sought help for my depression, I felt like I was breaking an unwritten rule.

> In our community, mental health issues are often dismissed as "just a phase." When my son started showing signs of anxiety, I hesitated to acknowledge it. The fear of judgment from extended family and neighbors held me back from seeking professional help.

> I come from a conservative background where mental health is associated with "madness." Opening up about my struggles with anxiety felt like admitting a personal failure. The fear of being ostracized kept me silent for years.

> As a professional, I feared the impact on my career if my struggle with bipolar disorder became public knowledge. The pressure to maintain a flawless image in our society made it incredibly challenging to seek the help I needed.

> In our community, mental health challenges are often attributed to a lack of religious faith. When I sought help for my anxiety, I faced resistance from my family, who believed that prayer alone could remedy the situation.

> Seeking therapy for my PTSD felt like admitting weakness in a culture that values resilience. The prevailing mindset that "strong people don't need help" hindered my ability to share my struggles with my community.

> As a Pakistani expatriate returning home, I found that mental health discussions were often hushed, especially within extended family circles. Sharing my experiences with anxiety was met with discomfort and avoidance.

The intersection of mental health and socioeconomic status creates formidable barriers. A middle-aged man recounts,

> I couldn't afford therapy, and mental health facilities are scarce in my neighborhood. The financial strain exacerbates the mental health challenges, creating a vicious cycle.

Further exploring the narratives of the general public regarding the socio-economic challenges, they shared:

> Being a daily wage laborer, affording mental health treatment seemed like a luxury. I had to prioritize putting food on the table over my mental well-being, perpetuating a cycle of distress.

> Living in a low-income neighborhood, mental health services were simply inaccessible. The cost of transportation to the nearest facility was often more than I could spare. It felt like the system was designed to exclude people like me.

> The economic downturn affected my family's financial stability. While grappling with increased stress, the inability to afford therapy became a harsh reality. Mental health care felt reserved for the privileged.

> In a society where mental health is not prioritized, insurance coverage for psychological services is rare. I found myself draining my savings to get the help I needed, pushing me further into financial turmoil.

> Living in a low-income neighborhood in Karachi, accessing mental health services was financially out of reach. The limited availability of affordable options exacerbated the challenges of addressing my mental health concerns.

> In the outskirts of Lahore, mental health facilities were scarce. The lack of government support and affordable clinics in rural areas made it difficult for me to access the necessary mental health care.

> Living in a small town, the cost of transportation to the nearest mental health clinic was a significant barrier. The financial burden of commuting became an additional obstacle to addressing my mental health needs.

## Impact of Gender Dynamics, Societal Expectations, and Family Structures in Pakistan

In the intricate tapestry of mental health challenges in Pakistan, an exploration of the role played by gender dynamics, societal expectations, and family structures is paramount. By extending our gaze beyond the individual to the broader societal and familial frameworks, we aim to illuminate the intersections of mental health with other social determinants, including poverty and education. Through this comprehensive lens, we seek to unravel the complex web of challenges faced by the Pakistani population in their mental health journeys.

## Gender Dynamics: Navigating Cultural Constructs

Gender dynamics in Pakistan are deeply entrenched in cultural constructs, influencing not only societal roles but also mental health perceptions. The prevailing expectations tied to masculinity and femininity create distinct pathways for how individuals navigate and express their mental health challenges.

### Impact on Mental Health Perception

In the context of mental health challenges, societal norms dictating acceptable behavior for men and women contribute to the stigmatization of certain mental health issues. A study conducted by Sokratis et al. (2004) highlighted that the presence of stigma acts as a formidable barrier, deterring numerous individuals grappling with mental illnesses from seeking the assistance they require. For instance, acknowledging vulnerability or seeking help may be perceived as a challenge to traditional gender roles, adding layers of complexity to mental health experiences.

Similarly, the study conducted by Kadri, Manoudi, Berrada, and Moussaoui (2004) observed that women, in particular, may face the weight of societal judgment concerning mental illness. This impact becomes evident in their potential for marriage, with an increased risk of divorce if their condition becomes public. The stigmatization of mental health issues becomes a significant hurdle for women, influencing their choices in seeking support and proper treatment. This societal attitude further complicates mental health experiences, where acknowledging vulnerability or seeking help can be perceived as a challenge to traditional gender roles.

## Societal Expectations: The Weight of Conformity

### Exploration of Prevailing Cultural Beliefs

Societal expectations, often rooted in cultural beliefs, play a significant role in shaping mental health narratives. The pressure to conform to societal norms and expectations can act as a substantial barrier, discouraging individuals from openly addressing their mental health concerns.

### Impact on Mental Health Attitudes

The stigma associated with mental health struggles is heightened when viewed through the lens of societal expectations. Fear of judgment and social ostracization may lead individuals to suppress their struggles, exacerbating the challenges associated with seeking help. In Pakistan, there is a common apprehension regarding privacy when it comes to seeking mental health care. This concern stems from the perceptions within their communities, with a prevailing fear that others may hesitate to marry into their families (Shafiq, 2020).

## Family Structures: The Crucible of Support or Strain

Family structures in Pakistan, characterized by close-knit bonds, wield considerable influence over an individual's mental health journey. While familial support can be a robust protective factor, strained family dynamics may contribute to the onset or exacerbation of mental health issues. In many developing countries, the narrative surrounding schizophrenia differs significantly from the frequent social challenges faced by individuals in the West, diminishing the likelihood of experiencing social defeat. This phenomenon is attributed to generally less harmful social conditions associated with the illness. Unlike Western perspectives, some interpretations in these regions view schizophrenia through non-medical lenses, conceiving it as a transient or even positive religious or spiritual encounter. Moreover, there is a notable trend of individuals returning to work after a psychotic episode, and community engagement remains high, often characterized by living with supportive families, marriage, and raising children.

However, it is crucial to acknowledge an opposing perspective. While close-knit family structures can provide significant support, there is a growing recognition that such structures may not always be conducive to optimal mental health outcomes. Close familial ties may inadvertently contribute to social pressures and expectations, intensifying the challenges associated with mental health. This perspective underscores the need for a nuanced understanding of the role of family structures in the mental health scenario. This observation aligns with the research conducted by Ahmad and Koncsol (2022) on cultural factors influencing mental health stigma, mainly focusing on the Perceptions of Mental Illness (POMI) among Pakistani adults.

## INTERSECTIONS WITH SOCIAL DETERMINANTS: POVERTY AND EDUCATION

The interplay of mental health with broader social determinants such as poverty and education adds layers of complexity. Limited access to resources, coupled with educational disparities, creates unique challenges that intersect with gender dynamics, societal expectations, and family structures.

The heightened exposure of impoverished communities to uncontrollable life events, such as the illness and demise of family members, job insecurity, and challenging work environments, significantly elevates their susceptibility to depression. A comprehensive study focusing on 260 women residing in a squatter settlement in Karachi revealed that approximately one in four women grappled with mental illness. Factors contributing to this mental health burden encompassed marital conflicts, the husband's unemployment, arguments with in-laws, the women's financial dependency, and a lack of autonomy in decision-making (Rabbani & Raja, 2000).

Living in conditions of poverty not only brings about economic challenges but can also be linked to a heightened risk of alcohol and drug abuse, as well as an increase in violent tendencies among men. The impact of education emerges as a potential catalyst in mitigating some of these societal issues. For instance, education plays a pivotal role in diminishing the likelihood of men engaging in abusive behavior toward their spouses or entering into multiple marriages. Moreover, empowerment through education extends to women, acting as a protective factor against mental distress. An illuminating example is drawn from a study conducted in Aleppo, Syria (Maziak et al., 2002). The research found that women who had completed twelve years of schooling were significantly less likely to experience mental distress compared to their illiterate counterparts. The likelihood of mental distress among Syrian women with a higher educational background was found to be only one-third of that among illiterate women (Maziak et al., 2002).

In the intricate landscape of mental health challenges in Pakistan, our exploration has unearthed the profound impact of gender dynamics, societal expectations, and family structures. Societal norms contribute to the stigma around mental health, deterring individuals from seeking assistance. Family structures, while offering support, can also pose challenges. Furthermore, the interplay with social determinants like poverty and education adds complexity. Poverty heightens susceptibility to mental health issues, while education emerges as a catalyst for resilience. Balancing familial support with recognizing potential strains deepens our understanding, emphasizing the need for nuanced approaches and comprehensive interventions in the pursuit of mental well-being.

### What People Say?

Gender dynamics play a pivotal role, influencing how mental health is perceived and addressed. A transgender individual reveals,

> As someone already marginalized, seeking mental health support adds another layer of vulnerability. Society expects us to be resilient, but we struggle like anyone else.

When the general public was reached to explore more about the resistance they face, they shared:

> As a woman, expressing vulnerability is often seen as a weakness. Seeking therapy for postpartum depression was met with judgment and raised eyebrows. Society expects mothers to be resilient without acknowledging their struggles.
>
> Gender norms dictate that men should be stoic and unyielding. Opening up about my battle with PTSD felt like a betrayal to my masculinity. The pressure to conform to these expectations hindered my journey to recovery.
>
> In our society, mental health issues are often trivialized as "women's problems." As a non-binary individual, finding acceptance and understanding for my struggles has been a constant battle against preconceived notions.
>
> As a Pakistani woman, discussing mental health issues was equated with airing family secrets. Seeking therapy for my postpartum depression was met with resistance, as the prevailing belief was that motherhood should be a source of joy.
>
> In a society where masculinity is associated with stoicism, my husband struggled to accept his anxiety. The societal expectations of men being the primary providers added an extra layer of pressure to cope silently.

Educational barriers compound the issue, limiting awareness and understanding. A university student expresses,

> In our textbooks, mental health is rarely discussed. There's a lack of awareness, and this ignorance perpetuates harmful stereotypes. It's challenging to seek help when you don't fully comprehend what you're facing.

Other members of general public also shared their thoughts on the barrier they faced:

> Growing up in Lahore, mental health education was conspicuously absent from our school curriculum. The lack of awareness contributed to the perpetuation of harmful stereotypes about mental health.

> As a university student in Multan, discussing mental health was considered a deviation from academic pursuits. The absence of awareness campaigns on campus made it challenging for students to recognize and address their mental health concerns.
>
> Being a teacher in a small town in Khyber Pakhtunkhwa, integrating mental health discussions into the classroom was met with resistance. The prevailing mindset prioritized academic achievements over the emotional well-being of students.
>
> In the educational landscape of Quetta, the lack of mental health resources on campus hindered my ability to access support. Recognizing my struggles and seeking help became a solo journey in an environment that overlooked mental health.
>
> As a teacher, addressing mental health in the classroom was met with resistance. The prevailing mindset is to prioritize academic achievements over the emotional well-being of students, perpetuating a harmful culture.

Family expectations can create internal struggles for those seeking help. A young professional shares:

> My family expects me to be resilient and strong. Opening up about mental health feels like admitting failure. Breaking this expectation is as challenging as confronting the mental health issue itself.

Further interviews explored the real-life struggles of the general community in seeking mental health because of family expectations:

> In our family, mental health discussions were considered taboo. Seeking therapy for my son's ADHD felt like challenging the family norms. The pressure to maintain an appearance of perfection added an extra layer of difficulty.
>
> Being the eldest son, my family expected me to be the pillar of strength. Acknowledging my battle with depression felt like I was betraying their expectations. The internal conflict added an extra layer of complexity to my journey.
>
> Our family values placed a strong emphasis on keeping personal struggles within the family. Opening up about my mental health issues felt like breaking an unspoken rule. The fear of disappointment and judgment was a significant barrier.

Being the eldest daughter in a family in Rawalpindi, there was a silent understanding that I should be a source of support. Opening up about my mental health challenges felt like challenging the traditional hierarchy within the family.

Growing up in a cosmopolitan family in Islamabad, mental health discussions were often dismissed as Western concepts. Admitting my struggles with PTSD felt like challenging the family's worldview and required navigating generational differences.

## STRATEGIES AND INTERVENTIONS TO ADDRESS MENTAL HEALTH CHALLENGES IN PAKISTAN

In navigating the complexities of mental health challenges in Pakistan, a proactive approach is vital. Our primary goal is to overcome these obstacles by raising awareness through targeted campaigns and workshops. Promoting research within academic institutions at both undergraduate and post-graduate levels is crucial. Increasing residency training programs is essential to strengthen mental health infrastructure. Opportunities for diplomas in mental health and specialized fellowships should be introduced to cultivate expertise. Allocating more budgetary resources to establish mental health care hospitals with dedicated units for various age groups is a critical step in enhancing mental health services (Javed et al., 2020). Continuing Education sessions, training programs, and certificate courses must be arranged for primary care providers and general physicians. Given that they often serve as the initial point of contact for individuals with mental health conditions, empowering them with the necessary knowledge and skills is paramount. Integrating screening for common mental illnesses into primary care programs designed for other health issues can streamline early detection. Recognizing the pivotal role of healthcare workers, efforts should be directed toward training them to identify symptoms of common mental illnesses. Equipping them to provide counseling, supportive psychotherapy, and manage psychosocial problems, particularly in remote and rural areas, can significantly broaden the reach of mental health support.

Collaboration with religious leaders and local community centers emerges as a promising avenue to encourage individuals to seek help for mental health concerns. By fostering alliances with influential figures in society, we can destigmatize mental health challenges and promote a more supportive environment. Furthermore, establishing mental health support groups for patients and caregivers can serve as a valuable resource. Non-Governmental Organizations (NGOs) working in underprivileged areas play a crucial role by providing free treatment and medications. A collaborative effort between healthcare providers and the government, grounded in a multi-disciplinary approach, is pivotal to overcoming challenges and optimizing care (Javed et al., 2020).

This comprehensive strategy not only enhances pathways to care but also refines treatment strategies, ultimately contributing to the attenuation of societal stigma surrounding mental health. By implementing these interventions collectively, we strive to usher in a transformative era where mental health is prioritized, understood, and supported within the diverse tapestry of Pakistani society.

The personal narratives of individuals who have navigated these interventions, shedding light on the diverse initiatives aimed at overcoming cultural, socioeconomic, gender-related, and educational obstacles:

> Participating in community-led mental health awareness programs in Lahore has been transformative. Learning about coping mechanisms and normalizing discussions around mental health has empowered me to support others facing similar challenges.

> Attending workshops in Karachi that aimed to destigmatize mental health struggles brought a positive change. The emphasis on education and open dialogue within the community helped break down barriers and encouraged seeking help.

> In Islamabad, community-driven campaigns have shifted perceptions. The inclusion of mental health education in local events has prompted conversations, fostering a more accepting environment for those grappling with mental health issues.

> Living in a remote area of Quetta, telemedicine has been a lifeline. Virtual consultations with mental health professionals have bridged the gap, providing much-needed support without the burden of travel.

> As a professional in Lahore, my workplace's mental health initiatives have been invaluable. Regular mindfulness sessions and employee assistance programs have created a supportive environment, emphasizing well-being alongside professional success.

> In a corporate setting in Islamabad, the implementation of mental health days has been a game-changer. Recognizing the importance of mental health in the workplace has enhanced the overall morale and productivity of the team.

> Working in Karachi, the availability of mental health resources at the workplace has positively impacted the work culture. The emphasis on work-life balance and mental health support has fostered a healthier and more compassionate environment.
>
> Benefiting from the services of nonprofit mental health organizations in Karachi has been a turning point. The commitment to providing affordable and accessible mental health care has been instrumental in my recovery.
>
> Living in Rawalpindi, the outreach programs of nonprofit mental health organizations have reached marginalized communities. The focus on inclusivity ensures that mental health support is extended to all, regardless of socio-economic background.

In confronting the intricate challenges of mental health in Pakistan, our proactive strategies converge on a multi-pronged approach. By amplifying awareness through targeted campaigns and fostering research at academic levels, we lay a foundation for informed action. Strengthening mental health infrastructure, empowering primary care providers, and engaging healthcare workers, especially in remote areas, widen the accessibility of support. Collaborative efforts with religious leaders and community centers destigmatize mental health, while support groups and NGO initiatives provide essential resources. This comprehensive strategy, anchored in a multi-disciplinary ethos, aspires to diminish societal stigma and usher in a transformative era of prioritized mental health support in Pakistani society.

## REFERENCES

Ahmad, S. S., & Koncsol, S. W. (2022). Cultural factors influencing mental health stigma: Perceptions of Mental Illness (POMI) in Pakistani emerging adults. *Religions, 13*(5), 401.

Ali, G., Lalani, N. S., & Charania, N. A. M. A. (2015). Community mental health initiatives in Pakistan. *Nursing Standard (2014+), 29*(22), 44.

Ali, N., McLachlan, N., Kanwar, S., & Randhawa, G. (2017). Pakistani young people's views on barriers to accessing mental health services. *International Journal of Culture and Mental Health, 10*(1), 33–43.

Asian Development Bank. (n.d.). Poverty in Pakistan. Retrieved from https://www.adb.org/where-we-work/pakistan/poverty.

Bhugra, D., & McKenzie, K. (2003). Expressed emotion across cultures. *Advances in Psychiatric treatment, 9*(5), 342–348.

Choudhry, F. R., Khan, N., & Munawar, K. (2021). Barriers and facilitators to mental health care: A systematic review in Pakistan. *International Journal of Mental Health, 52*(2), 124–162.

Ikram, A., Suhail, K., Jafery, S. Z., & Singh, S. (2011). Rates of expressed emotions in Pakistani relatives of patients with schizophrenia. *The Israel Journal of Psychiatry and Related Sciences*, *48*(2), 74–81.

Javed, A., Khan, M. N., Nasar, A., & Rasheed, A. (2020). Mental healthcare in Pakistan. *Taiwan Journal of Psychiatry, 34*, 6–14.

Kadri, N., Manoudi, F., Berrada, S., & Moussaoui, D. (2004). Stigma impact on Moroccan families of patients with schizophrenia. *The Canadian Journal of Psychiatry*, *49*(9), 625–629.

Khan, Q. U. A., & Sanober, A. (2016). "Jinn possession" and delirious mania in a Pakistani woman. *American Journal of Psychiatry, 173*(3), 219–220.

Maziak, W., Asfar, T., Mzayek, F., Fouad, F. M., & Kilzieh, N. (2002). Socio-demographic correlates of psychiatric morbidity among low-income women in Aleppo, Syria. *Social Science & Medicine*, *54*(9), 1419–1427.

Mirza, I., Mujtaba, M., Chaudhry, H., & Jenkins, R. (2006). Primary mental health care in rural Punjab, Pakistan: Providers, and user perspectives of the effectiveness of treatments. *Social Science & Medicine, 63*(3), 593–597.

Munawar, K., Abdul Khaiyom, J. H., Bokharey, I. Z., Park, M. S. A., & Choudhry, F. R. (2020). A systematic review of mental health literacy in Pakistan. *Asia-Pacific Psychiatry*, *12*(4), e12408.

PBS. (2023). *Press Release on Population*. Pakistan Bureau of Statistics. https://www.pbs.gov.pk/sites/default/files/population/2023/Press%20Release.pdf.

Rabbani, F., & Raja, F. F. (2000). The minds of mothers: Maternal mental health in an urban squatter settlement of Karachi. *Journal of the Pakistan Medical Association, 50*(9), 306–312.

Shafiq, S. (2020). Perceptions of Pakistani community toward their mental health problems: A systematic review. *Global Psychiatry, 3*(1), 28–50.

*Chapter 6*

# Contextual Correlates for the High Prevalence of HIV/AIDS at-Risk Behaviors in Transgender Community of Pakistan

Fahd Zulfiqar

The existing body of literature on male-female transgender persons in Pakistan covers a range of themes, from socio-economic discrimination, ostracization, violence, and HIV/AIDS. The intent of conducting current research was to explore the lives of male-female transgender persons in a way that connects their micro-narratives with the aforementioned themes. To explore this, a current study was conducted, theoretically grounded in transactional sexual relationships. Transactional relationships are essentially economic-based relationships in which one party instrumentalizes sex, sexual intimacy, and staged romantic love—all the factors that lead to securing cash, kind, and services from a man who plays a provider role. In the context of the current research, this man is called a *girya*, and the person who uses sex, sexual intimacy, and staged romance as instruments of securing finance, goods, and services is called a *khusra*[1] or a *zenana*[2]. The current study is about their relationship, socio-economic transactions, an instrumentality of love, and the actuality of HIV/AIDS at-risk behaviors between them and of *khusras* or *zenanas* and their clients.

The current methods include interviews and ethnographic techniques such as rapport building, participant observation, unstructured interviews, and focus group discussions. Data was analyzed using thematic analysis. The data for the current research was collected from three locales: Islamabad, Rawalpindi, and Kot Radha Kishan. Thirteen different sub-locales were selected from these locales, where respondents (*zenanas* and *khusras*) were sampled using purposive sampling. Data for the current research was collected from *zenanas*, *khusras*, *giryas*, social situations and events. For research ethics, original names have been replaced with pseudonyms. The data elicited from these units highlight the instrumentality of emotions, sex-for-money exchanges for basic needs and for raising social status, and financial security accrued from being in a steady or long-time relationship with a *girya*. The study shows that the instrumentality of emotion is typified by feigned romances, commodified expressions of love, and sexualized bodies, which work as an effective economic arrangement for *zenanas* and *khusras* but also create a space for them to negotiate, challenge, and question existing structures. The research highlights HIV/AIDS at-risk behaviors between *zenanas/khusras* and their *giryas*. Findings also suggest that in some cases, these relationships give power and agency to *zenanas* and *khusras* to practice safe sex, but this assertion does not hold for others, wherein sexual violence and unsafe sex are common occurrences. The study also highlights why it is important to have a cultural lens for HIV/AIDS intervention in Pakistan.

The current paper encapsulates the findings of HIV/AIDS at-risk behaviors and intends to respond to the research question on risky sexual practices. The chapter starts by explaining the risky sexual practices in general, especially for *khusras* and *zenanas* whose survival is dependent on *panpaisha* (prostitution). The chapter, furthermore, explains the sexual practices with a *girya*, the types of sexual acts performed in such relationships, the role of emotional proximity in sexual relationships with a *girya*, and the prevalence of violence in such relationships. The chapter concludes with a few findings detailing physical and oral violence as a precursor for sexual violence against the community and how that increases their vulnerabilities toward at-risk behaviors.

## ARE SEXUAL PRACTICES RISKY?

To elicit data on the sexual behaviors and practices of *khusras* and *zenanas* with their *giryas* and to explore how emotions of romance or feigned romance play out in describing the sexual relationships between them and their *giryas*, data related to risky sexual behaviors (in general) were elicited in individual interviews and focus group discussions. After having elicited data on such behaviors, more personalized questions on themes such as safe sex with *girya*, promiscuity of *giryas*, violence, sexual intercourse, romance and safe sex, and consensual, safe sex were asked.

## QUESTION OF SAFE SEX, IN GENERAL

Reema, an *uqwi guru* from Islamabad, asserts her take on the implausibility of safe sex for a *zenana* or a *khusra*. She explains that if a *moorat's*[3] single source of income is through prostitution, then how can she claim to have safe sex? She also comments on the sexual promiscuity of *khusras* and *zenanas* by explaining that if she wants to have safe sex, then she must have one man, not multiple ones, to be in these sexual relationships with.

[Verbatim]
*Reema:* Safe sex ko prostitute practice krty hai! Mjy to ye sawal herat zada kr rha hy! Prostitute to safe sex ko to ni na kr skti. Aik am insan ho, jis ne ek life partner rakha ho, woh already safe hy, safe sex kry gi. Ab jis ny din ke sou bndu se milna hy, wo safe kesay hy. Koe bnda din ky dus bees bandu ko mil rha ho aur kahay kehy bees bndu se safe sex kr rha ho . . . Agr usko safe sex krna hy to ek bndy se kry. Ek moorat jo bees bndu se mil rhy hay, usko safe sex ka nam kesay dia ja skta hy. Bees bndu ke sath woh kon si protection use key gi. Apko lgta hy keh bees bndu se milu aur phir bees bndu ke sath krny se pehly hath sanitize kru, phir usky kru, phir peechay se saf kru, phir krty hwe bhe usko kahu keh dekhay krty hwe phat na jae. Esa possible hy? Agr practically possible hy to bata dain mjy.

[Translated]
*Reema:* Prostitute will practice safe sex! REALLY! This question surprises me! A prostitute cannot have safe sex na! A person who has only one life partner is safe; she will have safe sex. The one who is promiscuous with a hundred men, how can she claim that she is safe? If she is sexually active with ten or twenty men per day and claims that she is having safe sex . . . she must be with one man if she wants safe sex. How can a woman be practising safe sex if she is active with twenty men per day? What protection can she practice with twenty men? Does it ring true to you if she is sanitizing herself and each one of [her customer's] hands, then she is cleaning herself from behind each time, then asks each client to make sure that [the condom] does not spill . . . Is it [all] possible? If it's practically possible then please illuminate me.

(Interview extract: Reema, 30, Islamabad)

Tina and Kajal, on the other hand, detailed during a focus group discussion conducted in Kot Radha Kishan, about various sexual acts they both perform. They both are vocal about sexual acts, but not many respondents were, including the ones I had developed close friendships with. Instead of vocal communication, they communicate meanings related to sexual acts through using their hands, fingers, mouths, lips, and tongues. For instance, encircling the first finger and thumb to make a circle shape, using the middle finger of the second hand, and inserting the middle finger into an encircled shape means anal sex is performed on a respondent. Broadening the palm of a hand and rubbing the middle finger of the second hand connotates a hand job performed by the respondent, and sucking a thumb means oral sex performed by a *zenana* or a *khusra*. In the excerpt below, Tina also shares that she plays an insertive role for her clients on demand. There is little negotiation power over safe sex and the choice of clients. Kajal, despite her dislike for older men, gives in sexually.

> [Verbatim]
> *Tina: Bund Marwa ky, bund maar ky, choopay wi landi aan. Fucking wi te sucking wi . . . Kajal: Gariyun walay choopay lagwaty hain. Me nahin lgati chupay, me sirf gand marwati hu, woh bhe majboori me. Munda sonrha lgy te free wi de dendi aan, babay menu zeher lgdy aan. Barhay umar de bandy zeher lgdy aan, unha nu me chunday mara . . .*
>
> [Translated]
> *Tina:* She gets inserted, she inserts, too, she gives blowjob too. Fucking and sucking, both.*Kajal:* The ones in cars are interested in oral sex. I don't give blowjobs; I am into anal sex only; that too when I am helpless. I give in when the man [client] is good-looking. I hate older men, and I wish to slap them.
>
> (Excerpt from Focus Group Discussion)

Most of the respondents from all the locales knew what HIV/AIDS was, how it can be transmitted, and how vulnerable *zenanas* and *khusras* are to the disease. They also knew that practising unsafe sex increases their vulnerability, but they could not afford to practice safe sex for three reasons. First, lack of negotiating power with clients over practising safe sex. Second, there is always another *zenana* or *khusra* who is ready to agree to unsafe sex because unsafe sex is preferred over safe sex by *chaamkay*[4] and *tamashbeen.*[5] Thirdly, insistence on safe sex led to sexual and physical violence against *zenanas* and *khusras* by their *chaamkay* and *tamashbeen.*

## QUESTION OF SAFE SEX, WITH GIRYA

The data presented so far is related to risky sexual acts and behaviors performed between the respondents and their *chaamkay* and *tamashbeen*. When leading and probing questions related to sexual intimacy, relational dynamics, sexual acts, and violence in *khusra/girya* relationships were asked, the respondents came up with the following replies.

Rano, for instance, cannot think of having safe sex with her *girya*. She found him at a dance function at a *mela* in a village. Since then, she has been in a relationship with him. She is in love; he loves her too, as she claims. It's a sixteen-year-long relationship, and she finds, in him a good, mature husband with whom practicing safe sex is out of the question, as she says during an interview:

> [Verbatim]
> *Rano: Jo paka dosy hai, uske sath nahin krty.*
>
> [Translated]
> *Rano:* [*I*] don't use [*condom*] with my man.
>
> (Interview extract: Rano, 23, Islamabad)

The issue arises when the same man who is married to a woman is also sexually active with other female sex workers. Rano herself practices unsafe sex with other men who come to her *dera* (a household unit of transgender persons) for *panpaisha.* In this way, risky sexual behavior increases the susceptibility of catching or transmitting sexually transmissible diseases such as syphilis and gonorrhea among risky groups, including transgender and female sex workers through their *giryas*.

Going in-depth about finding an articulation between *panpaisha* as a form of economic organization and sexual violence by a *girya*, Zamurat shared that her sexual promiscuity with other men is the only way for her survival, due to which her *girya* rapes her. This implies not only unsafe and condomless sex but also forced sex, which takes place alongside physical violence. Her *girya* also visits female sex workers, is married to a woman, and has three children. The *girya*, in this case, can become a transmitter of disease among two at-risk groups: transgender and female sex workers. He can also become a carrier of disease from these at-risk groups to a wider population by transmitting it to his wife and maybe to his children.

> [Verbatim]
> *Zamurat: O menu kharcha kurcha nahin denda, te me marwa lendi aan. Tey mera mard menu torda wi ay.*
>
> [Translated]
> *Zamurat:* Since he doesn't provide for me, I earn through prostitution [she performs unsafe anal intercourse]. In anger, my man rapes me.
>
> (Interview extract: Zamurat, 19, Mansehra)

Pinky, while commenting on a *girya* of her *shoormi saheli* (sisterly friend), also highlighted the commonality of forced sex in such relationships.

> [Verbatim]
> *Pinky:* Baji iss da honda girya tey iss da kut bharya janda si uj. Adi wi la lenrhi si. Hae wi painrha ki kalam wajun lagi saday ghar. Ay tey lotraan di moorat ay, parhi parhae.
>
> [Translated]
> *Pinky:* Baji, if her girya was here, he would have coerced her into sex. He would have penetrated her anally. Hae wi! What have you come to talk to us about? This seems to be an untouched moorat [and] learned, as well.
>
> (Interview extract: Pinky, 19, Rawalpindi)

Kaanchi's and Maira's conversation during an informal conversation highlights a few important points. First, it speaks of clientele expectations of sexual acts, which are not always about *zenanas* and *khusras* performing a passive sexual act in sexual intercourse. As Kaanchi details in the text below, the whole Twin City is full of men, irrespective of white-collar or student status, or those residing in domesticated or hostel settings, who want to be inserted. Switching this conversation to her *girya*, Maira explains her relational association. She is no longer in a relationship with him. She used to provide for him because she loved him. After breaking up with him, she is in love with a new *girya* (a policeman), to whom she gives fifteen thousand rupees each month. This conversation also speaks of the unfaithfulness of *giryas*. Many *zenanas* and *khusras* claimed that given a choice, they would not want to have multiple sexual partners. It is due to poverty and hunger that they must resort to *panpaisha* for survival. Giryas, on the other hand, are unfaithful, insatiable, and promiscuous. Kaanchi, in the text below, narrates that once, he forced her into sex because she refrained from paying extortion money. He left her bleeding. The last comment by Maira, "*khula khata*"[6] connotes the wideness of the anal hole and lack of pain due to multiple coerced sexual encounters.

> [Verbatim]
> *Kaanchi: Pura Islamabad Pindi gaanduu se barha parha hy. kia hostel, kia student, kia job walay, sab gaandu hain.*
>
> *Maira: Hae hwe the.*

*Kaanchi: Ek paka banda rakhya si, paka girya rakhya si.*

*Maira: Ek paka banda rakhya si, unhu me hi khawandi si. Wo Lahore ka tha. Ek idhar hy, police wala hy. usko maheeny ka dus pandra hazar bhe dete hu.*

*Kaanchi: Han han ye dete hy usko maheenay ka. Ek bar me paisahy pe the iska banda mjy utha ke le gaya. Mujhay esay choda, khoon o khoon hogae.*

*Maira: Ja way khoon o khoon, ithay tey khulay khatay aan.*

[Tranlated]
*Kaanchi:* The whole of Islamabad and Pindi is full of those who like to be inserted, including hostels, students, white collars, name anyone, all are *gandu.*[7]

*Maira:* Yes, I fell in love, once.

*Kaanchi:* I once fell for a man, he was my *paka girya.*

*Maira:* Yes, I once had a *paka girya*, I used to provide him. He was from Lahore. Now, I have one in Islamabad, he is a police officer. I give him ten fifteen thousand on a monthly basis.

*Kaanchi:* Yes, yes, she provides for him every month. One day when I was out for *paisha* his man forced me into sex, I was in blood after that encounter.

*Maira: Ja way* [go away], in blood! Her hole is wide open due to promiscuous sex.

(An extract from Focus Group Discussion)

Deedar, a *nirban* from Rawalpindi, describes the types of sexual acts she performs to her clientele. She also expresses how her body after undergoing multiple operations and surviving through many incidents of forced sex has become void of pain. The commonality of sexual violence is a recurrent narrative in her response, too.

[Verbatim]
*Deedar: Me char char companiyan dete hu. Ek idhar ikhatay kar ky, ek mu me, ek peechay, ek kus me.*

*Me: Dard nahin hota?*

*Deedar: Mujay koe dard nahin hota. Dard mere jism se urh gaya hy. Mujhay koe maray bhe to dard nahin hota. Gosht me gosht gaya to kia dard hoga, tum khud samjhdar ho. Mere me se dardy wurday khatam hogae hain. Zulm itny logu ne kye hain. Mujhay chuk ke le gae se, wah wah bunday tup gae si.*

[Translated]
*Deedar:* I can take in four men at a point in time. One man between the boobs, one from the ass, one in *chuchee* [the hole which appears after castration].

Me: Is it painful?

*Deedar:* I don't feel any pain. My body has become void of pain, now. I feel no pain even if I am beaten up. Sex is just like meat inserted into another meat, what is pain to do with it? You can surely understand that! I feel no pain. My body has borne so much pain. Many times, I am brutally forced into sex, and I have been raped multiple times.

(Interview extract: Deedar, 33, Rawalpindi)

## VIOLENCE: A PRECURSOR

The following excerpt is a conversation between Gori, her *saheli*[8] Mishi, and me. The conversation sparked a series of incidents from Gori's life. The incidents explain physical and sexual violence exercised against her by eight men who wanted her to sexually give in. Upon refusal, they not only chased her and cut her hair but also gang-raped her. Toward the end of the conversation, the respondent also shared that in addition to perpetuating physical and sexual violence against them, *zenanas* and *khusras* are also robbed. Hence, violence in its physical (chopping off hair), sexual (gang-rape), oral (oral abuse), and existential (violence because of a feminized identity) forms is practised against the community members.

[Verbatim]
*Me:* Koe badtameezi karta hy?

*Gori:* To ki hay na mere sath. Jab me function pe gae the.

Me: Kahan gae thee?

*Gori:* Lahore me.

Me: Phir?

*Gori:* Han. Mere bal kat dye function pe.

Me: Kiyun katay. Wajah kia the?

*Gori:* Function pe wo kehtay the, do. Sath aath janay the. Me ny kahan nahin. Me bhag gae. Unhu ne pakar lia.

Me: Phir? Bal kat dye?

*Gori:* Hmm. Wo dikhana meri tasveer.

[Her saheli gave her the photo frame]

*Gori:* Ye dekho.

Me: Bal kiyun katty hain?

Gori's saheli: Bal kat detay hain na.

*Gori:* Han han, functionu pe. Wo kehty hain, Idhar ao, choday tumhy. Kehty hain pura dalay gain.

*Mishi (Gori's saheli):* Sab se barhi kamzori to yehe hai na, bal.

*Gori:* Sab se barhi kamzori hay.

Me: Dobara a jae gy na.

*Gori:* A to jae gy, par ab kesay ae gay. Itni dair bad ae gy, ab me kia karu. Ab bus esay night dress pehan ke soti hu bas. Pehly bal the na to function wagera kar sakti the na.

Me: Ab bhe kar skteen hain na?

*Gori:* Ab kesay?

Me: Bal bahut zaruri hotay hain?

*Gori:* Han na. Ab kesay ghumao. Wig to utar jae gy phir.

Me: Unhu ne puray kat dye the bal?

*Gori:* Han na, meny thapar mara tha. Me bhag gae the. Lekin pakarh lia. Lahore ke qareeb gao tha. Pakarh ke le gae. Agay kutty, peechay mard.

*Mishi (Gori's saheli):* Kabhi do, kabhi teen. Pesay bhe cheen lety hain. Mobile bhe cheen lety hain. Martay hain. Jiyazti kartay hain.

[Translated]
*Me:* Do men misbehave?

*Gori:* Yes, they did. They misbehaved with me when I went to a function.

Me: Where did you go?

*Gori:* In Lahore.

Me: Then?

*Gori:* Yes, they forcefully cut my hair short.

Me: Why did they cut off? What was the reason?

*Gori:* They asked me to give in sexually at the function. There were seven, eight of them. I refused and tried to run, but they still found me.

Me: Then?

*Gori:* What then? They raped me.

Me: They also cut your hair?

*Gori:* Hmm. Give me that photo frame.

[Her saheli gave her the photo frame]

*Gori:* Look at this.

Me: Why do they cut hair?

Gori's saheli: They cut hair, na. It's common.

*Gori:* Yes yes, especially at functions. They expect us to comply to their sexual demands.

*Mishi (Gori's saheli):* Our biggest weakness is our hair.

*Gori:* The biggest weakness.

Me: They will grow again na.

*Gori:* They will, eventually but how will they? It is going to take a lot of time! What will I do till then? Now, these days I only sleep at night while wearing night dresses. I used to perform functions na when I had hair.

Me: You can still do na?

*Gori:* How?

Me: Is hair this important?

*Gori:* Absolutely *na*, how will I swirl my head now? The wig doesn't stay longer.

Me: Did they chop all your hair off?

*Gori:* Yes, I slapped one of them. I tried to run away but they found me. It was a village in the vicinity of Lahore. [They] took me to a dingy area. There were dogs ahead, and men behind.

*Mishi (Gori's saheli):* Sometimes two, sometimes three. They steal money from us. They also steal our mobile phones. They beat us. They rape us.

A similar view is shared by Katrina. She showed me the empty buildings and unvisited parks where men force *zenanas* and *khusras* into coerced sexual violence. When she was inquired about the possibility of safety measures, she responded with negation, stating that many among them are gang-raped by alcoholic men. It is very difficult to escape from such men. The interview extract is described in the text below.

[Verbatim]
*Katrina: Aur idhar mar peet bhe ziada hay. Le jatay side pe. Jhoot bol ke le gae hain. Humay leja ke martay hain. Hamaray pas jo bhe cheezain hain, pesay hain, mobile hain, woh bhe cheen letay hain. Jitnay banday hain woh ziaditi bhe karain gain. Kar ky phir kapru ke beghair hi bahir nikal de gain ya mar de gain.*

Me: *Aur koe hifazit?/*

*Katrina: / Kia honi hay. Ek idara tha. Wahan se latay the aur ek medical store hay wahan pe adhi qeemat par baich detay hain.*

[Translated]
*Katrina:* Violence is very common here. They forcefully take us to deserted areas. They trick us and take us to some deserted places. They beat us, they snatch things such as money and mobile from us. They take turns and rape us. After getting done, they throw us bare-bodied in an open space or will kill us.

Me: Any safety measures?

*Katrina:* What is there? Nothing. There was one center. They used to secure condoms from there and sell them in a nearby medical store at half price.

(Interview extract: Katrina, 30, Kot Radha Kishan)

Rekha also details one violent incident she experienced in Islamabad. The experience explains how duress and captivity create an extreme sense of fear. Physical violence in situations like these results in sexual violence and gang-rape. Such incidents of physical violence, threat, duress, and sexual violence by strangers were cited by respondents from other locales as well.

[Verbatim]
*Rekha:* Kaheen banday esay hotay hain jo galiyan detay hain. Bakwas karty hain. Kuch din pehlay ki bat hay. Hum donu tayar hoke nikleen theen. Ye bahut pyari lag rahi the, mujhay bhe ek larki ne bola aj tu into pyari lag rhy hay, utha lena hay tujay kisi ne. Esa hi hwa. Ye kam pe chali gae. Me ghar se wapas a rhy the. Mujhay bandu ne pakar lia. Kehty lay ke jae gy aj. Me ny kaha nahin jao gi. Do pathan mard the. F11 ke pas jungle sa hy wahan le gae. Ek ne kaha tujhay karu ga, me ny kaha chalo tum kar lo. Woh kehta dusra pesa de ga. Meny kaha

chal koe nahin tu de ya who de pese ek hi bat hay. woh ker ke gaya aur dusra aya. Kehta kry ga tujhy. Me ny kaha kar par pese de. Kehta hy me pathan hu, zaban ka paka hu. Usny kia. Me ny pese mangy to us ny pistol nikal li. Me ne kaha yar tu jo kuch krna chahta hy kr, bas mujhay mar na. Mere kapre phar de, mere kapre utar day, bas ye kam na kar. Usny jatay hwe mujhay kaha tum ye bees rupay rakh lo. Me ny usko dye aur kaha tum ye bhe rakh lo. Tumhary kisi kam ae gy. Mere us din koe kamae nahin hwe. Istarah bhe hota hay.

[Translated]
*Rekha:* Some men orally abuse us and call us with names. I will tell you what happened to me a few days ago. Both left home after getting ready. She looked gorgeous. On our way, one girl remarked, "You are looking so pretty today, you will be picked up today." This is exactly what happened that day. She went for *panpaisha*. I was on my way back to *dera* when two men blocked my way who wanted to pick me up. I told them that I wouldn't go with them. They were Pathan [one of the ethnicities in Pakistan] men. Using force on me, they took me to a jungle in F-11 [one of the sectors located in Islamabad]. One man said that he wanted to do me, and I replied to him to do it. He said I would be paid by the second one. I said that it was okay, as it would make no difference if he paid, or the other person did. After getting done, the second one came. He demanded the same. I asked him to pay me first. He said that he surely would as he is a Pathan and would never retract his words. After he got done with me, I demanded money to which he took his pistol out and pointed at me. I pleaded with him to not kill me, and he could do anything to me he wanted except kill me . . . he could tear my clothes, and he could take my clothes off. Whatever he wants. While leaving, he gave me a twenty rupee note. I handed those back to him and said, "These may be of some use to you! You keep it!." I did not earn a single rupee that day. Incidents like these are very common.(Interview extract: Rekha, 32, Islamabad)

Meher, again, speaks of physical violence in the excerpt below but exercised by her *girya* rather than by a stranger. Her *girya* once broke a water glass after getting drunk, which left a lifelong scar on her forehead. The scars left by cigarette burns on her chest, arms, and shoulders also haunt her of the ways he used to exercise violence on her. Eventually, she left him and the city of Lahore. The details are in the extract from an interview below.

[Verbatim]
*Meher:* Pyar kia hy yar. Hamari zindagi me agar wo bhe na ho to kia reh jata hy peechay. Me ny usay chorh dia tha. Jab us ny sharan peeni shuru kar di the. Marta tha sab kuch karta tha, mere chehry pe ye dekho Nishan uski wajah se hain. Ek din sharab pe ky itni ki mar pitae, mere sir par glass torh dia. Usi se pyar tha. Usky bad bus dillagi ki hy. Pyar nahin kia. Pyar bas ek bar hi hota hay.

> [Translated]
> *Meher:* I did fall in love *yar*. What else is left if we don't have a man in our lives? I left him since the time he started consuming alcohol. He used to beat me. Look at my face, all these scars are because of him. One day after getting drunk he beat me black and blue and broke a glass on my head. I loved him. After him, I haven't fallen in love, had been in temporary relationships but not love. Love happens once in a lifetime.
>
> (Interview extract: Meher, 20, Rawalpindi)

## CONCLUSION

The term MSM (Men who have Sex with Men) is used as an umbrella term for different communities throughout the world. The categorization of MSM into groups is important because it is within these groups that some are more vulnerable to HIV/AIDS than others with different causal factors. The Western world defines MSM in a way quite different from the non-Western world. The former, for the most part, is biologically framed and associates less with various social, familial, and institutional factors while defining MSM. Whereas in the latter, these features become more pronounced because the rise in HIV/AIDS is alleged to be intensely critical, particularly to MSM in the non-Western world.

Similar groups may exist with different names elsewhere in Western and non-Western countries. There has always been much controversy in defining MSM because it is not simply the bodily mannerisms and physical attributes that outrightly define MSM. For Chinese men, living as MSM is to decide between their own sexual identities and their familial and social obligations (getting married and producing children) (Zhou, 2006). Social scientists in the non-Western world view the Western take on MSM and homosexuality, in general, as technocratic and limited in scope due to the lack of societal norms and traditional values embedded in it (Zhou, 2006). Perhaps that is the reason that whenever MSM is defined from an "Asian" perspective, the "local" meaning is given prime importance (Zhou, 2006). In Asia, the definition of masculinity is not just associated with sexual behavior that defines sexual identity. Rather, it goes beyond, encapsulating diverse factors such as race, color, religion, and society. In Vietnam, a male may not be defined as MSM if he fulfills the socially constructed gender roles, although he has sexual links with other men (Bengtsson et al., 2013). Similarly, in Afghanistan, old men having insertive sexual intercourse with adolescent boys are considered real men (Naz Foundation International, 2008). In Vietnam, the men having sexual links with other men differ in their self-assertiveness of sexual identities ("*bonglo*" and "*bongkin*" both in sexual links with other men, both performing anal and insertive sexual roles interchangeably, but the former prefers to be more feminine in bodily mannerisms, whereas the latter may be married with children but tries to hide his male sexual preferences) (Ngo et al., 2009).

This chapter has defined MSM as a behavioral term, but the attempt is not to homogenize the population or to ignore the local contexts, sensibilities, and realities that shape sexualities. Local vernaculars of "*hijras*" in Pakistan and Bangladesh (Chan & Khan, 2007; Rajabali et al., 2008), "*alis*" in India (F.Go et al., 2004), or "*chungton*" in China (Zhou, 2006) may not completely fit into the Western construct of transsexuals, similarly *zenana* in Pakistan (Rajabali et al., 2008), "*kothi*" in Bangladesh (Chan & Khan, 2007) and India (F.Go et al., 2004), "*ponaya*" in Sri Lanka (Aggleton, 1999), or "*shuanxinglian*" in China (Zhou, 2006) may not fit into the construct of transgenderists. Khan in Aggleton (1999) defines "*kothi*" and "*panthi*" of Dhaka (Bangladesh) both as homosexually active people, but the former as feminine practicing anal intercourse with "*panthi*" and later as masculine practicing insertive intercourse with "*kothi.*" Involvement of "*kothi*" in sex work is driven by their poor socioeconomic status, but sexuality also plays an important role in becoming sex workers. In Thai gay bar culture, the complexity of multiple sexualities, whether "self-identified as gay or not," is documented in the literature. Those who self-identify as gays are more feminine than those who either do not identify or identify with certain resistance to their bi- or homosexuality. In Morocco, on the other hand, gigolos, despite having same-sex preferences, are not explicit in their self-identification as gays because of the taboo and homophobia linked to homosexuality. Among those are also included masculine gigolos who do not have to compromise on their masculinity as most of the clients (male/female) are passive (Aggleton, 1999). Contrary to gigolos are "prostitutes homosexuals" who are feminine and who, after running from their hostile social surroundings and families, became sex workers as a survival strategy.

Condom use among marginalized communities of MSM and FSWs (Female Sex Workers) can lead to a substantial fall in HIV/AIDS. However, current literature in developing countries poses a very relevant question of whether low condom use is a sufficient condition for high HIV prevalence. In Sub-Saharan African countries, HIV/AIDS transmission continues to persist despite high rates of condom use (Hearst & Chen, 2004). The transmission rates could have gone even higher without the use of condoms, but strictly resorting to high HIV prevalence to low condom use seems spurious, and there may be other influential factors to explain huge HIV prevalence despite high condom use in developing countries. The question of whether a condom is used consistently or not is very effectively posed by the current literature. The impact of inconsistent condom use on HIV prevalence is causing a rise in epidemic than no condom use. Interestingly, among MSM, low condom use is a sign of commitment and love, especially among those who are in emotional relationships with other people (Hearst & Chen, 2004). The *tongzhi* study by Zhou (2006) reveals that among cohabitating MSM, the need to use a condom by one partner is often regarded as a sign of distrust and less affection by the other partner. Similarly, the elements of "faithfulness and love" were recorded in a qualitative study conducted on Vietnamese MSM (Bengtsson et al., 2013). The study confirms that condom use becomes more implausible in love-based relationships with "steady partners" than with "casual partners." Research exposes that it is not always the stigma against these groups that limits their access to HIV/AIDS control programs or seeks information for reducing risky sexual behaviors; rather, it could be the personal choice among these groups to indulge in risky sexual behaviors through minimum condom use. In light of these important findings, it becomes important to assess whether condom use is always high (low) with casual partners or low (high) with steady partners and whether transmission is speedy through low condom use among casual partners or steady partners. A study on Chinese student MSM indicates that despite the provision of free HIV/AIDS-related information, accessibility to condoms, and acquisition of HIV/AIDS knowledge, MSM students practiced unprotected receptive intercourse with their "regular" (steady or non-casual) partners (Xu et al., 2011).

The project funded by the HIV Prevention Trials Network (HPTN) and conducted by the University of North Carolina (2012) analyzed the risky sexual behaviors among straight and gay African, Asian, North, and South American couples over six years. In each of the couples, one partner was infected, and the other was not infected. The research study, other than providing HIV testing, counseling, and analyzing sexual behaviors, also provided condoms, regular medical check-ups with proper confidentiality so that information did not leak out, and provided expensive HAART. Even after providing such coping mechanisms to control the cross-exchange of HIV/AIDS, twenty-eight cases of cross-exchange were reported. The reason was attributed to unprotected intercourse, due to which the other partners got infected. Among the causes of HIV/AIDS discussed previously, the lesser use of condoms among intimate partners or regular customers (for reasons varying from love and commitment) may not always strongly relate to stigma. As the study conducted by HPTN indicates, despite the provision of every possible treatment and information, the cross-exchange took place not due to stigma that constricted the infected people from getting medical assistance but due to unchanged risky sexual behaviors.

The study calls for the attention of two very important aspects. First, the importance of conducting time series rather than survey-based studies, especially when behavioral changes are to be introspected for better healthcare-related programmatic strategies in Asia and MENA. Secondly, due to a lack of data on cohabitating MSM partners in Pakistan, India, Nepal, Bangladesh, and MENA, such cross-HIV exchange research could never have been conducted in the past; also to what extent have love and personal choice have accounted for risky sexual behaviors among cohabitating MSM could never be researched upon.

Based on the literature on locating and identifying contextual correlates of high HIV/AIDS at-risk behaviors, as highlighted in the preceding text, the current research has detailed that unsafe sex is practiced with and by both strangers and *giryas*. Their male clientele are sexually active with other female sex workers and transgender sex workers. The situation is not different for *giryas*, as well; *giryas'* sexual promiscuity with female sex workers works as an intermediary of disease carrier between the two at-risk groups (transgender and female sex workers). The data also show that not only do *giryas* prefer unsafe sex, but the *khusras* and *zenanas* find practicing safe sex condescending to their *giryas*. For them, a wife cannot use a condom with her husband. I heard this anomaly many times during focus group discussions. The *giryas* are also sexually violent toward their *khusra* or *zenana* lovers, a situation which is not very different from experiencing sexual violence from a stranger as in both situations; safe sex is out of the question. Respondents also quoted excessive consumption of alcohol by violent male clientele, which compromised the decision of safe sex. A few respondents also cited greater consumption of alcohol before going for *panpaisha* because it aids in reducing the pain of unsafe anal intercourse.

## NOTES

1. Includes *nirban*—a castrated male-female transgender person who may also undergo injection of estrogen or breast enlargement or implant surgeries.
2. Includes *uqwi*- a feminized man who hasn't brought about any change in the physical attributes such as castration, injecting estrogen, or breast enlargement surgeries.
3. An umbrella term is used for male-female transgender persons in Pakistan.
4. Men who visit *zenanas* and *khusras* as regular clients.
5. Spectators who attend the events in which *zenanas* and *khusras* dance
6. Lexicographical meanings imply something which is open for public use and consumption
7. A derogatory slang in Punjabi language for a faggot.
8. A transgender friend.

## REFERENCES

Aggleton, P. (Ed.). (1999). *Men who sell sex: International perspectives on male prostitution and HIV/AIDS*. Temple University Press.

Bengtsson, L., Thorson, A., Thanh, V. P. N., Allebeck, P., & Popenoe, R. (2013). Sexual relationships among men who have sex with men in Hanoi, Vietnam: A qualitative interview study. *BMC Public Health*, *13*, 1–7.

Chan, P. A., & Khan, O. A. (2007). Risk factors for HIV infection in males who have sex with males (MSM) in Bangladesh. *BMC Public Health*, *7*, 1–8.

Hearst, N., & Chen, S. (2004). Condom promotion for AIDS prevention in the developing world:is it working?. *Studies in family planning*, *35*(1), 39–47.

Ngo, D. A., Ross, M. W., Phan, H., Ratliff, E. A., Trinh, T., & Sherburne, L. (2009). Male homosexual identities, relationships, and practices among young men who have sex with men in Vietnam: Implications for HIV prevention. *AIDS Education and Prevention*, *21*(3), 251–265.

Rajabali, A., Khan, S., Warraich, H. J., Khanani, M. R., & Ali, S. H. (2008). HIV and homosexuality in Pakistan. *The Lancet Infectious Diseases*, *8*(8), 511–515.

Xu, J. J., Reilly, K. H., Lu, C. M., Ma, N., Zhang, M., Chu, Z. X., . . . & Shang, H. (2011). A cross-sectional study of HIV and syphilis infections among male students who have sex with men (MSM) in northeast China: Implications for implementing HIV screening and intervention programs. *BMC Public Health*, *11*(1), 1–8.

Zhou, Y. R. (2006). Homosexuality, seropositivity, and family obligations: Perspectives of HIV-infected men who have sex with men in China. *Culture, Health & Sexuality*, *8*(6), 487–500.

*Section III*

# EMERGING CHALLENGES AND HEALTHCARE RESPONSE

*Chapter 7*

# Understanding the Sehat Sahulat Program

## *Insights from Public and Private Healthcare Providers in Pakistan*

Sumaira Yasmin and Hafsa Hina

Due to recent healthcare reforms, Pakistan has introduced social health insurance (SHI) through the Sehat Sahulat Program (SSP) to achieve universal health coverage (UHC). The program aims to provide cost-free healthcare to the economically disadvantaged, preventing them from falling below the poverty line due to excessive healthcare expenses (PIDE, 2021). Government spending on healthcare in Pakistan is low, at US$14 per citizen annually, well below the recommended threshold of US$86 per capita by the International Task Force (Mirza, 2022). The resultant high out-of-pocket expenditure (OOP) reaches around 60 percent, with 73 percent on outpatient and 20 percent on inpatient services, the majority of which is in the private sector (Pakistan Bureau of Statistics, 2021). In response to this alarming situation, the SSP was initiated as a significant public-private partnership, assigning the State Life Insurance Corporation (SLIC) responsibility for health benefit packages through an auction that empaneled public and private hospitals (Mirza, 2022). Global trends highlight the necessity of effective private-sector involvement in SHI for achieving UHC (Sieverding et al., 2018).

The success of SHI depends on the prudent design of the health financing mechanism, particularly in purchasing and pooling (Carrin & James, 2004). Provider accreditation, a result of purchasing decisions, is crucial for including public and private providers (McIntyre, 2007). Through strategic purchasing, the provider payment method (PPM) can incentivize improvements in quality, efficiency, and health service utilization (Phuong et al., 2015). However, issues arise in SHI schemes, such as delays in reimbursement, impacting provider performance to run the hospital in a negative way, and also causing changes in provider practices (Ogbuabor & Onwujekwe, 2018). Administrative challenges and unclear communication lines also lead to reluctance among private providers to participate in SHI (Obadha et al., 2019).

Despite the Sehat Sahulat Program's significant public-private partnership, only 800 hospitals got empanelment out of 1979 hospitals (International Trade Administration, 2022). This can further lead to persistence in challenges of bed capacity, healthcare accessibility, and out-of-pocket expenditure removal, which pose challenges to extending the program for universal healthcare. Understanding providers' perspectives on accreditation processes, requirements, incentives, and payment rates is crucial to overcoming these challenges and achieving UHC.

The observed discrepancy reveals that out of 1979 hospitals, only 800 public and private institutions have attained empanelment status (International Trade Administration, 2022). This situation presents challenges concerning bed capacity, accessibility, and eliminating out-of-pocket expenditures. Furthermore, it imposes constraints on the program's expansion to cover the entire population to achieve universal healthcare milestones (UHC). Concurrently, global literature underscores that the challenges faced by providers can adversely affect their engagement in social health insurance. Consequently, it is essential to comprehend providers' perspectives in both sectors regarding the obstacles in the inclusion process, focusing on accreditation procedures, requirements, incentive payment methods, and payment rates.

The research aims to explore the perspectives of public and private providers concerning their participation in the social health insurance scheme. The investigation delves into the factors influencing private providers' decisions on seeking accreditation within the social health insurance scheme. Additionally, it seeks insights into the experiences of private providers with the accreditation process and the SHI scheme, addressing challenges related to provider payment mechanisms.

## SALIENT FEATURES OF THE SEHAT SAHULAT PROGRAM SCHEME

### Enrollment Process

The Pakistan Social Health Insurance program was launched in December 2015 with the assistance of Pakistan's federal and provincial governments. This is the first step in the government's national vision to ensure universal indoor health coverage. Initially, the eligibility criteria were limited to the indigent group, whose poverty status was determined through the Benazir socioeconomic registry through NADRA (Mirza, 2021). However, later on, it was decided to expand its coverage to the whole of Pakistan without considering the socioeconomic strata of the population. Until now, the program has been launched in Islamabad capital territory (ICT), Azad Jammu and Kashmir (AJK), Gilgit–Baltistan, Khyber Pakhtunkhwa (KPK), Tharparkar-Sindh, and Punjab. So far, this program has benefitted 20 million families and entertained 6 million indoor patients, providing cost-free health services under its Sehat Qaumi Insaf Card (State Health., n.d.).

### Benefits of Sehat Sahulat Program

Under the Sehat Sahulat program, the beneficiaries are entitled to hospitalization for primary and secondary disease packages. The benefits packages under primary disease treatment packages included heart diseases, diabetes, end-stage kidney dialysis, chronic infection, all medical and surgical procedures, and cancer chemotherapy with initial coverage of 300,000 per family. However, for secondary packages, emergency cases required admission, and all maternity services, including C-sections and normal delivery, under the limit of 60,000 per family, were approved on a per-annum basis (PM Health Program, 2021). This scheme covered the upper limit for cardholders up to 720,000 annually, which can be topped up in case the patient suffers from any major disease. The ongoing treatment also could not be discontinued based on the insurance exhaustion limit, but the government will provide a further 360,000 in such cases (Bolo., n.d.). In addition to these medical facilities, this program also covered transportation allowances that include PKR 1,000 per family per visit, with a maximum of three visits permitted for a family on a yearly basis. This scheme also applies to pre-existing disease conditions without considering any age limit boundaries of patients that incorporate five days' post-hospitalization medicines expenses (Punjab Gov., 2023).

## LITERATURE REVIEW AND CONCEPTUAL FRAMEWORK

The emergence of the UHC concept spurred countries to reevaluate their health financing strategies to achieve this goal (Suchman, 2018; James et al., 2006). Social health insurance emerged as a promising international financing mechanism in response to the challenges posed by high healthcare costs (Dalinjong & Laar, 2012). In the context of reorienting health systems, health financing strategies focus on revenue collection, pooling, and purchasing decisions (McIntyre, 2007). Purchasing decisions, a critical aspect, involve various facets of provider payment mechanisms (Obadha et al., 2019). Robinson emphasized that the attributes of an effective payment mechanism include acceptability, sustainability, and economic viability, creating incentives for providers in terms of efficiency and equity (Robinson et al., 2005). Similarly, Water and Hussy (2004) explained that purchasers determine payment rates based on equipment costs, volumes, and costing information. Negotiation trends worldwide, such as those seen in Denmark, Hungary, Korea, and the Netherlands, play a role in these purchasing decisions (Mathauer, 2011). However, a major challenge is the absence of unit cost data in developing countries (Valdmanis et al., 2003).

Research in Kenya highlighted challenges of insufficient payment and under-capitation faced by providers. Complaints of out-of-pocket (OOP) charges were observed, impacting the participation rate of the poor (Suchman, 2018). Findings from Ghana's National Health Insurance (NHI) scheme underscored the negative effects of delayed reimbursement on provider behavior, patient satisfaction, and enrollment decisions (Severding, 2018).

Delayed reimbursement payments led providers to demand informal fees from patients, posing a challenge to social health insurance programs (Severding, 2018). A study in Karnataka, India, revealed difficulties in implementing the social health insurance scheme due to the lack of coordinated incentives between consultants and providers. Education and awareness were crucial for the effective implementation of the scheme (Rajasekhar et al., 2011). Barriers to private provider participation included administrative burdens and inadequate communication from higher management authorities regarding accreditation processes, fees, and incentives. There is a negative impact of unheard complaints, a lack of provider's voice, and low satisfaction with information provision on empanelment.

The Sehat Sahulat Program, inspired by working models in lower-middle-income countries like Ghana and Kenya, operates on a reimbursement model. Providers are paid on a fee-for-service basis, with SLIC handling reimbursements based on claims submitted by providers. The Sehat Sahulat program was recently launched in Pakistan to reduce out-of-pocket expenses and increase the disposable income capacity of Pakistani households. Until now, research has been conducted to check the impact of this program on the removal of out-of-pocket expenditures and patient experience regarding this program. Furthermore, even willingness to pay for such social health insurance schemes was also explored, but there needs to be more literature on behalf of providers with this scheme in terms of their experience.

Therefore, in this respect, our research examines the provider's feedback on the challenges they face with the program through primary data. This data will help us comprehend the on-ground realities providers face in getting empanelment. Their views will be determined based on which indicators they decide whether to apply for accreditation. These measures will help policymakers understand the business operation model, incentives, and motivation of public and private providers, as well as how to engage them, keeping such indexes in mind.

Mainly, this research covers three topics to achieve the research objectives: (1) reasons for participation in the Sehat Sahulat Program and the incentives provided by SLIC for inclusion, (2) difficulties encountered during the accreditation process, and (3) providers' experiences with the provider payment. We employ the Resilient and Responsive Health Systems (RESIST) consortium to examine providers' experiences with the Sehat Sahulat Program's provider payment mechanism. This payment mechanism further impacts the provider's behavior, creating efficiency, equity, and quality in the health system. We used this RESIST framework due to the absence of data on the experience of healthcare providers with the Sehat Sahulat payment mechanism.

This framework revolves around the characteristics of multiple funding flows (Ogbuabor & Onwujekwe, 2018). Therefore, it considers the attributes of adequacy, performance-based incentives, predictability of payment patterns, and autonomy. *Adequacy* is defined as whether the payment rates provided by the purchasing agency are sufficient and cover the service cost. Furthermore, *predictability* refers to the timing of reimbursement payment and its ultimate effect on the hospital operation process. Meanwhile, *autonomy* means the freedom to access funds used to purchase medicines and pay salaries. However, another attribute derived from this funding flow considers the element of strategic purchasing based on the provider's performance and incentives.

## RESEARCH METHODOLOGY

A qualitative research design is implemented, focusing exclusively on the Rawalpindi and Islamabad districts. Semi-structured interviews are conducted with key stakeholders, namely management staff, administrators, and SLIC representatives directly involved in the Sehat Sahulat Program affairs within hospitals, to gather comprehensive insights into providers' perspectives. A purposive sampling technique is employed to select providers. The initial criterion sampling stage narrows the research scope to Rawalpindi and Islamabad districts for practicality and efficiency. Subsequently, fifteen healthcare providers are randomly chosen from both the public and private sectors. Among these, ten are empaneled, evenly split between public and private, while five are not empaneled.

Data collection relies on semi-structured interviews, covering three key topics aligned with research objectives: (1) reasons for participation in the Sehat Sahulat Program and the incentives provided by SLIC for inclusion,

(2) difficulties encountered during the accreditation process, and (3) providers' experiences with the provider payment mechanism. These interviews, conducted in a blend of Urdu and English, involve eighteen respondents. The collected interviews are transcribed into Nvivo software for subsequent thematic data analysis.

We looked for the major themes from our data, with several sub-themes under each theme. The themes that emerged are categorized into public and private sectors based on their empanelment status, shedding light on the reasons for their participation in the Sehat Sahulat Program.

## COMMON REASON FOR INCLUSION IN SHI BY PUBLIC AND PRIVATE PROVIDERS

### Community Benefits

A prevalent theme from both public and private providers highlighted the community benefit as a pivotal factor influencing their participation decision. Respondents expressed a sense of obligation to attain accreditation, citing the inability of most citizens to access and afford healthcare services. One private healthcare provider emphasized their hospital's existing commitment to social welfare, positioning this project as an opportunity to contribute to societal well-being.

> The scenario with us was that one of our managing directors also has a social welfare cause. She was running a school and a hospital, where all the services were free. When we heard about this program, she stepped forward and offered that we would provide a free meal to Sehat card patients. Hence, her motivation encouraged the institute to go for accreditation. (Private Healthcare Provider, Rawalpindi, Pakistan)

### Customer Demand

Another significant factor prompting providers to opt for empanelment was customer demand. Public hospitals highlighted that most patients came from regions like Kashmir, KPK, and Gilgit-Baltistan, where the program had already been implemented. In response to government notifications, public hospitals promptly joined the initiative. Private providers also noted the impact of customer demand on their decision-making process.

> It started when one of our patients visited the hospital and asked the consultant if this Sehat card was applicable in our hospital. He was looking for dialysis treatment. Then, our doctor took a picture of that Sehat card and informed

> the director about this matter. That's how we decided to get empanelment. Even before this event, our marketing committee presented a proposal before the director, but he rejected it. (Private Healthcare Provider, Rawalpindi, Pakistan)

## OTHER REASONS OF PUBLIC AND PRIVATE PROVIDERS FOR INCLUSION

### To Attract Private Customers

Respondents from private empaneled facilities disclosed their aim to attract private customers, particularly from the middle-class demographic in their vicinity. Their strategy involved leveraging the Sehat Card option as an appealing healthcare solution for potential private customers.

> Now, look, if this Sehat card is an option in front of people, they will prefer it. Our patients were also decreasing due to this, so ultimately, we were bound to move towards this to attract the private customer. (Private Providers, Islamabad, Pakistan)

### Indirect Advertisement

Certain private healthcare providers, particularly in Islamabad, view empanelment as an indirect method of advertising their hospital. They conveyed that their hospital's visibility expanded, drawing patients not just from the city but also from regions like Kashmir.

> As you know, this Sehat Card has been launched everywhere. One of our patients from the upper areas of Kashmir mentioned that he visited our hospital on the recommendation of someone who got treatment last week. Therefore, it is a source of indirect advertisement for our health facility too. (Private Healthcare Provider, Islamabad, Pakistan)

### Program Nature to Achieve UHC

Several respondents from both public and private hospitals expressed participation in the program based on its inclusive nature for the future.

> As you know, soon this program will be universal, and universalism indirectly means that this card will be in everyone's pocket in the coming future. Everyone would get this facility, so why shouldn't we get the empanelment status? What is wrong in it? (Public-Private Providers, Rawalpindi, Islamabad, Pakistan)

Contrastingly, the motivation behind the public sector's integration into the scheme differed. Their primary incentive was the government's enforcement policy.

> We had received the notification from the government of Punjab, and they recommended getting accreditation with this program as soon as possible, so in return, we completed all our initial documentation and got the empanelment status at its initial phase. (Public Providers, Rawalpindi, Pakistan)

### Public Sector Privatization

Public providers anticipated that the government's initiative signaled the privatization of the public sector. They perceived it as a deliberate attempt to shift the public sector into a private mode, raising concerns about budget cuts and prompting their enrollment in the Sehat Sahulat Program.

> We knew that we would not receive any funds very soon in the future. It's the government's deliberate attempt to shift the public sector into private mode. (Public Providers, Rawalpindi, Islamabad, Pakistan)

Private healthcare providers are motivated to participate in the Sehat Sahulat Program (SSP) due to a commitment to community benefit, responding to customer demand, and aiming to attract private customers. They see the program as a source of advertisement and a means to contribute to the universality of healthcare services. On the other hand, public healthcare providers are inclined to join SSP primarily because of government policy directives driven by customer demand and, interestingly, to prevent potential privatization of the public sector. The motivations highlight distinct considerations for private and public providers in their decision-making regarding SSP involvement.

## THE DECISION TO NOT PARTICIPATE IN THE SEHAT SAHULAT PROGRAM

In this section, we discuss the public providers' reasons for non-empanelment. While the primary driver for public providers' participation was government policy, a substantial number still needed to secure accreditation. Only 300 public hospitals out of 1,200 were empaneled, comprising thirty percent of total public health providers. Challenges, such as legal processing, hindered enrollment.

## Complex Process

Public providers cited complex procedures, lack of costing techniques, and price ascertainment as reasons for non-empanelment. Hierarchy-related delays in approval processes were also identified as a constraint.

> The Sehat Sahulat Program's main condition for the public sector is the existence of a non-lapsable account, which means the account would remain continuous and never end on any financial year. Meanwhile, earlier, the finance division banned government hospitals from opening any non-lapsable account, especially in a commercial bank. Hence, to meet this condition, we sent an application to the finance division, and they further forwarded it to the federal cabinet, and the process took one year. (Public Provider, Islamabad, Pakistan)

## Cost Determination

Providers highlighted challenges in determining prices for the health benefit package within the government-defined limit.

> If I had exposed the truth, we would have been fighting how to determine the cost of this package, like, the surgical procedure price is 20,000 while a C-section is 15,000. How would we meet this rate? Normally, our cost goes beyond this limit. So, we were working on the cost of this package. (Public Provider, Islamabad, Not Empaneled)

## Absence of Budgeting System

Public providers expressed reservations about technical issues in the budgeting system, emphasizing the need for a proper backup system and transparency in budget utilization.

> One of our reservations was that they did not have any proper budgeting, which means a backup system. For example, if we would do 500 operations in the month, will they clear its payment in the next month, and if they held our payment for the next six months, then how would we survive under this system. (Public Providers, Islamabad, Not Empaneled)

## Program Sustainability

Concerns were raised about the program's sustainability due to SLIC's payment reimbursement capacity. Public providers monitored an extension in payment return time, worrying about survival under the evolving system.

> We kept our eyes on this system; we analyzed when this program started, its reimbursement time limit was 15 days for the public hospitals. Now it's reached 45 to 50 days. If you look at the data, only 20 percent of the public hospitals have been empaneled yet. If this empanelment ratio reaches 60 percent, then this payment return time will be extended to 180 days. Then how would we survive under this system? (Public Providers, Islamabad, Not Empaneled)

## Private Providers' Reason for Non-Empanelment

The primary reasons cited by both providers for not applying for accreditation were similar. Nearly all providers avoided empanelment due to concerns about the lowest rates and budgeting factors. Another shared concern was their apprehension about the program's long-term sustainability, attributed to State Life's capacity to finance it. Additionally, some providers declined membership due to the stringent criteria set by State Life Insurance.

They explained that being smaller health centers, they had limited patient service packages, with only three-bed capacities restricted to C-section patients, limited physician availability, and a constrained range of services. Consequently, they expressed disinterest in the empanelment process. Criticism was directed at some hospitals for refusing empanelment due to the low rates offered by the authorities. Providers characterized these rates as insufficient to sustain hospital operations. Furthermore, they affirmed that the process of obtaining registration at reasonable rates is challenging for smaller institutions. They accused authorities of discrimination and claimed that due to favoritism, a few hospitals received ideal rates despite being smaller institutions.

> We have tried, but it's not easy for the smaller hospital to get empanelment. It's all the game of references, especially in the establishment of rates. (Private Providers, Rawalpindi, Pakistan)

Contrastingly, one respondent emphasized their renowned health services and the inability to compromise quality at low rates.

> We have never thought about it because we have our set-up and customers who visited our hospital due to the standard of quality services. (Private Providers, Islamabad, Pakistan)

However, one informant clarified that, being a fund-based institution, all services are unpaid, rendering empanelment pointless. Private providers cited limitations in health services, concerns about the lowest rates, quality issues, corruption, and uncertainties about the program's sustainability as reasons for not applying to the Sehat Sahulat Program (SSP). In contrast, public providers highlighted challenges in cost determination, the absence of a budgeting system, lack of feedback, uncertainties about program sustainability, and the complexity of the enrollment process as factors influencing their decision not to apply to SSP.

## Experience Regarding Empanelment Process Challenges

Experience regarding challenges in the empanelment process has varying impacts on providers' participation decisions, both negatively and positively. This section presents perspectives from both public and private providers on the obstacles encountered during the enrollment process.

## Challenges Regarding Approval Length of Time

The comparative analysis highlighted differences in the challenges faced by hospitals from both sectors during the enrollment process in the Sehat Sahulat Program. Private sector informants found the process straightforward, with applications, documentation completion, and contract signing. Some interviewees visited the SLIC directly to discuss rates and bed allocation for Sehat Card patients.

In contrast, public sector hospitals in Islamabad faced a more complex process involving various bureaucracies, leading to delays in approval. They had to fulfill documentation and legal contracts separately with the Ministry of Health (MOH), the Sehat Sahulat Program (SSP), and the State Life Insurance Corporation. Both sectors were obliged to open non-lapsable treasury accounts, with public hospitals restricted to the National Bank of Pakistan (NBP). In contrast, the private sector had more flexibility in choosing a bank.

> We went through different contracts; every ministry had its terms and conditions necessary to meet, like the condition to open the treasury account set by the Sehat Sahulat Program (SSP), while the State Life Insurance Corporation put forth the placement of claim management staff in the hospital. (Public-provider, Islamabad, Empaneled)

In contrast, the procedure in Rawalpindi was more straightforward, with the Ministry of Punjab handling all contracts with the State Life Insurance Corporation.

## Challenges Related to Conditions to Change

Private providers were not required to modify their health center equipment, water connections, staff, or buildings, as the project was implemented on their existing infrastructure. Public providers that acquired accreditation initially had to fulfill conditions like building a model pharmacy, hiring staff, creating space for Sehat Card administration, and displaying banners. State Life officials investigated but did not enforce these changes.

> We have not gone through any changes in facilities; nobody mentioned us on inspection; you are failing in some particular departments, so do changes; the fact was, the program implements on us, on our existing infrastructure. (Private-provider, Rawalpindi, Pakistan, Empaneled)

## Provider Payment Mechanism Challenges

The prominent feature of the provider's payment mechanism in the Sehat Sahulat Program is strategic purchasing, which has the potential to create incentives for improved efficiency, quality, and utilization of health services. However, the program operated on a "fee for services" model, covering all services such as bed stay fees, laboratory tests, medication, and payment for the health benefits package. The process for payment rate settlement was generally similar in both sector hospitals, except for specific institutions. Rates were based on State Life's self-assessment approach and facilities available in the hospital. Some rates were finalized based on tender, with the lowest bidder rates implemented after State Life evaluation.

> After going through all the documentation and contract, their team visited, checked all the facilities, and then defined our class based on primary, secondary, and tertiary. If we had a 500-bed capacity in our hospital, then the given rates would be full, which means we could get a handsome package, such as having a 40-bed capacity and falling in the primary category. That was the reason we had five to ten thousand differences due to bed capacity issues. (Private-provider, Rawalpindi, Pakistan, Empaneled)

Moreover, a few providers revealed that the finalization of rates was based on the tender process, wherein the rates of the lowest bidder were implemented. They characterized these rates as subsidized, settled post-State Life evaluation. However, our analysis of interviewee responses brought to light significant aspects of the provider's payment mechanism within the resilient framework approach.

## Insufficient Payment Rates

Providers expressed deep concern about the inadequacy of payment rates, emphasizing that these rates failed to cover the costs allocated for health services. They specifically identified certain packages, such as female replacement implants, where the costs were deemed unacceptable.

> Some cases like female replacement implants were so expensive, and if institutions entertained such patients, then it means we didn't have any advantage; we hardly meet the cost of such packages and work on a no-profit, no-loss condition. (Private-provider, Rawalpindi, *Pakistan*, Empaneled)

A public provider echoed these concerns, highlighting the rate deficiency that hindered the delivery of standard services, especially in cardiac procedures.

> There were some procedures like cardiac-related disease, which were known as totally lifesaving procedures, in which one could die too. It's not like others' general procedures like the appendix, benign tumor surgery, or polypectomy-type procedures. So, we couldn't compromise on the quality level and the usage of standard products in the procedure. So, how could we compromise on such low rates? If we do, we have to compromise on these quality procedures, which we cannot in any case. (Public-provider, Rawalpindi, Pakistan, Empaneled)

## Absence of Incentives for the Consultant

Another critical concern highlighted by providers in the SSP payment mechanism is the absence of incentives for consultants in service delivery. Providers emphasized that consultants operate as independent entities, making it challenging to influence their collaboration with the institution without appropriate incentives. The perceived lack of incentives not only complicates matters for the consultant but also triggers conflicts between hospitals and State Life, with allegations of consultant bribery contributing to the discord.

## Absence of Self-Determination on Funds Utilization

The autonomy for healthcare providers to utilize funds in a self-directed manner is of paramount importance to ensure standard services. Our research explored the contrast between private and public providers in fund collection and utilization. Providers objected to the restrictions imposed by the new policy of the government of Punjab, which mandates hospitals to deposit all revenue generated from serving Sehat patients into the national fund. The allocation formula suggests that 80 percent of this revenue returns to the government, with 65 percent retained by them. Additionally, 15 percent is earmarked for the institution to enhance infrastructure, equipment, and quality. However, the hospital is granted only 20 percent authority to utilize the collection for patient entertainment, which is deemed discouraging.

### Absence of Feedback in Rate Settlement

Providers expressed distress over the rate settlement process, noting that rates were decided without their feedback. They found this approach offensive and emphasized the need for responsible authorities to consider their opinions by involving all stakeholders in the decision-making process.

> The problem with this program is that the authorities didn't consider our concerns; they made all the decisions by themselves. By saying the market rates already are too high, and they want to break this chain.

### Delayed Claim Reimbursement and Cumbersome System

The claims management process, initiated upon the patient's arrival with ID confirmation, involves the preparation of a claim sheet sent for verification and approval to state life health officers, district health officers, and Sehat Sahulat DMS. Initially, the reimbursement timeframe was fifteen days for private and thirty days for public providers. However, it was later extended to forty-five days for public and thirty days for private providers. Public providers expressed distress over a two to three-month delay in claim reimbursement, receiving only a fraction of the total claims even after the delay. Likewise, one public provider respondent criticized and communicated that they only received one-third of the total claims, even after a delay.

> Like look, we are in May. Unfortunately, they only paid us up to January. Even though we sent claims weekly, we sent the first claim on 15th January. However, in May, we only sent 1310 claims but till now haven't received even one-third amount of it. (Public providers, Rawalpindi, empaneled)

In comparison, private providers also complained about the delay in claim reimbursement, but they provided reasons for such delays. They mentioned that due to the absence of supporting paperwork, the authorities of State Life raised objections, leading to delays in payment. For instance, in cases involving gynecology, the absence of an ultrasound report, or for neuro patients, the necessity of an MRI report, and for spinal cord patients, a stool test report was deemed mandatory.

## DISCUSSION

Achieving the goal of UHC by introducing a new health financing system like social health insurance (SHI) is considered significant (Kruk, 2013). The success of a social health insurance scheme relies on the effective involvement of both public and private sectors (Prata N et al., 2005). In line with this, Pakistan has implemented the Sehat Sahulat Program based on the SHI model, where providers are selected through a tendering process (Morgan, 2019). This research identifies critical factors for the effective participation of providers in the context of the SLIC managing both public and private engagement.

Our findings highlight that both public and private providers recognized the importance of public health values and were motivated to participate in the SHI scheme. Community benefit and customer demand emerged as common reasons for their participation, emphasizing the societal significance of the Sehat Sahulat Program. Notably, private hospitals were driven by business motives, viewing inclusion as a form of indirect advertisement and a strategy to counteract patient migration to hospitals offering Sehat cards.

A comparative analysis revealed that government policy was the primary driver for public sector inclusion. However, challenges faced by public providers during enrollment, such as bureaucratic hierarchies, prolonged waiting times, and issues related to health benefits package cost determination, highlighted obstacles unique to the public sector. Discriminatory practices were observed, as public hospitals were required to make infrastructure changes, while private providers faced a straightforward accreditation process.

Furthermore, challenges emerged in the provider payment mechanism, notably the inadequacy of payment rates. Providers expressed concerns about insufficient rates to cover costs, particularly for specialized procedures like female replacement implants and cardiac-related surgeries. The low rates were perceived as negatively impacting healthcare quality, leading to difficulties in sustaining quality services. Similar findings were detected during the Burkina Faso CBHI scheme, where they found that capitation rates paid were inadequate to cover the basic service cost (Robyn et al., 2014). Nevertheless, in another research, the rationality of the capitation amount was pointed out for other chronic conditions like hypertension and diabetes (Obadha et al., 2019).

An additional concern was the absence of incentives for consultants, affecting the motivation of healthcare professionals. Providers argued that incentives were necessary to attract experienced consultants, especially for critical procedures. The lack of incentives also contributed to allegations of informal payments against consultants. Providers also expressed frustration with the rate settlement process and advocated for a visible accreditation score policy on the SLIC website. The delay in claim reimbursement further compounded challenges, with payment delays extending from two to six months. This unpredictability in payment patterns had repercussions, including difficulties in managing expenses, especially for pharmaceutical companies.

However, another issue highlighted by both providers was the delay in claims reimbursement, extending from two to six months, considered nominal compared to Low and Middle-Income Countries (LMICs). They conveyed that these overdue payments posed challenges in settling dues with pharmaceutical companies. Private providers mentioned attempting to manage these expenses through their Outpatient Department (OPD).

This unpredictability in payment patterns mirrors observations in Nigeria's maternal and child healthcare scheme, leading to medicine stockouts and the emergence of informal payments (Ogbuabor & Onwujekwe, 2018). Similarly, delays in the Indian National Health Insurance Scheme disappointed providers to the extent that some considered transitioning to Direct Empanelment (DE) (Rajasekhar et al., 2011). Interestingly, a parallel pattern was noted in the Sehat Sahulat Program, where a public provider contemplated withdrawing due to prolonged payment delays.

Public hospitals also expressed concern about delayed payment reimbursement despite receiving operational costs from the government. Their worry stemmed from negative anticipation regarding the government's future intentions, suspecting a deliberate move toward privatizing the public sector through this program.

Another emerging theme was the impact on providers' self-determination due to the Punjab government's policy to return funds to the national revenue. Providers argued that delivering quality services and competing with the private sector becomes challenging without adequate funds. This echoes observations in Kenya, where public providers lost autonomy at the start of devolution. In contrast, Tanzania granted liberty to public health facilities to receive funds directly into their accounts instead of relying on district managers (Mayumana et al., 2017). The discussion underscores the complexity of implementing a social health insurance scheme like the Sehat Sahulat Program in Pakistan. It highlights the diverse motivations and challenges faced by both public and private providers, emphasizing the need for a balanced and inclusive approach to ensure the program's success and contribute to achieving UHC. The discussion underscores the complexity of implementing a social health insurance scheme like the Sehat Sahulat Program in Pakistan. It highlights the diverse motivations and challenges faced by both public and private providers, emphasizing the need for a balanced and inclusive approach to ensure the program's success and contribute to achieving UHC.

## CONCLUSION AND POLICY RECOMMENDATION

This research aimed to investigate providers' experiences with the Sehat Sahulat social health insurance program. This marked the first research endeavor in Pakistan to explore the motivations behind providers' participation in the scheme and the challenges they encountered in its implementation.

The research findings demonstrated that public and private providers recognized the significance of the Social Health Insurance (SHI) scheme as a financing mechanism. They acknowledged its importance and sought accreditation, driven by considerations of community benefit and customer requirements. Some providers also had a business motive, perceiving enrollment status as an indirect form of advertisement for their institutions.

The comparative analysis highlighted various constraints public providers face during empanelment, including challenges such as the absence of proper budgeting, difficulty in cost determination, low rates, lack of feedback mechanisms for rate settlements, and existing bureaucratic hierarchies. The limited autonomy in fund utilization further discouraged public providers. Private providers, too, expressed dissatisfaction due to low rates and the absence of incentives for consultants. To prevent frustration related to corruption and favoritism, it is essential to involve all stakeholders in the rate settlement process.

Considering the importance of provider inclusion, further research could delve into the quantitative aspects of challenges related to claims reimbursement and explore costing techniques for health benefit packages. Providers often show reluctance to provide data due to restrictions imposed by purchasing agencies. Involving the purchasing agency in research discussions could address this issue.

Several policy viewpoints need consideration to enhance efficiency, accessibility, and provider loyalty to the Sehat Sahulat scheme. Firstly, consultants, nurses, and health workers should be allocated incentives to keep them motivated in service provision. Policymakers should monitor consultants through the Pakistan Medical and Dental Council (PMDC) in cases where complaints regarding informal payments are received. Issuing warnings and canceling PMDC status for such consultants could improve the situation.

Additionally, providers' feedback before payment settlement should be a crucial factor. Adopting an explicit accrediting scoring policy would prevent allegations of favoritism in the payment settlement process. Providing autonomy to public providers for fund utilization would enable them to improve their health centers and compete effectively in the market. Reducing bureaucratic hierarchies would also minimize waiting times for approval.

Furthermore, ensuring timely claims disbursement would facilitate providers' day-to-day functioning, allowing them to cover operating costs and make timely payments to pharmaceutical companies.

## REFERENCES

Bolo. (n.d.). How to apply for Qaumi Sehat Card in Pakistan. Retrieved from https://www.bolo-pk.info/en-us/articles/4404094839703.

Carrin, G., & James, C. (2004). *Reaching universal coverage via social health insurance: Key design features in the transition period.* Geneva: World Health Organization, 13.

Dalinjong, P. A., & Laar, A. S. (2012). The national health insurance scheme: perceptions and experiences of health care providers and clients in two districts of Ghana. *Health Economics Review*, *2*(1), 1–13.

Figueras, J., Robinson, R., & Jakubowski, E. (2005). *Purchasing to improve health systems performance*. London: McGraw-Hill Education (UK).

Kruk, M. E. (2013). Universal health coverage: A policy whose time has come. *Bmj*, *347*: f6360 doi: 10.1136/bmj.f6360

Mathauer, I. (2011). Setting health insurance remuneration rates of private providers in Kenya: The role of costing, challenges and implications. *The International Journal of Health Planning and Management*, *26*(1), e30–e47.

Mayumana, I., Borghi, J., Anselmi, L., Mamdani, M., & Lange, S. (2017). Effects of payment for performance on accountability mechanisms: evidence from Pwani, Tanzania. *Social Science & Medicine*, *179*, 61–73.

McIntyre, D. (2007, July). *Learning from experience: Health care financing in low- and middle-income countries*. Geneva: Global forum for health research.

Mirza, Z. (2021, July 9). Unpacking social health insurance. *Dawn*. https://www.dawn.com/news/1634058.

Morgan, L. (ILO). (2019). *Actuarial analysis of the federal sehat sahulat program. April*. www.ilo.org/publns.

Obadha, M., Chuma, J., Kazungu, J., & Barasa, E. (2019). Health care purchasing in Kenya: Experiences of health care providers with capitation and fee-for-service provider payment mechanisms. *The International Journal of Health Planning and Management*, *34*(1), e917–e933.

Ogbuabor, D. C., & Onwujekwe, O. E. (2018). Scaling-up strategic purchasing: Analysis of health system governance imperatives for strategic purchasing in a free maternal and child healthcare programme in Enugu State, Nigeria. *BMC Health Services Research*, *18*(1), 1–12.

Pakistan Bureau of Statistics. (2021). *National Health Accounts-Pakistan 2017–18*. Ministry of Planning, Development & Special Initiatives, Government of Pakistan.

Phuong, N. K., Oanh, T. T. M., Phuong, H. T., Tien, T. V., & Cashin, C. (2015). Assessment of systems for paying health care providers in Vietnam: implications for equity, efficiency and expanding effective health coverage. *Global Public Health*, *10*(sup1), S80–S94.

PIDE (2021). *Sehat Sahulat program Webinar brief.* Pakistan Institute of Development Economics. https://file.pide.org.pk/pdf/brief/Sehat-Sahulat-Program-Webinar-Brief-28.pdf.

PM Health Program. (2021). Title of the charter document. Retrieved from https://pmhealthprogram.gov.pk/downloads/charter.pdf.

Prata, N., Montagu, D., & Jefferys, E. (2005). Private sector, human resources and health franchising in Africa. *Bulletin of the World Health Organization*, *83*(4), 274–279.

Punjab Gov. (2023). Punjab health initiative management company. Retrieved from https://phimc.punjab.gov.pk/faqe.

Rajasekhar, D., Berg, E., Ghatak, M., Manjula, R., & Roy, S. (2011). Implementing health insurance: The rollout of Rashtriya Swasthya Bima Yojana in Karnataka. *Economic and Political Weekly*, *46*(20), 56–63.

Robyn, P. J., Bärnighausen, T., Souares, A., Traoré, A., Bicaba, B., Sié, A., & Sauerborn, R. (2014). Provider payment methods and health worker motivation in community-based health insurance: a mixed-methods study. *Social Science & Medicine*, *108*, 223–236.-

Sieverding, M., Onyango, C., & Suchman, L. (2018). Private healthcare provider experiences with social health insurance schemes: Findings from a qualitative study in Ghana and Kenya. *PLoS One*, *13*(2), e0192973.

State Health. (n.d.). Sehat Sahulat Program. Retrieved from https://statehealth.com.pk/sehat_sahulat_program.php.

Suchman, L. (2018). Accrediting private providers with National Health Insurance to better serve low-income populations in Kenya and Ghana: a qualitative study. *International Journal for Equity in Health*, *17*, 1–18.

U.S. Department of Commerce. (n.d.). *Healthcare Resource Guide: Pakistan.* International Trade Administration. Retrieved from https://www.trade.gov/healthcare-resource-guide-pakistan.

Valdmanis, V., Walker, D., & Fox-Rushby, J. (2003). Are vaccination sites in Bangladesh scale efficient? *International Journal of Technology Assessment in Health Care*, *19*(4), 692–697.

Waters, H. R., & Hussey, P. (2004). Pricing health services for purchasers—a review of methods and experiences. *Health Policy*, *70*(2), 175–184.

*Chapter 8*

# Prevalence and Risk Factors Associated with Hepatitis B and Hepatitis C in Sindh Province, Pakistan

Ayaz Ali Samo, Zulfiqar Ali Laghari, Husan Bano Channar, and Arsalan Ahmed Uqaili

Viral hepatitis is a serious global public health problem. Hepatitis B (HBV) and C (HCV) are blood-borne and transmissible diseases. HBV and HCV are transmitted from an already infected person to a normal healthy person through blood and other body fluids via pricking, piercing, surgical instruments, reused syringes, shaving razors, sexual intercourse, mother-to-child transmission, sexual contact, and use of contaminated blood (Samo et al., 2021). The incubation time for the HBV and HCV viruses ranges from two weeks to two to three months. However, an HBV and HCV-infected person may remain asymptomatic for years. Symptoms begin to appear when there is enough damage to the liver caused by the hepatitis virus. These symptoms vary from mild to severe, depending on whether the infection is acute or chronic. The common symptoms of HBV and HCV viral infections include jaundice, fatigue, abdominal pain, loss of appetite, nausea, vomiting, fever, muscle and joint pain, dark urine, and clay-colored stools (Hoofnagle, 1997; Liang, 2009). A World Health Organization (WHO) report indicates that approximately 257 million persons are chronically infected with HBV, and 71 million individuals are infected with HCV. It is estimated that 20 million deaths will occur between 2015 and 2030 (World Health Organization, 2023). The impact is particularly severe in regions with limited healthcare and mass-level health awareness. Pakistan is included in the low-middle-income countries, facing multiple challenges, including increasing cost of living, unemployment, socio-economic inequalities, and illiteracy. Viral hepatitis, associated with morbidity and mortality, has led to a rise in the economic burden on the healthcare system and society at large. It will continue to do so if steps to eliminate HBV and HCV are not taken (Chhatwal et al., 2019). All four provinces of Pakistan, that is, Punjab, Sindh, Baluchistan, and Khyber Pakhtunkhwa, are different ethnically, culturally, and economically. Understanding the dynamics of HBV and HCV sets the stage for a comprehensive examination of their prevalence and associated risk factors in the specific context of Sindh Province. As we uncover more, it will become apparent that there is a need to do more for surveillance, prevention, and intervention to eliminate HBV and HCV.

## PREVALENCE OF HBV AND HCV AMONG THE HIGH-RISK POPULATIONS IN SINDH

The investigation into the prevalence of Hepatitis B Virus (HBV), particularly among high-risk groups, has been systematically conducted in various regions of Sindh. Within the province, distinct prevalence rates of HBV have been identified among specific high-risk populations. Specifically, the prevalence of HBV among pregnant women in Karachi varies from 4.5 percent to 20 percent (Naseeb et al., 2023; Sami et al., 2009). Furthermore, in Naushahro Feroz and Hyderabad, the prevalence rate of HBV among pregnant women is reported as 5.14 percent (Ghanghro & Jokhio, 2016), and 4.2 percent (Qazi et al., 2019), respectively. The weighted average prevalence of HBV among pregnant women in Sindh is calculated to be 13.72 percent. For individuals with blood disorders, including hemophilia and thalassemia, residing in Karachi, the prevalence of HBV ranges widely from 1 percent to 51 percent (Afreen et al., 2023; Ansari et al., 2012; Borhany et al., 2011; Hussain et al., 2018; Riaz et al., 2010; Sultan et al., 2016). In Larkana, the prevalence of HBV among thalassemia patients specifically is noted to be 13.08 percent (Puno et al., 2021). The weighted average prevalence of HBV among individuals with blood disorders is calculated at 34.95 percent.

Among injection drug users in Karachi, the prevalence of HBV ranges from 3.17 percent to 7.5 percent (Altaf et al., 2007; Abdul et al., 2012), with a weighted average prevalence rate of 6.21 percent. Additionally, for surgery patients in various locations, the prevalence rates of HBV range from 2.14 percent to 14 percent (Daudpota & Soomro, 2008; Lohano et al., 2016; Moosa et al., 2009; Naeem et al., 2012; Surahio et al., 2012). The weighted average prevalence rate of HBV among surgery patients is calculated to be 13.72 percent. This comprehensive exploration provides valuable insights into the distinct prevalence rates of HBV within specific high-risk groups in Sindh, contributing to the understanding of the epidemiological landscape (table 8.1).

In the epidemiological landscape of hepatitis, the prevalence of HCV has been investigated among high-risk groups. The prevalence of HCV among

**Table 8.1 Prevalence of Hepatitis B among High-Risk Groups in Sindh Province**

| Author Citation | Year | City | Population | Sample Size | HBV Prevalence | Prevalence/ 100=Weightage | Prevalence X Weightage | Weighted Average |
|---|---|---|---|---|---|---|---|---|
| (Hussain et al., 2018) | 2015–2016 | Karachi | Blood disorder/ Hemophilia and other blood disorders | 1497 | 1 | 0.01 | 0.01 | |
| (Munira et al., 2011) | 2011 | Karachi | Blood disorder/ Hemophilia Patients | 173 | 1.73 | 0.0173 | 0.029929 | |
| (Sultan., 2016) | 2016 | Karachi | Blood disorder/ Thalassemia | 100 | 3 | 0.03 | 0.0 | |
| (Puno et al., 2021) | 2021 | Larkana | Blood disorder/ Thalassemia | 237 | 13.08 | 0.1308 | 1.710864 | |
| Afreen et al., 2023) | 2023 | Karachi | Blood disorder/ Thalassemia | 328 | 15.85 | 0.1585 | 2.512225 | |
| (Riaz et al., 2010) | 2011 | Karachi | Blood Disorder/ Thalassemia | 79 | 51 | 0.51 | 26.01 | |
| (Ansari et al., 2012) | 2012 | Karachi | Blood disorder/ Thalassemia Patients | 5717 | 1.25 | 0.0125 | 0.015625 | |
| | | | | | | 0.8691 | 30.37864 | 34.95414 |
| (Altaf et al., 2007) | 2003 | Karachi | Injection Drugs Users | 161 | 7.5 | 0.075 | 0.5625 | |
| (Abdul et al., 2012) | 2012 | Karachi | Injection Drug Users Prisoners, Healthcare workers, | 4202 | 3.17 | 0.0317 | 0.100489 | |
| | | | Security staff | | 0.1067 | 0.662989 | 6.21358 | |

(Continued)

**Table 8.1 (Continued)**

| *Author Citation* | *Year* | *City* | *Population* | *Sample Size* | *HBV Prevalence* | *Prevalence/ 100=Weightage* | *Prevalence X Weightage* | *Weighted Average* |
|---|---|---|---|---|---|---|---|---|
| (Shehla., 2009) | 2005 | Karachi | Pregnant females | 5902 | 4.5 | 0.045 | 0.2025 | |
| (Ghanghro., 2016) | 2014 | Naushahro | Pregnant females Feroz | 175 | 5.14 | 0.0514 | 0.264196 | |
| (Qazi et., 2019) | 2019 | Hyderabad | Pregnant females | 500 | 4.2 | 0.042 | 0.1764 | |
| (Naseeb et al., 2023) | 2023 | Karachi | Pregnant females | 332 | 20 | 0.2 | 4 | |
| | | | | | | 0.3384 | 4.643096 | 13.72073 |
| (Naeem et al., 2012) | 2010–2011 | Karachi | Surgery patients/ Cataracts | 337 | 2.1 | 0.021 | 0.0441 | |
| (Abdul et al.,2008) | 2008 | Jacobabad | Surgery patients Elective | 150 | 14 | 0.14 | 1.96 | |
| (Surahio et al., 2012) | 2012 | Hyderabad | Surgery patients/ Emergency | 1716 | 4.7 | 0.047 | 0.2209 | |
| | (Mossa et al., 2010) | 2010 | Karachi | Surgery patients/Eye | 496 | 5 | 0.05 | |
| (Lohano et., 2010) | 2010 | Hyderabad | Surgery patients/ | 2200 | 2.54 | 0.0254 | 0.064516 | |
| | | | | | | 0.2834 | 2.539516 | 8.960889 |

*Source*: Google Scholar.

**Table 8.2 Prevalence of Hepatitis C among the High-Risk Groups in Sindh Province**

| *Author Citation* | *Year* | *City* | *Population* | *Sample Size* | *HCV Prevalence* | *Prevalence/ 100=Weightage* | *Prevalence X Weightage* | *Weighted Average* |
|---|---|---|---|---|---|---|---|---|
| (Hussain et al., 2018) | 2015–2016 | Karachi | Blood disorder/ Hemophilia and other blood disorders | 1497 | 28 | 0.28 | 7.84 | |
| (Munira et al., 2011) | 2011 | Karachi | Blood disorder/ Hemophilia patients | 183 | 51.4 | 0.541 | 26.4196 | |
| (Sultan et al., 2016) | 2016 | Karachi | Blood disorder/ Thalassemia | 100 | 27 | 0.27 | 7.29 | |
| (Puno et al., 2021) | 2021 | Larkana | Blood disorder/ Thalassemia patients | 237 | 30.8 | 0.308 | 9.4864 | |
| (Arfeen at al., 2023) | 2023 | Karachi | Blood disorder/ Thalassemia patients | 328 | 85.9 | 0.859 | 73.7881 | |
| (Riaz et al., 2010) | 2011 | Karachi | Blood disorder/ Thalassemia patients | 79 | 43 | 0.43 | 18.49 | |
| (Ansari et al., 2012) | 2012 | Karachi | Blood disorder/ Thalassemia patients | 5717 | 13.1 | 0.131 | 1.7161 | |
| | | | | | | 2.792 | 145.0302 | 51.94491404 |
| (Altaf et al., 2007) | 2003 | Karachi | Injection Drug Users | 161 | 94.3 | 0.943 | 88.9249 | |
| (Abdul et al., 2012) | 2012 | Karachi | Injection Drug Users, Prisoners, Healthcare workers | 4202 | 13 | 0.13 | 1.69 | |
| | | | Security staff | | | 1.073 | 90.6149 | 84.4500466 |
| (Shehla et al., 2009) | 2005 | Karachi | Pregnant | 5902 | 1.8 | 0.018 | 0.0324 | |
| (Ghanghro et al., 2016) | 2014 | Naushahro Feroz | Pregnant females | 175 | 7 | 0.07 | 0.49 | |

(*Continued*)

**Table 8.2 (Continued)**

| *Author Citation* | *Year* | *City* | *Population* | *Sample Size* | *HCV Prevalence* | *Prevalence/ 100=Weightage* | *Prevalence X Weightage* | *Weighted Average* |
|---|---|---|---|---|---|---|---|---|
| (Qazi et. al, 2019) | 2019 | Hyderabad | Pregnant females | 500 | 7 | 0.07 | 0.49 | |
| (Naseeb et al,. 2023) | 2023 | Karachi | Pregnant | 332 | 14.5 | 0.145 | 2.1025 | |
| (Bibi et al., 2013) | 2010 | Hyderabad | Pregnant females | 343 | 4.7 | 0.047 | 0.2209 | |
| | | | | | | 0.35 | 3.3358 | 9.5305857143 |
| (Abdul et al., 2008) | 2008 | Jacobabad | Surgery patients | 150 | 14 | 0.14 | 1.96 | |
| (Moosa et al., 2010) | 2010 | Karachi | Surgery patients | 496 | 12 | 0.12 | 1.44 | |
| (Lohano et., 2010) | 2010 | Hyderabad | Surgery patients | 2200 | 12.81 | 0.1281 | 1.640961 | |
| (Naeem et al., 2012) | 2010–20211 | Karachi | Surgery patients/ Cataract | 337 | 11 | 0.11 | 1.21 | |
| (Surahio et al., 2012) | 2012 | Hyderabad | Surgery patients/ Emergency | 1716 | 11.94 | 0.1194 | 1.425636 | |
| | | | | | | 0.6175 | 7.676597 | 12.43173603 |

*Source*: Google Scholar.

pregnant women of Karachi, Hyderabad, and Naushahro Feroz ranged from 1.8 percent to 14.5 percent (Bibi et al., 2013; Ghanghro & Jokhio, 2016; Naseeb et al., 2023; Qazi et al., 2019; Sami et al., 2009) and the weighted average prevalence rate was 9.53 percent. The prevalence of HCV among people with blood disorders in Karachi, Sindh ranged from 13.1 percent to 85.9 percent (Afreen et al., 2023; Ansari et al., 2012; Borhany et al., 2011; Hussain et al., 2018; Riaz et al., 2010; Sultan et al., 2016) and in Larkana, Sindh, the prevalence rate was noticed as 30.8 percent (Puno et al., 2021). The weighted average prevalence of HCV among people with blood disorders in Karachi and Larkana was noticed as 51.9 percent. Two separate studies independently reported the prevalence rate of HCV among injection drug users in Karachi, with one study identifying it as 13 percent (Memon et al., 2012) and the other noting a prevalence rate of 94.3 percent (Altaf et al., 2007). The weighted average prevalence rate of HCV among injection drug users in Karachi was noted as 84.45 percent. The prevalence of HCV among surgery patients in Karachi, Hyderabad, and Jacobabad ranged from 11 percent to 14 percent (Daudpota & Soomro, 2008; Lohano et al., 2016; Moosa et al., 2009; Naeem et al., 2012; Surahio et al., 2012). The weighted average prevalence of HCV among Karachi, Hyderabad, and Jacobabad was 12.43 percent (table 8.2).

## PREVALENCE OF HBV AND HCV AMONG THE GENERAL POPULATION IN SINDH

The prevalence of the Hepatitis B Virus (HBV) exhibits variability across districts in Sindh. In the Karachi division, the prevalence rate of HBV ranges from 1 percent to 7 percent (Mujeeb et al., 2006; Abdullah et al., 2012; Akhtar et al., 2005; Aziz et al., 2002; Irfan et al., 2013; Jafri et al., 2006; Mujeeb & Pearce, 2008; Naeem et al., 2012; Noorali et al., 2008). The district-specific prevalence of HBV in Sindh is as follows: Thatta, 3.1 percent (Aziz et al., 2010); Hyderabad, 2.28 percent (Kakepoto et al., 1996); Larkana, 8 percent (Mir et al., 2020); Mirpur Khas, 6.75 percent (Arain et al., 2020); Naushahro Feroz, 7 percent to 9.9 percent (Aziz et al., 2010; Ghanghro & Jokhio, 2016); Nawab Shah District, 6.7 percent (Samo et al., 2021); Sukkur, 5 percent (Abbas et al., 2008); Tando Muhammad Khan District, 17 percent (Kumar et al., 2010). These studies account for variations in sample sizes and population heterogeneity. The weighted average of prevalence of HBV is calculated to be 7.79 percent in the Sindh province (table 8.3).

The prevalence of Hepatitis C Virus (HCV) exhibits considerable variation across districts in the Sindh region. In the Karachi division, the prevalence

**Table 8.3 Prevalence of Hepatitis B among the General Population of Sindh Province.**

| *Author Citation* | *Year* | *City* | *Population* | *Sample Size* | *HBV prevalence* | *Prevalence/ 100=weightage* | *Prevalence X weightage* | *Weighted average* |
|---|---|---|---|---|---|---|---|---|
| (Kakepoto et al., 1996) | 1996 | Hyderabad Karachi | Blood donors | 51257 | 2.28 | 0.0228 | 0.051984 | |
| (Baqi et al., 1999) | 1999 | Karachi | Transgenders | 300 | 3.4 | 0.034 | 0.1156 | |
| (S. A. Mujeeb & M. S. Pearce, 2008) | 2000 | Karachi | Blood donors | 312 | 2.21 | 0.0221 | 0.048841 | |
| (Akhtar et al., 2005) | 1998–2002 | Karachi | Blood donors | 351309 | 2 | 0.02 | 0.04 | |
| (Mujeeb et al., 2008) | 2004–2007 | Karachi | Blood donors | 5345 | 6.2 | 0.036 | 0.3844 | |
| (Kazi et al.,2010) | 2010 | Karachi | Prisoners | 357 | 5.9 | 0.059 | 0.3481 | |
| (Irfan et al., 2013) | 2004–2011 | Karachi | Blood donors | 108598 | 1.9 | 0.019 | 0.1361 | |
| (Arshad et al., 2016) | 2016 | Karachi | Blood donors | 16602 | 1.84 | 0.0184 | 0.033856 | |
| (Ghanghro et al., 2016) | 2014 | Naushahro Feroz | Blood donors | 656 | 9.9 | 0.099 | 0.9801 | |
| (Jafri et al., 2006) | 2006 | Karachi | Children | 3533 | 108 | 0.018 | 0.0324 | |
| (Mir et al., 2020) | 2019 | Larkana | Children | 31239 | 8 | 0.08 | 0.64 | |
| (Mujeeb et al., 1998) | 1998 | Karachi | Healthcare workers | 114 | 7.5 | 0.075 | 0.5625 | |
| (S. Aziz et al., 2002) | 2002 | Karachi | Healthcare workers | 250 | 2.4 | 0.024 | 0.0576 | |
| (S. Aziz et al., 2010) | 2007–2008 | Gharo, Thatta | Healthy Adults | 573 | 3.1 | 0.031 | 0.0961 | |

| | | | | | | | | |
|---|---|---|---|---|---|---|---|---|
| (Noorali, et al.,2008) | 2002–2006 | Karachi | Healthy Adults | 4000 | 4.5 | 0.045 | 0.2025 | |
| (Abdullah et al., 2012) | 2009–2011 | Karachi | Healthy Adults | 8648 | 6.4 | 0.064 | 0.4096 | |
| (Arain et al., 2020) | 2019 | Mirpur Khas | Healthy Adults | 311 | 6.75 | 0.0675 | 0.455625 | |
| (Samo et al., 2021) | 2019 | Nawabshah | Healthy Adults | 514 | 6.7 | 0.067 | 0.4489 | |
| ( Abbas et al., 2008) | 2007 | Sukkur | Healthy Adults | 873 | 5 | 0.05 | 0.25 | |
| (Kumar et al., 2010) | 2010 | Tando Muhammad Khan | Healthy Adults | 5989 | 17 | 0.17 | 2.89 | |
| (Aziz et al., 2010) | 2007–2008 | Tharoshah, Naushahro Feroz | Healthy Adults | 573 | 7 | 0.07 | 0.49 | |
| | | | | | | 1.1178 | 8.574206 | 7.670608338 |

*Source*: Google Scholar.

rates of HCV range from 1.7 percent to 13.5 percent, according to multiple studies (Arshad et al., 2016; Irfan et al., 2013; Mansoor et al., 2023; Naeem et al., 2012). Further breakdown by district reveals varying prevalence rates, including 13.8 percent in Dadu, 15.6 percent in Ghotki, 12.7 percent in Hyderabad, 21.7 percent in Jamshoro, 15.9 percent in Kashmore at Kandhkot, 18 percent in Khairpur Mirs, 18.3 percent in Noushahro Feroz, 19 percent in Sanghar, 16 percent in Sukkur, and 10.2 percent in Tharparkar (Ujjan et al., 2021). Additional district-specific rates include 14.64 percent in Mirpur Khas (Arain et al., 2020), 12.1 percent to 28 percent in Naushahro Feroz (Aziz et al., 2010; Ghanghro & Jokhio, 2016), 14.3 percent in Nawabshah (Samo et al., 2021), 8 percent in Tando Muhammad Khan (Kumar et al., 2010), 3 percent in Larkana (Mir et al., 2020), and 3.9 percent in the Gharo area of the Thatta district (Aziz et al., 2010). The weighted average prevalence of HCV in the Sindh province is estimated at 16.92 percent, providing a comprehensive overview of the regional distribution of HCV prevalence (Arshad et al., 2016; Irfan et al., 2013; Mansoor et al., 2023; Naeem et al., 2012; Ujjan et al. 2021; Arain et al., 2020; Aziz et al., 2010; Ghanghro & Jokhio, 2016; Samo et al., 2021; Kumar et al., 2010; Mir et al., 2020; Aziz et al., 2010) (table 8.4).

This epidemiological data highlights the increased susceptibility of the identified subpopulations to Hepatitis B Virus (HBV) and Hepatitis C Virus (HCV) in various cities of Sindh. These findings underscore the essential need for targeted preventive and intervention strategies within these specific high-risk groups to reduce the prevalence of HBV and HCV and improve public health outcomes. The effectiveness of such strategies is contingent upon the financial resources allocated to the healthcare system.

The Pakistani government is currently facing an economic crisis. In 2022, Pakistan's estimated debt-to-GDP ratio stood at 75 percent, and its external debt was projected to reach US$125.7 billion by March 2023. The targeted revenue collection for 2023–2024 is expected to range between Rs. 8.6 trillion and Rs. 9.2 trillion, but a significant portion exceeding Rs. 7.3 trillion is anticipated to be absorbed by debt servicing costs (Waheed, 2023). Other critical budget allocations include defense, pensions, salaries, the development budget, and subsidies.

To meet these financial challenges, the government of Pakistan imposes taxes on gas, electricity, and fuel, aiming to generate revenue for the payment of the International Monetary Fund's debt. However, this increase in taxation has downstream effects, leading to elevated prices of essential commodities like food and medicine. The rise in medicine prices particularly impacts patients, who may either forego necessary treatments due to financial constraints or turn to alternative remedies such as homeopathic or herbal solutions.

**Table 8.4 Prevalence of Hepatitis C among General Population of Sindh Province.**

| *Author Citation* | *Year* | *City* | *Population* | *Sample Size* | *HBV prevalence* | *Prevalence/ 100=weightage* | *Prevalence X weightage* | *Weighted average* |
|---|---|---|---|---|---|---|---|---|
| (Arshad et al., 2016) | 2016 | Karachi | Blood donors | 16602 | 1.7 | 0.017 | 0.0289 | |
| (Irfan et al., 2013) | 2004–2011 | Karachi | Blood donors | 108598 | 2.61 | 0.0261 | 0.0681 | |
| (Mir et al., 2020) | 2019 | Larkana | Children | 31239 | 3 | 0.03 | 0.09 | |
| (Aziz et al., 2010) | 2007–2008 | Gharo, Thatta | Healthy Adults | 573 | 3.9 | 0.039 | 0.1521 | |
| (Kazi et al., 2010) | 2010 | Karachi | Prisoners | 357 | 15.2 | 0.152 | 2.3104 | |
| (Janjua et al., 2010) | 2010 | Karachi | Healthy Adults | 1997 | 23.8 | 0.238 | 5.6644 | |
| (Kumar et al.,2010) | 2010 | Tando Muhammad Khan | Healthy Adults | 5989 | 8 | 0.08 | 0.64 | |
| (Ujjan et al., 2021) | 2021 | Tharparkar | Healthy Adults/OPD | 818 | 10.2 | 0.102 | 1.0404 | |
| (Mansoor et al., 2023) | 2023 | Karachi | General Population | 1303 | 13.5 | 0.135 | 1.8225 | |
| (Ghanghro et al., 2016) | 2014 | Naushahro Feroz | Blood donors | 656 | 12.1 | 0.121 | 1.4641 | |
| (Ujjan et al., 2021) | 2021 | Hyderabad | Healthy Adults/OPD | 51622 | 12.7 | 0.127 | 1.6129 | |
| (Ujjan et al., 2021) | 2021 | Dadu OPD | Healthy Adults | 2755 | 13.8 | 0.138 | 1.9044 | |
| (Samo et al., 2021) | 2019 | Nawabshah | Healthy Adults | 514 | 14.3 | 0.143 | 2.0449 | |

(Continued)

**Table 8.4 (Continued)**

| *Author Citation* | *Year* | *City* | *Population* | *Sample Size* | *HBV prevalence* | *Prevalence/ 100=weightage* | *Prevalence X weightage* | *Weighted average* |
|---|---|---|---|---|---|---|---|---|
| (Arain et al., 2020) | 2019 | Mirpur Khas | Healthy Adults | 311 | 14.64 | 0.1464 | 2.1433 | |
| (Ujjan et al., 2021) | 2021 | Ghotki | Healthy Adults/OPD | 867 | 15.6 | 0.156 | 2.4336 | |
| (Ujjan et al., 2021) | 2021 | Kashmore | Healthy Adults/OPD | 2016 | 15.9 | 0.159 | 2.5281 | |
| (Ujjan et al., 2021) | 2021 | Sukkur | Healthy Adults/OPD | 5102 | 16 | 0.16 | 2.56 | |
| (Ujjan et al., 2021) | 2021 | Kahirpur Mirs | Healthy Adults/OPD | 1258 | 18 | 0.18 | 3.24 | |
| (Ujjan et al., 2021) | 2021 | Noshahro Feroz | Healthy Adults/OPD | 2251 | 18.3 | 0.183 | 3.3489 | |
| (Ujjan et al., 2021) | 2021 | Sanhar | Healthy Adults/OPD | 3471 | 19 | 0.19 | 3.61 | |
| (Ujjan et al., 2021) | 2021 | Jamshoro | Healthy Adults/OPD | 4242 | 21.7 | 0.217 | 4.7089 | |
| ( Aziz et al., 2010) | 2007–2008 | Tharoshah, Naushahro Feroz | Healthy AdultsOPD | 573 | 28.6 | 0.286 | 8.1796 | |
| | | | | | | 3.0255 | 51.596 | 17.05355049 |

*Source*: Google Scholar.

The healthcare scenario in Pakistan is further complicated by the government's expenditure of US$38 per capita, significantly lower than other developing countries like India, Ghana, and the Philippines, which allocate US$57, US$165, and US$85 per capita, respectively. This constrained per capita healthcare expenditure limits the ability of Pakistan's government to provide adequate health infrastructure, medicines, medical equipment, and a proficient healthcare workforce (Khan et al., 2023).

In Sindh province, the government has set the minimum wage for unskilled workers at Rs32,000 (equivalent to US$114) per month (Employers' Federation of Pakistan, 2023). However, the prevailing high inflation and escalating cost of living contribute to increased unemployment, income inequality, and reduced purchasing power, affecting access to essential needs such as nutrition, education, and healthcare (United Nations Development Programme, 2023; Chaudhry & Chaudhry, 2008; Zehra, 2023).

Under these challenging circumstances, individuals with limited financial resources may seek more affordable healthcare options, creating space for unregulated medical practices like quackery (Khan et al., 2021). Despite the existence of an Anti-quackery law, patients seeking cost-effective and rapid relief at both regulated and unregulated medical centers are at risk of exposure to excessive therapeutic injections. Reuse of injections poses a substantial threat of transmitting Hepatitis B Virus (HBV) and Hepatitis C Virus (HCV). This chapter aims to comprehensively discuss the hospital-based and non-hospital-based risk factors associated with HBV and HCV.

## Awareness of Hepatitis B and Hepatitis C among Population of Sindh

Healthcare awareness among the population is a crucial part of public health. Public health education aims to make individuals aware of different health-related issues, including infectious diseases such as hepatitis, preventive measures, vaccination, and why timely medical care seeking is essential, so that they can access, understand, and utilize health information to make informed decisions about their well-being. Illiteracy in the general population and lack of awareness in the illiterate and literate populations about the risk factors that contribute to infection by HBV and HCV is a major barrier to the eradication of hepatitis B and hepatitis C and other infectious diseases. Pakistan has a public health component in its federal and provincial health ministries, though it could have performed better in raising people's health literacy. Hospitals are hubs for risk factors of transmission of HBV and HCV. Medical practice watchdogs such as provincial healthcare commissions have failed to force hospital staff to enforce strict infection prevention control practices. Several reports from Sindh province indicate that a substantial percentage of the population is unaware of the risk factors of HBV and HCV. Khowaja and coworkers assessed the knowledge of people attending family clinics and reported that 60 percent of the people believed that HCV is vaccine-preventable, and a majority believed that bad dietary habits are the cause of infection by HBV and HCV (Khuwaja et al., 2002). Mansoor and his workmates from Karachi have reported that 60 percent of participants in a community-based study do not know any ways a person can avoid getting hepatitis C (Mansoor et al., 2023). Majid and colleagues have reported that 68 percent of the urban population was unaware of the risk factors for chronic liver disease. Among this 68 percent, 51.4 percent of the participants don't know that HBV can be transmitted through sexual contact and from mother to baby (Majid et al., 2019). A study conducted in Hyderabad to assess the knowledge of risk factors of HBV and HCV among barbers reported that 64 percent were unaware of the transmission risk factors (Jokhio et al., 2010). This indicates how unregulated professions in the hands of low-literate people can play with lives. Khan et al. have assessed the knowledge about transmission, diagnosis, prevention, and vaccine availability among medical students. They found that 40 percent of medical students have poor knowledge about HBV and HCV spread, 15.9 percent have poor knowledge about diagnosis, 30 percent believe that hepatitis B is completely curable, and 27 percent believe that HCV is not curable (Khan et al., 2010).

## HOSPITAL-BASED RISK FACTORS ASSOCIATED WITH TRANSMISSION OF HEPATITIS B AND HEPATITIS C IN SINDH

### Hospitalization

There are increased cases of hospitalization due to overpopulation and a lack of hospitals in relation to the population (Muhammad et al., 2023; Nawaz et al., 2021). The wards in the hospitals are full of patients; in a few cases, the patients are even accommodated in the same bed. This higher number of patients in the hospitals exposes them to infectious diseases. The longer the stay, the higher the chances; the more repeated the stay, the higher the chances, and this has been documented in several studies. Samo and colleagues reported that among 6.7 percent of HBsAg-positive participants, 2.86 percent had a history of hospitalization. Samo and colleagues, in their same report, have noted that among a total of 14.3 percent of HCV-positive participants, 8.60 percent had a history of hospitalization. Janjua and colleagues reported that among a total of 23.83 percent of the HCV-positive participants, 8.71 percent of the participants had a history of hospitalization. Janjua and colleagues, in their same report, have noted that among a total of 23.83 percent of HCV-positive participants, 6 percent of participants had a history of hospitalization for the treatment of an injury. Abbas and colleagues reported that among a total of 21.10 percent of HCV-positive participants, 2.90 percent had a history of hospitalization, and 8.44 percent of participants had a history of intravenous infusion use (Abbas et al., 2008; Janjua et al., 2009; Mansoor et al., 2023; Samo et al., 2021).

## Reuse of Syringes

The directorate of anti-quackery at Sindh Healthcare Commission, Government of Sindh, Karachi, has inspected 4,315 private practitioners, out of which 3,022 (70 percent) were unlicensed health practitioners of various categories. They observed poor infection control and prevention practices in 89.4 percent (3,861/4,315) of all health providers. The report showed that the reuse of syringes and intravenous drip sets was observed among 78.7 percent (1,916/2,432) of the untrained providers across the province. Authors also found that 155 MBBS doctors had given their names on rent to be used as a signboard outside the clinics of some of the unlicensed practitioners (Khan & Mustufa, 2023; Khan et al., 2020; Mustufa et al., 2021).

Pricking with the needle as a factor has previously been documented in a number of studies. These pricks are usually accidental. Pakistani hospitals are overburdened with patients, having insufficient and untrained staff, which makes it possible either to have a self-prick or prick patients either unknowingly or due to careless handling. A study on needle stick injuries from a tertiary care hospital in Karachi has reported that out of 497, 63 percent of healthcare workers have at least one needle stick injury, 72.8 percent have more than two needle stick injuries, and only 33.2 percent of healthcare workers were vaccinated for HBV. Among those who were injured due by needle, 41 percent were injured while injecting medicine/drawing blood, 36.6 percent were injured while recapping the needle, 21.3 percent were injured during surgical procedure and 13.9 percent were injured due to handling uncooperative patients (Afridi et al., 2013; Soomro, 2005). Samo and colleagues reported that among the total of 6.7 percent of HBsAg-positive participants, 3.49 percent of participants had a history of syringe use. Janjua and colleagues reported that among the total 23.83 percent of HCV-positive participants, 6.35 percent of participants had a history of injection use. Abbas et al. (2008) have reported that among the total of 21.10 percent of HCV-positive participants, 15.83 percent of participants had a history of injection use. Samo and co-workers reported that among a total of 14.3 percent of HCV-positive participants, 11.47 percent had a history of injection use; Mansoor and others reported that 26.1 percent of HCV-positive participants,

17 percent of the participants had a history of therapeutic injection use in the last 12 months (Abbas et al., 2008; Janjua et al., 2009; Mansoor et al., 2023; Samo et al., 2021).

## Dental Treatment

Increased prevalence of HBV and HCV in dental patients can be associated with various practices such as dental procedures involving contact with blood and oral fluids, needlestick injuries or sharps exposure during procedures, and inadequate handling and disposal of sharps. Several studies from different areas of Sindh Province have associated dental treatment with HBV and HCV transmission. Samo and colleagues reported that among 6.7 percent of HBsAg-positive participants, 2.86 percent of participants had a history of dental treatment. Janjua and colleagues reported that among the total of 23.83 percent of HCV-positive participants, 6.05 percent had a history of dental treatment. Abbas et al. (2008) have reported that among the total of 21.10 percent of the HCV-positive participants, 6.33 percent had a history of dental treatment. Samo and co-workers reported that among the total of 14.3 percent of HCV-positive participants, 9.56 percent had a history of dental treatment. Mansoor and others reported that among the total of 32.27 percent of HCV-infected participants, 21.7 percent of participants had a history of dental treatment (Abbas et al., 2008; Janjua et al., 2009; Mansoor et al., 2023; Samo et al., 2021).

## Unsafe Blood Transfusion

Blood transfusion services in Pakistan face challenges, particularly due to the existence of private blood banks engaged in the buying and selling of blood in several cities of Sindh (Butt & Butt, 2015; Kassi et al., 2011). A study conducted in Hyderabad revealed that among blood donors, the seropositivity rates for HCV infection, HBV infection, human immunodeficiency virus infection, and syphilis were 5.1 percent, 1.1 percent, 0.8 percent, and 2.3 percent, respectively (Samo, 2021).

In Karachi, a study involving 173 multi-transfused male hemophilia patients found that 51.4 percent were HBV positive and 1.73 percent were HCV positive (Kiani et al., 2016). Another study by Kiani et al. reported that out of 1,253 multi-transfused thalassemia major patients, 21.7 percent, 3 percent, and 0.5 percent were infected with HCV, HBV, and human immunodeficiency virus infection, respectively (Kiani et al., 2016).

Samo and colleagues discovered that among 6.7 percent of HBsAg-positive participants, 2.86 percent had a history of blood transfusion. Similarly,

Janjua and colleagues reported that out of the total of 23.83 percent of HCV-positive participants, 2.65 percent had a history of blood transfusion. Additionally, Samo and colleagues found that among the total of 14.3 percent of HCV-positive participants, 6.69 percent had a history of blood transfusion. Furthermore, Mansoor and colleagues reported that among 35.6 percent of HCV-positive participants, 23.9 percent had a history of transfusion (Janjua et al., 2009; Mansoor et al., 2023; Samo et al., 2021).

## Marriage, C-section, and Birth

HBV and HCV can potentially be transmitted through sexual intercourse as both viruses can be spread through the exchange of bodily fluids such as blood, semen, and vaginal fluids. If an HBV or HCV-positive person marries a healthy person, the chance of transmission would be increased. Though there is a pre-marital screening program for screening hemoglobinopathies, this program does not screen individuals for infectious diseases such as HIV, HBV, and HCV. This could have impacted prevention efforts negatively. Currently, there is no data that could show the prevalence of HBV or HCV among married couples in Sindh or Pakistan. The cultural barrier is a major hindrance to achieving pre-marital screening for HBV and HCV (Saleem et al., 2017). Janjua and colleagues reported that among the total of 26.03 percent of HCV-positive females, 17.4 percent of females had a history of hospitalization for childbirth (Janjua et al., 2009). A study from the Gynae and Obstetrics Department of Civil Hospital Karachi and Abbasi Shaheed Hospital reported that the prevalence of HCV among pregnant females was 5.79 percent, and 215 babies (age range three months to three years) were also HCV positive. This study reported that the HCV vertical transmission rate was 1.39 percent (Aziz et al., 2010).

## Hemodialysis

Kidney patients need dialysis to remove waste products from their blood, a process called hemodialysis. This process is done by a medical instrument called a dialysis machine. If the healthcare staff involved in dialysis ignores or breaches infection control practices, there is a risk of HCV transmission. Previously, at Larkana, a breach in infection control practices at a tertiary care hospital during dialysis infected fifty-four normal persons with HIV (Dawn, 2016). A recently published meta-analysis showed that the prevalence of HCV in hemodialysis patients in Sindh was 27.11 percent (95 percent CI: 15.81–40.12; I2 = 94.5, $p < 0.01$) (Sohail Akhtar et al., 2020).

### No Vaccination

The vaccine for HBV is available in Pakistan, and an uninfected person can be immunized through three shots of the HBV vaccine. Pakistan has started vaccinating its population against HBV. However, there is no publicly accessible data on how much of the Pakistani population of different age groups is unvaccinated. In the context of HBV, the unvaccinated person is at risk of HBV infection. Abbas and colleagues reported that among the total of 21.10 percent of HCV-positive participants, 13.19 percent of participants were unvaccinated for HBV (Abbas et al., 2008). There is no vaccination available for HCV; however, through therapeutic treatment, HCV can be completely cured.

## NON-HOSPITAL-BASED RISK FACTORS ASSOCIATED WITH HBV AND HCV IN SINDH

### Multiple Sexual Contacts

The context of having sex with multiple sexual partners is complex and may depend on cultural, societal, individual, and interpersonal factors. Social influences, such as peer dynamics, societal trends, or media portrayal of relationships, can shape a person's choices regarding the number of sexual partners (Faisal et al., 2022). Some partners have a strong desire for sexual sensation, which is diminished by condoms; this often leads to unprotected sex, which can be a risk factor for HBV and HCV transmission. Samo and colleagues reported that among the total of 6.7 percent of HBsAg-positive participants, 0.95 percent had a history of sex with more than one partner. Janjua and colleagues reported that among the total of 19.37 percent of HCV-positive males, 1.86 percent of the male participants had a history of sexual intercourse with women other than their spouse (Janjua et al., 2009; Samo et al., 2021).

### Barbershops

The majority of the Pakistani population goes to barbershops for shaving and haircuts. Most barbers are unaware of the routes of transmission of HBV and HCV. They use unsterilized razors, scissors, or clippers between infected and uninfected clients, which can contribute to the transmission of hepatitis. Samo and co-workers reported that 6.7 percent of HBsAg-positive participants, 3.82 percent, have a history of shaving at barbershops. Samo and his colleagues, in their same report, noted that among the total of 14.3

percent of HCV-positive participants, 8.60 percent have a history of shaving at a barbershop. Janjua and colleagues reported that among the total 19.37 percent of HCV-positive males, 19.22 percent of the male participants had a history of shaving at barbershops. Abbas and colleagues reported that among the total 21.10 percent of HCV-positive participants, 7.65 percent had a history of shaving at barbershops (Abbas et al., 2008; Janjua et al., 2009; Samo et al., 2021).

### Piercing

Piercing has been associated as a risk factor for the transmission of HBV and HCV. Piercing ear and nose has a cultural and aesthetic value, and it is considered to symbolize marriage. Compared to urban areas, the trend is common in rural areas. Unprofessional piercers in rural areas lack education about health, including routes of transmission of HBV and HCV. Piercers use contaminated needles to prick and make an opening in the nose and ear of females for jewelry. This could be a potential source of HBV and HCV transmission. (Sajjad & Jafree, 2023; Trickey et al., 2017). Janjua and colleagues reported that among 26.06 percent of HCV-positive female participants, 25.66 percent of the females had a history of ear/nose piercing. Abbas and co-workers reported that among 21.10 percent of HCV-positive participants, 12.13 percent had a history of ear piercing (Zaigham et al., 2008; Janjua et al., 2009).

## DEMOGRAPHIC FACTORS ASSOCIATED WITH HBV AND HCV IN SINDH

The demographic factors associated with HBV and HCV prevalence in Sindh are severely underreported in existing literature. Very few reports have noted such associations. A study conducted in rural areas of Upper Sindh has reported that factors such as increasing age and the male population are associated with an increased prevalence of HBV and HCV (Zaigham et al., 2008). Three other studies from Karachi, Mirpur Khas, and Nawab Shah reported a positive association of demographic factors such as age, male population, marriage, and illiteracy with increased prevalence of HBV and HCV (Arain et al., 2020; Mansoor et al., 2023; Samo et al., 2021). The findings of these studies regarding increasing age, male gender, and illiteracy are consistent; however, one study from Karachi has noted that the female population has been associated with an increased prevalence of HCV (Janjua et al., 2009).

## DISCUSSION

In the context of developing countries like Pakistan, the HBV and HCV incidence is mainly driven by two factors: (1) hospital-based risk factors and (2) non-hospital-based risk factors. The hospital-based risk factors include the use of unsafe hospitals, reused syringes, needle pricking, dental pricking treatment, pregnancy, c-section, birth, hemodialysis, and vaccination, which is regarded as invasive medical practice. Non-hospital-based risk factors include shaving and haircutting at barbershops, piercing, multiple sexual contacts, and circumcisions. The relationship between the noted hospital-based and non-hospital-based factors and the transmission of HBV and HCV underscores a significant concern within healthcare settings. The prevalence rates of HBV and HCV are high among the high-risk population and the public also. This highlights the substantial risk posed by the above medical procedures followed by non-hospital-based risk factors. From this understanding of transmission dynamics, it becomes imperative to implement strict protocols to safeguard healthcare providers and patients from HBV and HCV infections.

Addressing the challenges posed by HBV and HCV in the context of hospital-based and non-hospital-based risk factors necessitates a comprehensive approach, starting with mass-level screening of HBV and HCV vaccination against HBV, improved infection prevention strategies in all healthcare settings, and ongoing research initiatives. By fostering a commitment to proactive infection control measures, we can eradicate the risk of HBV and HCV transmission in all settings. We need to ensure the safety of individuals seeking medical care in hospitals. Educating people about non-hospital-based risk factors and regulating barbers and piercers are key steps to prevent non-hospital-based transmission of HBV and HCV.

## RECOMMENDATIONS TO THE GOVERNMENT OF SINDH

(1) The Hepatitis Control Program of the Government of Sindh, in collaboration with the Pakistan Telecom Authority, should send text messages to people providing information about the nearest vaccination centers for HBV and treatment centers for HCV. Hepatitis control programs should visit each union council of Sindh for mass screening and immunize unvaccinated individuals against HBV. These statistics on Union Council-level immunization should be publicly accessible to the community and healthcare staff.

(2) The health department of the Government of Sindh should reduce the severe shortage of qualified doctors, nurses, and paramedical staff

in public hospitals by employing competent staff who have sound knowledge and experience about safe and infection-free medical procedures such as injection use, intravenous infusion, hemodialysis, and blood transfusion. Hospital administrators should ensure an adequate supply of new syringes, gloves, goggles, and protective face shields for staff involved in pricking. Healthcare staff should mark the hemodialysis machine separately for HBV, HCV, HBV+HCV coinfection, HIV, HIV+HBV, HIV+HCV, and HIV+HVB+HCV coinfected individuals.

(3) The unregulated blood banks are involved in activities like lack of donor screening, inadequate testing practices, poor quality control measures, absence of training and education, lack of reporting mechanisms, illegal blood trade, and transmission of HIV, HBV, and HCV through contaminated equipment and facilities. The Sindh Healthcare Commission should strictly regulate the blood banks as per the standard protocols set by the World Health Organization for blood banks.

(4) Injectable drug abuse is a matter of concern in Pakistan. Despite having anti-narcotics departments, drug abuse is rising in Pakistan, so if the anti-narcotics department does not control drug abuse, the Government of Sindh should provide medically regulated safe spaces to individuals who consume drugs. Adopting this model will help to prevent not only HBV and HCV but also HIV.

(5) The government of Sindh has a pre-marital screening program for hemoglobinopathies; it should also include infectious diseases to screen unmarried people. Adopting will help in reducing vertical and horizontal transmission.

(6) The Sindh Healthcare Commission should introduce the mobile application "Sindh Health App" for medical records. This app should be accessible to individuals and healthcare providers. All the physicians, surgeons, and hospital administrators should enter patients' medical histories in this mobile app. Sindh Health App should have the person's vaccination status and medical history. By viewing medical history, the healthcare staff should take precautionary measures to control vertical and horizontal transmission of infections. This app should also alert a person to nearby regulated and unregulated hospitals.

(7) Sindh province is rich in natural resources. There are many multinational and national companies operating in Sindh province extracting oil, gas, minerals, and other natural resources. Constitutionally, such companies are bound to perform their corporate social responsibilities. Through its District Commissioners, the Government of Sindh should bind these companies to provide hemodialysis machines to district and taluka hospitals and free mobile temperature-controlled vehicles

equipped with screening kits and HBV vaccines. Companies should immunize all the uninfected individuals and provide screening and treatment services to HCV-infected people.

(8) Public health education is necessary to prevent communicable and non-communicable diseases. Research publications are continuously reporting that HBV and HCV are increasing among males, the illiterate population, and married and young adults. Through its Health Department, the Government of Sindh should design a District Public Health Education Program. This program, in collaboration with academic institutions and the directorate of health, should hire graduates of Public Health, Physiology, and Microbiology as "Health Education Officers." The duty of these health education officers would be to make the district population aware of the threats Pakistan and Sindh face due to communicable and non-communicable diseases, screening, immunization, and treatment of diseases. The Government of Sindh, through its School Education Department, should introduce public health lessons to make the leaders of tomorrow aware of health issues.

## REFERENCES

Aamir, K., & Mehmood, K. (2000). Seroprevalence of HBV, HCV and HIV infections among college going first time voluntary blood donors. *JPMA. The Journal of the Pakistan Medical Association*, *50*(8), 269–270.

Abbas, Z., Jeswani, N. L., Kakepoto, G. N., Islam, M., Mehdi, K., & Jafri, W. (2008). Prevalence and mode of spread of hepatitis B and C in rural Sindh, Pakistan. *Trop Gastroenterol*, *29*(4), 210–216.

Abdullah, F. E., Memon, A. A., Mushtaq, A., Adil, S. E. E. R., & Kazmi, S. U. (2012). Frequency of HBsAg positivity: A laboratory data analysis. *Journal of the College of Physicians and Surgeons Pakistan*, *22*(11), 742–743.

Afreen, H., Sheikh, M., Jamal, D. E. N., Butt, H. O., Wadood, M., & Ali, A. (2023). Assessment of the infectious status of transmissible transfusion infections (Hepatitis B and C) among β-Thalassemia major patients of Karachi; A multicenter study by SBTA (Sindh Blood Transfusion Authority). *Pakistan Journal of Medical & Health Sciences*, *17*(01), 675–675.

Afridi, A. A. K., Kumar, A., & Sayani, R. (2013). Needle stick injuries–risk and preventive factors: A study among health care workers in tertiary care hospitals in Pakistan. *Global Journal of Health Science*, *5*(4), 85.

Ahmed Kiani, R., Anwar, M., Waheed, U., Asad, M. J., Abbasi, S., & Abbas Zaheer, H. (2016). Epidemiology of transfusion transmitted infection among patients with β-thalassaemia major in Pakistan. *Journal of Blood Transfusion*, *2016*, 8135649.

Akhtar, S., Nasir, J. A., Usman, M., Sarwar, A., Majeed, R., & Billah, B. (2020). The prevalence of hepatitis C virus in hemodialysis patients in Pakistan: A systematic review and meta-analysis. *PLoS One*, *15*(5), e0232931.

Akhtar, S., Younus, M., Adil, S., Hassan, F., & Jafri, S. H. (2005). Epidemiologic study of chronic hepatitis B virus infection in male volunteer blood donors in Karachi, Pakistan. *BMC gastroenterology*, *5*, 1–9.

Altaf, A., Shah, S. A., Zaidi, N. A., Memon, A., & Wray, N. (2007). High risk behaviors of injection drug users registered with harm reduction programme in Karachi, Pakistan. *Harm Reduction Journal*, *4*(1), 1–6.

Ansari, S. H., Shamsi, T. S., Khan, M. T., Perveen, K., Farzana, T., Erum, S., & Ansari, I. (2012). Seropositivity of Hepatitis C, Hepatitis B and HIV in chronically transfused ββ-thalassaemia major patients. *Journal of College of Physicians and Surgeons Pakistan*, *22*(9), 610–611.

Arain, M. A., Laghari, Z. A., Samo, A. A., Memon, S. F., Shaikh, S. A., & Warsi, J. (2020). Prevalence and risk factors associated with Hepatitis B and Hepatitis C infection in Mirpurkhas, Sindh, Pakistan. *Rawal Medical Journal*, *45*(4), 750–750.

Arshad, A., Borhany, M., Anwar, N., Naseer, I., Ansari, R., Boota, S., . . . & Shamsi, T. (2016). Prevalence of transfusion transmissible infections in blood donors of Pakistan. *BMC Hematology*, *16*, 1–6.

Aziz, S., Hossain, N., Karim, S. A., Rajper, J., Soomro, N., Noorulain, W., . . . & Khanani, R. (2011). Vertical transmission of hepatitis C virus in low to middle socioeconomic pregnant population of Karachi. *Hepatology International*, *5*, 677–680.

Aziz, S., Khanani, R., Noorulain, W., & Rajper, J. (2010). Frequency of hepatitis B and C in rural and periurban Sindh. *JPMA-Journal of the Pakistan Medical Association*, *60*(10), 853.

Aziz, S., Memon, A., Tily, H. I., Rasheed, K., Jehangir, K., & Quraishy, M. S. (2002). Prevalence of HIV, hepatitis B and C amongst health workers of Civil Hospital Karachi. *Journal-Pakistan Medical Association*, *52*(3), 92–94.

Bibi, S., Dars, S., Ashfaq, S., Qazi, R. A., & Akhund, S. (2013). Seroprevalence and risk factors for hepatitis C virus (HCV) infection in pregnant women attending public sector tertiary care hospital in Hyderabad Sindh. *Pakistan Journal of Medical Sciences*, *29*(2), 505.

Borhany, M., Shamsi, T., Boota, S., Ali, H., Tahir, N., Naz, A., . . . & Sangji, Z. (2011). Transfusion transmitted infections in patients with hemophilia of Karachi, Pakistan. *Clinical and Applied Thrombosis/Hemostasis*, *17*(6), 651–655.

Butt, M., & Butt, M. A. (2015). Illegal blood banks are causing morbidity and mortality due to unsafe blood transfusions in Pakistan-increasing the number of regular unpaid volunteer donors is the solution to this problem. *An Experience of the Bangladeshi Garment Industry*. Retrieved from https://platform.almanhal.com /Files/Articles/74075.

Chaudhry, A., & Chaudhry, T. T. (2008). The effects of rising food and fuel costs in Pakistan. *The Lahore Journal of Economics, Special Edition*, 117–138.

Chhatwal, J., Chen, Q., Wang, X., Ayer, T., Zhuo, Y., Janjua, N. Z., & Kanwal, F. (2019). Assessment of the feasibility and cost of hepatitis C elimination in Pakistan. *JAMA Network Open*, 2(5), e193613–e193613.

Daudpota, A. Q., & Soomro, A. W. (2008). Sero prevalence of hepatitis B and C in surgical patients. *Pakistan Journal of Medical Sciences*, *24*(3), 483.

Dawn. (2016, October 12). The code of conduct for armed forces. Retrieved from https://www.dawn.com/news/1289582.

Employers' Federation of Pakistan. (2023). Sindh Minimum Wages (Unskilled Workers) Notification 2023. Retrieved from https://lhr.sindh.gov.pk/notifications.

Faisal, K., Rashid, A., & Khan, S. (2022). What leads to premarital sex among young males in Pakistan. *Journal of Professional & Applied Psychology*, *3*(1), 69–84.

Ghanghro, A. A., & Jokhio, P. (2016). High prevalence of hepatitis C and hepatitis B infection among pregnant women and their blood donors attending a surgical referral clinic in District Naushahro Feroze, Sindh, Pakistan 2014. *International Journal of Infectious Diseases*, *45*, 437.

Hoofnagle, J. H. (1997). Hepatitis C: The clinical spectrum of disease. *Hepatology*, *26*(S3), 15S–20S.

Hussain, S., Baloch, S., Parvin, A., Najmuddin, A., Musheer, F., Junaid, M., . . . & Moiz, B. (2018). Inherited bleeding disorders—Experience of a not-for-profit organization in Pakistan. *Clinical and Applied Thrombosis/Hemostasis*, *24*(8), 1241–1248.

Irfan, S. M., Uddin, J., Zaheer, H. A., Sultan, S., & Baig, A. (2013). Trends in transfusion-transmitted infections among replacement blood donors in Karachi, Pakistan. *Turkish Journal of Hematology, 30*(2), 163–167. https://doi.org/10.4274/Tjh.2012.0132.

Jafri, W., Jafri, N., Yakoob, J., Islam, M., Tirmizi, S. F. A., Jafar, T., . . . & Nizami, S. Q. (2006). Hepatitis B and C: Prevalence and risk factors associated with seropositivity among children in Karachi, Pakistan. *BMC Infectious Diseases*, *6*(1), 1–10.

Janjua, N. Z., Hamza, H. B., Islam, M., Tirmizi, S. F. A., Siddiqui, A., Jafri, W., & Hamid, S. (2010). Health care risk factors among women and personal behaviors among men explain the high prevalence of hepatitis C virus infection in Karachi, Pakistan. *Journal of Viral Hepatitis*, *17*(5), 317–326.

Jokhio, A. H., Bhatti, T. A., & Memon, M. S. (2010). Knowledge, attitudes and practices of barbers about hepatitis B and C transmission in Hyderabad, Pakistan. *EMHJ-Eastern Mediterranean Health Journal, 16*(10), 1079–1084.

Kakepoto, G. N., Bhally, H. S., Khaliq, G., Kayani, N., Burney, I. A., Siddiqui, T., & Khurshid, M. (1996). Epidemiology of blood-borne viruses: A study of healthy blood donors in Southern Pakistan. *The Southeast Asian Journal of Tropical Medicine and Public Health*, *27*(4), 703–706.

Kassi, M., Afghan, A. K., Khanani, M. R., Khan, I. A., & Ali, S. H. (2011). Safe blood transfusion practices in blood banks of Karachi, Pakistan. *Transfusion Medicine*, *21*(1), 57–62.

Khan, K. A., Iftikhar, T., Anwar, S., Ahmad, A., & Anwar, S. (2021). An assessment of major factors contributing towards choosing alternate healers (Hakeem, Dispenser, Spiritual Healer) over Registered Medical Practitioner (RMP). *Pakistan Journal of Public Health*, *11*(4), 268–273.

Khan, N., Ahmed, S. M., Khalid, M. M., Siddiqui, S. H., & Merchant, A. A. (2010). Effect of gender and age on the knowledge, attitude and practice regarding hepatitis

B and C and vaccination status of hepatitis B among medical students of Karachi. *Pakistan. Journal of Pakistan Medical Association*, *60*(6), 450–455.

Khan, R., & Mustufa, M. A. (2023). An empirical research study on deluging quackery outlets across Sindh, Pakistan and propositions to deal with confounding factors of rising quackery. *JPMA. The Journal of the Pakistan Medical Association*, *73*(1), 135–138.

Khan, R., Mustufa, M. A., & Hussain, S. (2020). Factors contributing to the public proneness towards quacks in Sindh. *Pan African Medical Journal*, *37*(1), 1–5.

Khan, S. J., Asif, M., Aslam, S., Khan, W. J., & Hamza, S. A. (2023). Pakistan's healthcare system: A review of major challenges and the first comprehensive universal health coverage initiative. *Cureus*, *15*(9).

Khuwaja, A. K., Qureshi, R., & Fatmi, Z. (2002). Knowledge about hepatitis B and C among patients attending family medicine clinics in Karachi. *Eastern Mediterranean Health Journal*, *8*(6), 787.

Kumar, A., Lalani, S., Afridi, A. A. K., & Khuwaja, A. K. (2010). Screening of hepatitis B and C among people visiting general practice clinics in a rural district of Sindh, Pakistan. *Journal of Ayub Medical College*, *22*(4), 143.

Liang, T. J. (2009). Hepatitis B: The virus and disease. *Hepatology*, *49*(S5), S13–S21.

Lohano, M. K., Su, L., Narsani, A. K., Jawed, M., & Naveed, H. (2016). Frequency of Hepatitis B surface antigen (HBsAg) and Hepatitis C antibody (HCVAb) seropositivity among preoperative eye surgery patients. *British Journal of Medical Practitioners*, *9*(2), 5–9.

Majid, B., Khan, R., Junaid, Z., Khurshid, O., Rehman, S. H., Jaffri, S. N., . . . & Safina, F. (2019). Assessment of knowledge about the risk Factors for chronic liver disease in patients admitted in Civil Hospital Karachi. *Cureus*, *11*(10):e5945. DOI 10.7759/cureus.594

Mansoor, M., De Glanville, W. A., Alam, R., Aslam, K., Ahmed, M., Isaakidis, P., & Pasha, A. (2023). Prevalence and risk factors for hepatitis C virus infection in an informal settlement in Karachi, Pakistan. *PLOS Global Public Health*, *3*(9), e0002076.

Memon, A. R., Shafique, K., Memon, A., Draz, A. U., Rauf, M. U. A., & Afsar, S. (2012). Hepatitis B and C prevalence among the high risk groups of Pakistani population. A cross sectional study. *Archives of Public Health*, *70*, 1–6.

Mir, F., Mahmood, F., Siddiqui, A. R., Baqi, S., Abidi, S. H., Kazi, A. M., . . . & Ferrand, R. A. (2020). HIV infection predominantly affecting children in Sindh, Pakistan, 2019: A cross-sectional study of an outbreak. *The Lancet Infectious Diseases*, *20*(3), 362–370.

Moosa, F. A., Shaikh, B. A., Choudhry, M. S., Zuberi, B. F., Khan, F. W., & Sultan, N. (2009). Frequency of hepatitis B and C in pre-operative patients for elective surgery. *JLUMHS*, *8*(2), 150–152.

Muhammad, Q., Eiman, H., Fazal, F., Ibrahim, M., & Gondal, M. F. (2023). Healthcare in Pakistan: Navigating challenges and building a brighter future. *Cureus*, *15*(6): e40218. DOI 10.7759/cureus.40218

Mujeeb, S. A., & Pearce, M. S. (2008). Temporal trends in hepatitis B and C infection in family blood donors from interior Sindh, Pakistan. *BMC Infectious Diseases*, *8*, 1–6.

Mustufa, M. A., Khan, R., Hussain, S., & Qidwai, M. A. (2021). Regulation of quackery amid unprecedented HIV outbreak in Sindh, Pakistan. *JPMA. The Journal of the Pakistan Medical Association*, *71*(8), S22–S25.

Naeem, S. S., Siddiqui, E. U., Kazi, A. N., Khan, S., Abdullah, F. E., & Adhi, I. (2012). Prevalence of Hepatitis "B"and Hepatitis "C"among preoperative cataract patients in Karachi. *BMC Research Notes*, *5*(1), 1–4.

Naseeb, S., Rashid, S., & Dehar, S. (2023). The frequency of Hepatitis B and C and its risk factors in pregnant women presenting at Jinnah Postgraduate medical center, Karachi: Hepatitis B and C and its risk factors in pregnant women. *Pakistan Journal of Health Sciences*, 83–87.

Nawaz, R., Zhou, Z., Khalid, N., Cao, D., Liu, G., Ren, Y., . . . & Chen, Y. (2021). Income-related inequality in distribution of health human resource among districts of Pakistan. *BMC Health Services Research*, *21*, 1–15.

Noorali, S., Hakim, S. T., McLean, D., Kazmi, S. U., & Bagasra, O. (2008). Prevalence of Hepatitis B virus genotype D in females in Karachi, Pakistan. *The Journal of Infection in Developing Countries*, *2*(05), 373–378.

Puno, S. N., Gemnani, V. K., Parkash, O., Naz, L., Kumar, R., & Abro, K. (2021, May). Prevalence of Hepatitis B and Hepatitis C among patients of thalassemia major at a teaching hospital in Larkana. *Medical Forum, 32*(5), 44.

Qazi, A., Shanker, B., Rathi, R., & Kumar, N. (2019). Seroprevalence of Hepatitis-B virus and Hepatitis-C virus in pregnant women in Hyderabad. *Journal of Muhammad Medical College*, *10*(2), 59–61. Retrieved from https://blog-pfm.imf.org/en/pfmblog/2023/08/pakistan-s-debt-.

Riaz, H., Riaz, T., Ullah, F., Aziz, S., Khan, M. U., Pervaiz, R., . . . & Naqvi, S. A. A. (2011). Assessment of the seroprevalence of viral hepatitis B, viral hepatitis C and HIV in multitransfused thalassaemia major patients in Karachi, Pakistan. *Tropical Doctor*, *41*(1), 23–25.

Sajjad, T., & Jafree, S. R. (2023). A qualitative exploration of the health awareness and social challenges facing Pakistani youth engaging in body piercing and tattooing. *International Journal of Natural Medicine and Health Sciences*, 2(3), 1–8.

Saleem, H., Khan, M., Ali, S. I., Khan, A. A., Iqbal, S., Khan, M., . . . & Ali, S. A. (2017). Premarital screening–awareness and acceptability among the population of Hyderabad, Pakistan. *Madinat Al-Hikmah*, *60*(3), 41.

Sami, S., Korejo, R., & Bhutta, S. Z. (2009). Prevalence of hepatitis B and C: a Jinnah Postgraduate Medical Centre experience. *Journal of Obstetrics and Gynaecology Research*, *35*(3), 533–538.

Samo, A. A., Baig, N. M., Sidhu, A., Shaikh, S. N., & Laghari, Z. A. (2021). Seropositivity of Hepatitis B, Hepatitis C, human immunodeficiency virus and syphilis in blood donors of Hyderabad, Sindh, Pakistan. *Sindh University Research Journal*, 53(2), 155–158.

Samo, A. A., Laghari, Z. A., Baig, N. M., & Khoso, G. M. (2021). Prevalence and risk factors associated with hepatitis B and C in Nawabshah, Sindh, Pakistan. *The American Journal of Tropical Medicine and Hygiene*, *104*(3), 1101.

Soomro, F. R. (2005). HIV/AIDS control in Larkana/Kamber Shahdadkot district, Sindh. Perspectives. *Infectious Diseases Journal of Pakistan, 2*(1), 66–67.

Sultan, S., Irfan, S. M., Siddiqui, M., & Zaidi, S. M. (2016). Current trends of seroprevalence of transfusion transmitted infections in Pakistani β-thalassaemic patients. *The Malaysian Journal of Pathology*, *38*(3), 251.

Surahio, A. R., Talpur, A. A., Kella, N. L., & Memon, A. S. (2012). Prevalence of Hepatitis B & C in patients for emergency surgery: An institutional experience. *Medical Channel*, *18*(1), 84–86

Trickey, A., May, M. T., Davies, C., Qureshi, H., Hamid, S., Mahmood, H., . . . & Vickerman, P. (2017). Importance and contribution of community, social, and healthcare risk factors for hepatitis C infection in Pakistan. *The American Journal of Tropical Medicine and Hygiene*, *97*(6), 1920.

Ujjan, I. D., Khan, D., Ujjan, A. A., Abro, A. A., Kandhro, F., Khokhar, N. A., & Nizamani, R. N. (2021). Prevalence of hepatitis c virus antibodies: A case study of outpatients in sindh, pakistan. *International Journal of Biology and Biotechnology*, 18(1), 45–64.

United Nations Development Programme. (2023). Choosing Development: DAP—Volume 10, Issue 2. Retrieved from https://www.undp.org/sites/g/files/zskgke326/files/2023-08/dap_-_volume_10_issue_2_-_choosing_development_14-08-2023.pdf.

Waheed, A. (2023). Pakistan's Debt Dilemma. IMF Public Financial Management Blog.

World Health Organization. (2023). Prevention & control of hepatitis. Retrieved from https://www.emro.who.int/pak/programmes/prevention-a-control-of-hepatitis.html.

Zehra, N. (2023). Consequences of uncertain food prices on household health and education living in urban areas of Pakistan. *Human Nature Journal of Social Sciences*, *4*(3), 242–255.

## *Chapter 9*

# Social and Economic Burden of Non-Communicable Diseases (NCDs) in Pakistan

Muhammad Ashar Malik, Shehzad Ali, and Mohammad Wasay

With over 241 million inhabitants, Pakistan is the fifth most populous country in the world (Pakistan Bureau of Statistics, 2023), with approximately 50 percent of the population suffering from one or more non-communicable diseases (NCDs) such as cardiovascular diseases (including stroke and heart disease), diabetes, mental health disorders, cancers, and chronic airway diseases (Jafar et al., 2013). Deaths due to NCDs now far outnumber deaths due to communicable diseases. The Global Burden of Disease 2010 data suggests that NCDs and injuries account for 77 percent of age-standardized deaths in Pakistan (Lozano et al., 2010).

The infant mortality rate for Pakistan in 2023 was 55.7 deaths per 1,000 live births, a 1.95 percent decline from 2022. Maternal mortality is high, with 154 women dying for every 100,000 live births, mainly due to socioeconomic status and barriers to healthcare access in rural areas. The current life expectancy for Pakistan in 2024 is 67.94 years, a 0.22 percent increase from 2023. A study from 2013 reported that an estimated 40 million individuals in Pakistan suffer from high blood pressure, 32 million from heart disease, 24 million from obesity, 18 million from high cholesterol, 8 million from diabetes, and about 50 million from mental health disorders out of a 180 million population (Jafar et al., 2013). At the current rate, the burden is expected to increase by 10–15 percent over the next ten years. Using population-level mortality rates, Jafar et al. (2013) have projected that between 2010 and 2025, 3.87 million Pakistanis will die due to NCDs like cardiovascular diseases, cancers, and chronic respiratory diseases. They projected that the economic burden associated with NCD deaths will rise from US$152 million in the year

2010 to US$296 million in 2025 (Jafar et al., 2013). If disabilities and mental health disorders are added to Jafar et al.'s (2013) estimates, this number would be far greater.

In the post-devolution era, provincial governments constitute a substantial share of public sector spending compared with the federal government. Since devolution, the share of health allocation by the provincial governments has increased from 4 percent to 6 percent of the budget in 2010 to 8–11 percent of the budget in 2012–2013 (Lozano et al., 2010). However, most of the allocations are for curative services, leaving few resources for health promotion and prevention of NCDs (Lakha KS, 2013).

Researchers have identified key risk factors that, if addressed, will avert more than six hundred thousand deaths due to major NCDs in the next ten years. These include simple measures such as a 30 percent reduction in tobacco use, a 3 mm reduction in systolic blood pressure, increased consumption of fruits and vegetables, and an increase in physical activity, to name a few (Jafar et al., 2013; Nishtar et al., 2013). Four cost-effective interventions, including low salt intake, tobacco cessation, exercise, and recommended pharmacotherapy, are known to reduce NCD-related mortality and morbidity in Pakistan (Wasay et al., 2009). What is needed now are functional platforms for providing stewardship on NCD control and a multi-pronged approach involving regulation, primary care interventions, awareness, and surveillance to reduce NCDs on a national scale. Pakistan is fortunate to have experts in both the public and private sectors who can actively contribute toward a health system's response to NCDs (Zaidi et al., 2012). Primary prevention programs with the least cost and higher benefits should be prioritized in national and provincial resource allocation. Population-based, cost-effective interventions must become a priority agenda for future research (Malik et al., 2013).

The current focus of policy and planning is disease-oriented, but it must become health-oriented with an enhanced focus on primary care, prevention, and health promotion. The best strategy to handle NCDs is primary prevention. This editorial suggests many interventions, including government taxation and law enforcement, in addition to using part of philanthropic funding for primary care. Despite decades of health promotion, education, and advocacy work, mental health remains a neglected area in Pakistan (Sohail et al., 2017). A recent Global Burden of Disease study found that depressive disorders alone are one of the top three causes of years lost due to disability in Pakistan (Hafeez et al., 2023). Estimates suggest that the economic burden of mental illnesses in Pakistan is approximately £2.97 billion (or 1 trillion 55 billion PKR; Alvi et al., 2023). This contrasts with the budgetary allocation of 2.4 billion PKR (0.4 percent of the health budget) for mental health, a reflection of the lack of priority for policymakers.

Non-communicable diseases (NCDs) are emerging threats to health systems and economies. Over the past two decades, the burden of NCDs has escalated. The spread of NCDs in low- and low-middle-income countries (LMICs) is unprecedented and needs the urgent attention of local policymakers and development partners. Pakistan is a low-middle-income country. With a weak economic base, the management of NCDs in Pakistan is challenging yet crucial to the country's economic development. In this chapter, the economics of NCDs in Pakistan is discussed with supporting evidence. Where appropriate, local and international scientific literature is used, while further analysis of existing data on health systems and healthcare financing is carried out. We first discuss the global perspective of the economics of NCDs, followed by sections on the local context, local evidence on the economics of NCDs, a review of health systems and healthcare financing in the context of NCDs, and financing planning and fiscal space for funding NCDs in Pakistan. Lastly, a set of mitigation strategies is proposed for the attention of health policymakers and planners, prior to the conclusion.

## GLOBAL PERSPECTIVE

The global perspective on the economics of NCDs encompasses two aspects: the economic consequences of NCDs and the costs of inaction toward the management of NCDs. Firstly, the economic burden of NCDs studied by the World Economic Forum and Harvard University is among the few systematic efforts sensitizing political economists on the threat NCDs pose to the global economy in the form of lost productivity (Bloom and Cafiero et al., 2011). Using the value of lost output, it provides the economic consequences of five major NCDs: Cancer, Cardiovascular Diseases (CVDs), Chronic Obstructive Pulmonary Diseases (COPD), diabetes, and Mental Disorders in 2010, with projections for 2030. The projected cost estimates stood at US$ 46.7 trillion, with a major share attributed to CVDs and mental disorders both in high-income and low- and low-middle-income countries (LMICs). The economic burden of NCDs borne by LMICs was US$ 21.3 trillion (Bloom and Cafiero et al., 2012).

Secondly, the study commissioned by the Lancet estimated a US$ 85 billion loss of economic productivity as the cost of inaction on three major NCDs: heart disease, stroke, and diabetes in twenty-three LMICs over 2006–2015 (Abegunde et al., 2007). Applying an economic perspective on NCDs highlighted the economic and social costs surpassing the treatment cost of managing the NCDs. The underlying objective of estimating the economic consequences of NCDs was realizing the shared responsibility for the control of NCDs among the economic policymakers besides the health policymakers (Abegunde et al., 2007).

## THE LOCAL CONTEXT

Like other emerging economies, Pakistan is facing the emerging threat of NCDs. Pakistan is experiencing similar NCD prevalence pathways that are globally established, such as rapid urbanization, stressful lifestyles, changes in dietary intake, and lack of physical activity (Oni et al., 2020). Besides many positive effects of the emerging middle class, these lifestyle modifications are known for developing risk factors such as raised blood pressure, raised blood glucose levels, and mental distress that, if unchecked, will progress to heart diseases, diabetes, pulmonary disorders, malignant neoplasms, and mental disorders (Oni et al., 2020).

In Pakistan, 38 percent of the population currently lives in urban areas. Over the last two decades, the rate of urbanization in Pakistan has been among the highest in South Asia and is projected to be 50 percent by the year 2025 (UNDP, 2024). Parallel to this trend is the declining pattern of the share of the agriculture sector in the national income, which currently stands at 22 percent of GDP, moving down from 25 percent in the year 2000 (Government of Pakistan, 2020). The indicators of a sedentary lifestyle, for example, the use of the internet and mobile phones, have substantially heightened in the last two decades. The proportion of internet users increased from 1 percent in 2000 to 25 percent in 2022, and subscribers of mobile phones increased from >1 million in 2000 to 189 million in 2021 (World Bank, 2024). During a similar period (2004–2018), the population living below the poverty line declined from 52 percent to 22 percent (Haque et al., 2021). Recent research on unhealthy lifestyles reported that more than 80 percent of the respondents consumed an unhealthy diet. The same study reported that more than 50 percent of adolescents were physically inactive during the recall period of the survey (Rao & Shah, 2015).

An economic perspective on emerging NCDs hints that infectious and communicable diseases are managed with low-cost treatment regimes, while the cost of non-communicable diseases is often high and recurring over the lifespan. To highlight the economic consequences of NCDS, a study estimated out-of-pocket health expenditure for communicable diseases and NCDs. The findings showed stark differences in households' OPHE of PKR 405 (US$ 6.77) and PKR 3,935 (USUS$ 65.80) in the treatment of NCDs (Nishtar et al., 2005).

The economic consequences of non-communicable diseases (NCDs) are twofold: the loss of productivity and income and the cost of treatment of NCDs. The productivity losses of NCDs adversely impact the national income, whereas the treatment cost increases financial pressure on healthcare delivery systems. Moreover, the productivity losses are more immense than the health system costs of NCD management, especially for mental disorders (table 9.1).

**Table 9.1 Health System and Economy of NCDs**

| Non-Communicable Diseases | Global Economic Burden in Billion US$ | | |
|---|---|---|---|
| | Health Systems | Economy | Total |
| Cancers | 154 | 67 | 221 |
| CVDs | 474 | 389 | 863 |
| COPDs | 1878 | 230 | 2108 |
| Diabetes | 376 | 124 | 500 |
| Mental disorders | 823 | 1671 | 2494 |
| Total | 3705 | 2481 | 6186 |

*Source*: Authors analysis on Bloom and Cafiero (2011).

## DOMESTIC SCIENTIFIC EVIDENCE ON COSTS OF NCDS

Scientific evidence on the cost of NCDs in Pakistan indicates exorbitant costs of managing NCDs (Gillani et al., 2018) that is often paid out of pocket, contribute to financial distress, and are unaffordable to families (Datta et al., 2019; Khealani et al., 2003; Zaid & Ansari, 2012) which mostly living in urban areas. Moreover, the economic consequences of NCDs are beyond the healthcare system, adversely affecting economic activity in the form of lost productivity of the patient and their caregivers (Gillani et al., 2018).

A study of the financial implication of the management of type 2 diabetes among patients (n=399) seeking care estimated cost of US$ 27.6 and social costs (productivity losses of patients and caregivers) of US$18.61 in 2016 in the southern Punjab province of Pakistan (Gillani et al., 2018). Extrapolating the results to the population of Pakistan in 2016 and the prevalence of type 2 diabetes at 6.9 percent, they arrived at an economic burden of healthcare costs for type 2 diabetes of 37.9 billion (Gillani et al., 2018). Their findings suggest higher healthcare and social costs for patients from rural areas compared to their urban counterparts. Moreover, the study finds a high share of urbanites seeking healthcare (61.9 percent of the patients).

A hospital-based study analyzed the medical bills of patients paid for the treatment of acute stroke (in 1998–2001) and estimated an average cost of 70,714 rupees (US$ 1179). Comparing this estimate with the average annual per capita earning of 4,881 rupees (US$ 85) in Pakistan in the year 2000–2001, the authors concluded that most of the population could not afford treatment for an episode of acute stroke in the household and argued for enhanced allocation in the health sector that was 135 million rupees (1.8 percent of the budget) in the year 2000–2001 (Khealani et al., 2003).

A study on financing the treatment of breast cancer (n=200) at public hospitals (n=2) in an urban city in Pakistan reported a mean cost of US$ 1846.44 (PKR 189,762) in 2015. Travel and accommodation costs were US$ 310.88

(PKR 31,950), and productivity losses were US$ 273.38 (PKR 28,096). Delayed diagnosis was one of the critical findings of the study. Most of the study participants (54 percent) reported noticing symptoms of breast cancer more than a year ago (average 13.5 months). The reasons for not using public diagnostic facilities were inapposite locations (33.5 percent), delays in getting reports (30 percent), and quality/untrustworthy findings (30 percent). With an average monthly income of the family of US$ 228.17, a large proportion of the patients reported distressed self-financing (over 80 percent) using their savings (42 percent) or sold assets (41.5 percent) to finance their treatment (Mahmood et al., 2018).

A study on the treatment cost of breast cancer and head and neck cancer in an expensive private tertiary care setting in Karachi during 2009–2010 reported a monthly cost of US$ 946.42 over a mean duration of 7.8 months for breast cancer and 5.04 months for head and neck cancer. Though the cancer patients belonged to a high-income segment (median family income of US$996.4 per month), 67 percent of them reported financial distress as significant and unmanageable. Most patients (94 percent) had financed their healthcare from their resources (Zaid & Ansari, 2012).

Using data from the Pakistan labor force survey, Mushtaq et al. (2015) estimated the economic consequences of occupational injuries to the injured and society. The productivity loss framework quantified the income with the number of work-lost days. They estimated that the lost productivity of all types of occupational injuries was PKR 186.5 billion, including PKR 141 billion for permanent injuries and PKR 44.5 billion for temporary occupational injuries in 2012–2013. Similarly, Datta and Hussain et al. (2019), using national survey data from 2015 to 2016, reported that the incidence of financial catastrophe of OPHE (OPHE >10 percent of the household income) was found to be 6.7 percentage points higher for households consuming medication for hypertension and diabetes than for those with other types of OPHE.

## ECONOMIC BURDEN OF MENTAL ILLNESS

Due to pervasive social stigma, individuals with mental health conditions are frequently perceived as less competent for formal employment and deemed high-risk, requiring supervision, resulting in a burden of unemployment, underemployment, illness absence, and reduced productivity (Brouwers, 2020). Moreover, individuals themselves often feel that work environments are stigmatized and not accommodating for those with mental health challenges. In a study of 432 psychiatric patients in Peshawar, 27 percent reported being discriminated against at the workplace due to their mental health condition, and 20 percent reported that they were thinking of quitting their job due to their illness (Daniel et al., 2021).

Individuals with known mental health challenges are often relegated to low-skilled and low-paid positions (Muhammad et al., 2010). This, in turn, negatively impacts their socioeconomic capacity and causes a loss of productivity for society. Furthermore, financial dependence leads to significant social stigma, both from family members and society (Shah et al., 2020).

Comprehensive estimates of the long-term cost of lost productivity attributable to mental health challenges are not available for Pakistan. However, a study conducted in Faisalabad city of Pakistan has estimated an annual income loss of 58,439 PKR (i.e., PKR 4869.9 x 12) associated with depression, including productivity loss for the patient and caregivers (Sadaf et al., 2022). Another study estimated that 59 percent of the total economic cost among mental health patients seeking hospital outpatient and inpatient care is attributed to productivity loss—this was estimated to be US$2,514.59 million per year (Malik & Khan, 2016), or 9.02 billion PKR in 2021/2022 after adjusting for inflation. Further accounting for the cost of under-unemployment and low productivity over the lifetime will push these estimates much higher.

## BURDEN OF HEALTHCARE EXPENDITURE

Given the dominant nature of out-of-pocket healthcare expenditures in Pakistan, there is significant underutilization of healthcare. As a result, mental healthcare costs, based on observed expenditure, should be interpreted in light of unmet needs. The cost of care varies significantly among those who use care, depending on the condition, type and duration of care, provider, facility, and geography. Malik and Khan (2016) estimated the average annual cost of medical care among private hospital patients in Karachi to be PKR 81,922 (US$ 1394.65) and PKR 19,592 (US$ 333.54) for admitted and ambulatory care patients, respectively. In another study conducted in Peshawar, Hamdani et al. (2020) estimated the cost of mental health care among primary care patients with psychological distress to be 2,445 PKR; this includes the cost of medical professionals, inpatient care, medications, traditional healers, and community health workers. Another study conducted in Faisalabad estimated the direct cost of care-seeking for depression to be 11,108 PKR, with variation based on gender, income, age, and education (Sadaf et al., 2022). While cost estimates differ across settings, these costs significantly deter care-seeking, resulting in a significant treatment gap.

## SOCIAL BURDEN OF MENTAL ILLNESS

Patients with mental illnesses are socially stigmatized and often considered "mad" or "insane," particularly those with severe mental illnesses (Rastogi et al., 2014), while those with common mental disorders, that is, depression and anxiety, are often seen as weak, pitiful, ungrateful, and lacking religious faith (Shah et al., 2019). In societies with a lack of education, mental health patients, particularly those with schizophrenia, are seen as "possessed" (Rathod et al., 2023). Mental health-related social stigmatization leads to discrimination that affects the social health of both patients and their caregivers. In a survey of fifty caregivers of patients receiving in-hospital psychiatric care in Islamabad, Shah et al. (2019) reported significant public stigma related to the perception that "receiving mental health treatment is a sign of personal failure" and that "most people think less of a person who has received mental health treatment."

Patients are often excluded from social participation, leading to social isolation and further exacerbation of mental health challenges. Another important domain of social impact is the depletion of social capital, that is, the network of dependable individuals with interpersonal trust who can provide both material and emotional support in a time of need. In a study of 146 elderly respondents in Punjab, Tariq et al. (2019) found that low levels of social capital were strongly associated with higher levels of depression.

Among children with mental health conditions, self-stigmatization is widespread. In a study on (n=110) children receiving psychiatric care (aged 8–12) in Lahore, Khalil et al. (2020) found that most children experienced trust issues, rejection by other children, avoidance, discrimination and bullying at school, and feeling embarrassed about their own mental health. This stigmatization has long-term implications for self-confidence, educational achievement, social participation, and economic productivity. Mental health problems may also be associated with engagement in peer violence, particularly if children have witnessed paternal violence (Asad et al., 2007). Parental mental health problems also lead to low self-esteem among children, both due to domestic abuse and neglect, as well as societal discrimination.

## HEALTH SYSTEM AND HEALTHCARE FINANCING

The health system in Pakistan is a mix of public and private sectors. However, the private sector dominates in financing as more than 50 percent of total health expenditure is managed by the patients and families from their out-of-pocket resources, and over 60 percent of the health-seeking is catered by private healthcare providers. Secondary and tertiary care in Pakistan have expanded in the last two decades; however, except for an increase in the doctor-to-population ratio (0.6 doctor/1000 population in 2000 to 1.1 doctor/1000 population in 2019), this absolute increase is offset by rapid population growth (World Bank, 2024). For example, in absolute terms, the number of hospital beds has increased (figure 9.1) from 103,000, beds in 2008 to 134,000 beds in 2019 (Pakistan Bureau of Statistics, 2019). Nevertheless, the hospital bed ratio remained stagnant, from 0.7 bed/1000 in 2000 to 0.6 bed/1000 in 2017 (World Bank, 2024). Similarly, the specialist surgical workforce and nurse-to-population ratios have stagnated over the same period.

An alarming situation prevails in the role of the primary healthcare setup in the delivery of health services in the country. There are around ten thousand primary healthcare facilities. An additional one hundred thousand community health workers provide door-to-door primary healthcare covering the whole country. However, the utilization rates of PHC facilities are stagnant at around 5–6 percent, the rest of health seeking is from the private sector and public hospitals (Pakistan Bureau of Statistics, 2005; Pakistan Bureau of Statistics, 2020). Under the influence of bilateral and multilateral donors, the primary healthcare setup is overburdened with projects focusing on infectious disease and maternal and child health. Moreover, the medical staff do not have relevant training and are ill-equipped to manage NCDs at the primary healthcare level, often referring patients to the next level of care.

Two aspects of health systems are critical in the context of NCDs. Firstly, NCD patients are referred to secondary and tertiary levels of care that are concentrated in ten large cities in Pakistan, where 70 percent of hospital beds are available. This type of treatment is costly, time-consuming, and delayed

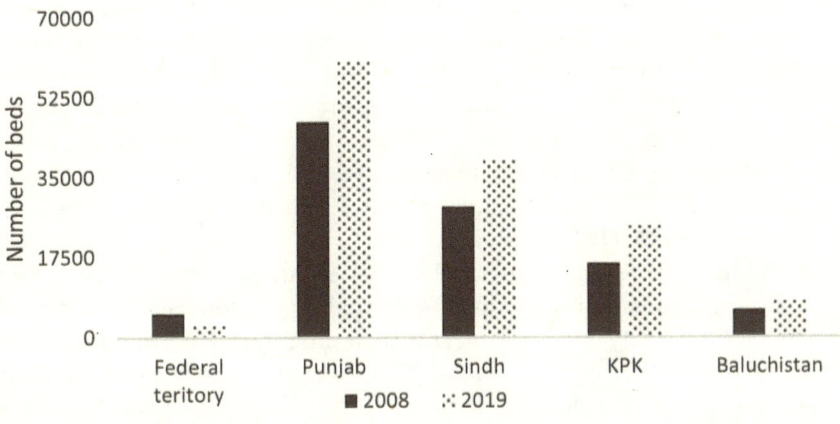


**Figure 9.1. Hospital Beds in Pakistan.** *Source*: Data from Pakistan Bureau of Statistics, 2019.

compared to management at the primary healthcare level with a proper referral system to the next level of care. Secondly, expenditure on the treatment of NCDs is made from the household's resources. A major reason for this trend is the primary focus of inland health policies and priorities, and development partners have remained on infectious diseases and maternal and child health. While efforts are underway to cover the cost of NCDs with financial risk protection schemes, the scope of such initiatives covers hospitalization.

Since 2015, a health financing scheme that protects families from the cost of hospitalization has been operating in the country. The Sehat Sahulat Program (SSP) provides financial risk protection to families with a claim cap of PKR 240,000–400,000 per family per year. The NCDs covered in the scheme's benefit package include hospitalization for heart diseases, complications of diabetes, end-stage kidney disease, road traffic injuries, cancers, and neurosurgical procedures (Saeed, 2023). Due to embedded limitations of financial risk protection schemes, except for the quality of healthcare and accreditation of healthcare providers, these schemes have limited scope for removing physical barriers to access and use of health services. The metropolitan concentration of healthcare is one of the factors that compromise many people's access to health services. The non-medical travel and stay costs are often excluded from health insurance packages such as SSP. A recent study on NCDs revealed that poor access and longer health-seeking duration are major reasons that hamper the medical management of NCDs (Gowani et al., 2016).

## FINANCING PLANNING AND FISCAL SPACE

Management of NCDs is resource-intensive and requires substantial funding from the public sector. The National Action Framework of the government of Pakistan has estimated the per-person cost (inclusive of health system costs) of US$ 28.5, ranging across provinces/regions at a minimum of US$ 24.8/person/year in Punjab and a maximum of US$ 31.8/person/year in the Gilgit-Baltistan region. With a population of 241.5 million (Pakistan Bureau of Statistics, 2023), the total financial outlay for financing NCDs in Pakistan is US$ 6.9 billion (MNHSRC, 2021).

According to the recent report of National Health Accounts, the per capita health expenditure is US$ 40, with a substantial proportion paid out of pocket (54 percent) privately by patients and their families (Pakistan Bureau of Statistics, 2020b). Treatment costs of NCDs by the patient and their families account for greater than 50 percent of OOP payments, with 25 percent of OOP on cardiovascular disorders, followed by diabetes (7.09 percent of OOP) and liver/kidney diseases (6.82 percent of OOP), injuries/fractures

(5.12 percent of OOP), and cancers (4.14 percent of OOP). Non-medical social costs of seeking care are around 17 percent of the OOP payments by the patient and their families. This includes a substantial portion of OOP spent on transportation of patients to health facilities (7.71 percent of OOP), followed by food (2.06 percent of OOP), tips/bribes (0.23 percent of OOP), accompanying person cost (0.55 percent of OOP), and others (6.21 percent of OOP) (Pakistan Bureau of Statistics, 2020b).

Considering the current fiscal space of the public sector in the backdrop of the fact that the economy of the country is on the verge of bankruptcy, consistently requiring bailout packages from the International Monetary Fund, it is less likely that the dominant out-of-pocket nature of financing NCDs will improve by replacing it with public sector allocations to the management of NCDs.

## MITIGATION STRATEGIES

The National Action Framework (2021–2030), endorsed by national and provincial health ministers, proposed strategies to combat NCDs in five areas: governance, prevention and reduction in risk, NCDs-related healthcare services, mental health services, and surveillance, monitoring, and evaluation. The Universal Health Coverage monitoring framework included four areas: Blood Pressure, Diabetes Mellitus, Cervical Cancer Screening, and Tobacco Control in the services package index for NCDs. The financial implications of the recommendation on NCDs discussed in the previous section are beyond the existing means. With this background, reliance on available resources is the only viable option. In the remaining part of this section, four policy directions are proposed that will rely on strengthening the existing healthcare delivery system, addressing social determinants of health, and working on risk factors of NCDs.

### Timely Screening and Early Diagnosis

Screening and early diagnosis programs in public health not only contribute to better clinical management of NCDs but also save costs by avoiding complications and minimizing the severity of the disease. Participatory strategies to ensure the involvement of community and civil society organizations in health screening programs can improve the outcomes of these programs.

### Strengthening Primary Healthcare

Health delivery in Pakistan favors PHC in terms of numbers and secondary and tertiary care in terms of utilization. Investing in the PHC sector for the management of NCDs will save resources for the health system. This will require expanding the mandate of primary healthcare by training the PHC providers with the skill set of NCD management and an effective referral to the next level of care.

### Social Determinants of Health

The role of social determinants of health in improving health is well established. This can be pushed by aligning health investment with investment in social sectors such as improving literacy, providing clean water supply, and improving hygienic sanitation services. Investment in water supply and sanitation schemes has multiple returns, including improving health with resource implications for the health sector.

### Tobacco Control through Public Health

Tobacco addiction is the single most important contributor to the burden of NCDs. In Pakistan, all forms of tobacco addiction exist, including smokeless tobacco. While economic policies such as tobacco taxation are highly effective in controlling tobacco consumption, smokeless tobacco use is alarmingly high in Pakistan. Due to the informal nature of the smokeless tobacco industry, the role of public health intervention is over the taxation policies.

## CONCLUSION

The economic and social burden of non-communicable diseases in Pakistan is significant and multifaceted and is exacerbated by the lack of public funding. The economic burden manifests through various channels, including unemployment, underemployment, and work absences. The long-term costs of lost productivity and substantial healthcare expenditures contribute to a profound economic impact. The social burden of mental illnesses is equally significant, with patients facing stigmatization and discrimination that extend beyond the individual to impact caregivers. Social exclusion, self-stigmatization, and the depletion of social capital further compound these challenges.

There is an urgent need for a re-evaluation of resource allocation, policy frameworks, and societal attitudes toward mental health in Pakistan. Prioritizing mental health in national agendas, investing in comprehensive mental health care, and fostering societal awareness and acceptance are imperative steps toward mitigating economic and social burdens. Failure to address these issues not only hampers the well-being of individuals and families but also impedes the overall socioeconomic development of the nation. The economic perspective on NCDs is a realization that disease management is an economic and social issue that needs collective efforts by all stakeholders, including healthcare providers, public health experts, economic policymakers, and civil society. This chapter provides the economic perspective of NCDs with recommendations using existing resources and a set of proven cost-effective strategies and greater public good in the domain of NCDs.

## REFERENCES


Abegunde, D. O., Mathers, C. D., Adam, T., Ortegon, M., & Strong, K. (2007). The burden and costs of chronic diseases in low-income and middle-income countries. *The Lancet, 370*(9603), 1929–1938.

Alvi, M. H., Ashraf, T., Kiran, T., Iqbal, N., Gumber, A., Patel, A., & Husain, N. (2023). Economic burden of mental illness in Pakistan: An estimation for the year 2020 from existing evidence. *BJPsych International, 20*(3), 54–56.

Asad, N., Karmaliani, R., McFarlane, J., Bhamani, S. S., Somani, Y., Chirwa, E., & Jewkes, R. (2017). The intersection of adolescent depression and peer violence: Baseline results from a randomized controlled trial of 1752 youth in Pakistan. *Child and Adolescent Mental Health, 22*(4), 232–241.

Bloom, D. E., Cafiero, E., Jané-Llopis, E., Abrahams-Gessel, S., Bloom, L. R., Fathima, S., . . . & Weiss, J. (2012). *The global economic burden of noncommunicable diseases* (No. 8712). Program on the Global Demography of Aging.

Brouwers, E. P. (2020). Social stigma is an underestimated contributing factor to unemployment in people with mental illness or mental health issues: position paper and future directions. *BMC Psychologyy, 8*, 1–7.

Daniel, F., Ghani, N., Ali, S., & Suliman, M. (2021). Impact of mental disorders in terms of discrimination and stigmatization: A cross-sectional study in Peshawar, Khyber Pakhtunkhwa. *Journal of Saidu Medical College, Swat, 11*(2), 96–102.

Datta, B. K., Husain, M. J., & Asma, S. (2019). Assessing the relationship between out-of-pocket spending on blood pressure and diabetes medication and household catastrophic health expenditure: evidence from Pakistan. *International Journal for Equity in Health, 18*(1), 1–12.

Gillani, A. H., Aziz, M. M., Masood, I., Saqib, A., Yang, C., Chang, J., . . . & Fang, Y. (2018). Direct and indirect cost of diabetes care among patients with type 2 diabetes in private clinics: A multicenter study in Punjab, Pakistan. *Expert Review of Pharmacoeconomics & Outcomes Research, 18*(6), 647–653

Government of Pakistan. (2020). *Pakistan economic survey 2020*, Islamabad: Ministry of Finance.

Gowani, A., Ahmed, H. I., Khalid, W., Muqeet, A., Abdullah, S., Khoja, S., & Kamal, A. K. (2016). Facilitators and barriers to NCD prevention in Pakistanis–invincibility or inevitability: A qualitative research study. *BMC Research Notes, 9*(1), 1–9.

Hafeez, A., Dangel, W. J., Ostroff, S. M., Kiani, A. G., Glenn, S. D., Abbas, J., . . . & Mokdad, A. H. (2023). The state of health in Pakistan and its provinces and territories, 1990–2019: A systematic analysis for the Global Burden of Disease Study 2019. *The Lancet Global Health, 11*(2), e229–e243.

Hamdani, S. U., Rahman, A., Wang, D., Chen, T., van Ommeren, M., Chisholm, D., & Farooq, S. (2020). Cost-effectiveness of WHO Problem Management Plus for adults with mood and anxiety disorders in a post-conflict area of Pakistan: Randomised controlled trial. *The British Journal of Psychiatry, 217*(5), 623–629.

Haque, N. U., Nazuk, A., Burgess, R., Rasul, I., Albasit, S. J., Ahsan, H., . . . & Zulfiqar, F. (2021). *The State of Poverty in Pakistan* (No. 2021: 12). Pakistan Institute of Development Economics.

Jafar, T. H., Haaland, B. A., Rahman, A., Razzak, J. A., Bilger, M., Naghavi, M., . . . & Hyder, A. A. (2013). Non-communicable diseases and injuries in Pakistan: Strategic priorities. *The Lancet, 381*(9885), 2281–2290.

Kassim-Lakha, S., & Bennett, J. (2013). Philanthropic funding for health in Pakistan. *The Lancet, 381*(9885), 2236–2237.

Khalil, A., Gondal, F., Imran, N., & Azeem, M. W. (2020). Self-Stigmatization in children receiving mental health treatment in Lahore, Pakistan. *Asian Journal of Psychiatry, 47*, 101,839.

Khan, M. M. (2016). Economic burden of mental illnesses in Pakistan. *Journal of Mental Health Policy and Economics, 19*(3), 155.

Khealani, B. A., Javed, Z. F., Syed, N. A., Shafqat, S., & Wasay, M. (2003). Cost of acute stroke care at a tertiary care hospital in Karachi, Pakistan. *Journal of Pakistan Medical Association, 53*(11), 552.

Lozano, R., Naghavi, M., Foreman, K., Lim, S., Shibuya, K., Aboyans, V., . . . & Remuzzi, G. (2012). Global and regional mortality from 235 causes of death for 20 age groups in 1990 and 2010: A systematic analysis for the Global Burden of Disease Study 2010. *The Lancet, 380*(9859), 2095–2128.

Mahmood, H. Z., Khaliq, I. H., Iqbal Bhatti, Z., J Wilson, K., Gondal, K. M., Malik, S., & Zaman, S. (2018). Household costs of breast cancer morbidity: An empirical assessment from Pakistan. *JBUON, 23*(Suppl 1), S28–S33.

Malik, M. A., & Wasay, M. (2013). Economics of health and health care in Pakistan. *Journal of Pakistan Medical Association, seven*, 814–815.

Ministry of National Health Services Regulation and Coordination. (2021). *National action framework for non-communicable disease and mental health 2021–30*. Islamabad.

Muhammad, N., Shah, M., Ahmad, M., & Alam, I. (2010). Mental disorders: A glance at its socio-economic pushing factors in Peshawar. *Pakistan Journal of Life and Social Sciences (Pakistan)*.8(1), 49–53

Mushtaq, F. (2015). Economic impact of occupational injuries in Pakistan (Doctoral dissertation, Pakistan Institute of Development Economics).

Nishtar, S., Bhutta, Z. A., Jafar, T. H., Ghaffar, A., Akhtar, T., Bengali, K., . . . & Rahim, E. (2013). Health reform in Pakistan: A call to action. *The Lancet, 381*(9885), 2291–2297.

Nishtar, S., Bile, K. M., Ahmed, A., Amjad, S., & Iqbal, A. (2005). Integrated population-based surveillance of noncommunicable diseases: The Pakistan model. *American Journal of Preventive Medicine, 29*(5), 102–106.

Oni, T., Assah, F., Erzse, A., Foley, L., Govia, I., Hofman, K. J., . . . & Wareham, N. J. (2020). The global diet and activity research (GDAR) network: A global public health partnership to address upstream NCD risk factors in urban low and middle-income contexts. *Globalization and Health*, *16*, 1–11.

Pakistan Bureau of Statistics. (2005). Pakistan social and living standard measurement survey. Retrieved from https://www.pbs.gov.pk/content/pakistan-social-and-living-standards-measurement.

Pakistan Bureau of Statistics. (2020a). Pakistan social and living standard measurement survey. Retrieved from https://www.pbs.gov.pk/content/pakistan-social-and-living-standards-measurement.

Pakistan Bureau of Statistics. (2020b). Pakistan national health accounts 2019–20. Retrieved from https://www.pbs.gov.pk/publication/national-health-accounts-pakistan-2019–20.

Pakistan Bureau of Statistics. (2023). Final results 7th population and housing census 2023 (Digital Census). Retrieved from https://www.pbs.gov.pk/content/announcement-results-seventh-population-and-housing-census-2023-digital-census.

Rao, S., Shah, N., Jawed, N., Inam, S., & Shafique, K. (2015). Nutritional and lifestyle risk behaviors and their association with mental health and violence among Pakistani adolescents: Results from the National Survey of 4583 individuals. *BMC Public Health*, *15*(1), 1–9.

Rastogi, P., Khushalani, S., Dhawan, S., Goga, J., Hemanth, N., Kosi, R., . . . & Rao, V. (2014). Understanding clinician perception of common presentations in South Asians seeking mental health treatment and determining barriers and facilitators to treatment. *Asian Journal of Psychiatry*, *7*, 15–21.

Rathod, S., Javed, A., Iqbal, R., Al-Sudani, A., Vaswani-Bye, A., Haider, I., & Phiri, P. (2023). Results of a qualitative study of patient, carer and clinician views on the experience of caring for individuals with psychosis in Pakistan. *The Cognitive Behaviour Therapist*, *16*, e17.

Sadaf, T., Iqbal, M. A., Jamil, F., Raza, M. H., & Nazir, A. (2022). Cost of mental illness and depression in developing countries: A case study of Pakistan. *Journal of Education and Social Studies*, *3*(2), 84–94.

Saeed. (2023). Policy making and implementation processes of public health interventions: A case study of Sehat Sahulat program (MPhil Public Policy dissertation). Pakistan Institute of Development Economics. Retrieved from https://file-thesis.pide.org.pk/pdf/mphil-public-policy-2020-asim-saeed--policy-making-and-implementation-processes-of-public-health-interventions-a-case-study-of-sehat-sahulat-program.pdf.

Shah, I., Khalily, M. T., Ahmad, I., & Hallahan, B. (2019). Impact of conventional beliefs and social stigma on attitude toward access to mental health Services in Pakistan. *Community Mental Health Journal*, *55*, 527–533.

Shah, R., Jafeer, Q. U. A., Saeed, S., Aslam, S., & Ali, I. (2020). Unemployment and social stigma: Naming, blaming and shaming of educated youth in rural Khyber Pakhtunkhwa province of Pakistan. *International Journal of Sociology and Social Policy*, *40*(7/8), 543–558.

Sohail, S. A., Syed, A. A., & Rahman, A. (2017). Mental health in Pakistan: Yesterday, today and tomorrow. *Mental Health in Asia and the Pacific: Historical and Cultural Perspectives*, 17–37.

Tariq, A., Beihai, T., Ali, S., Abbas, N., & Ilyas, A. (2019). Mediating effect of cognitive social capital on the relationship between physical disability and depression in elderly people of rural Pakistan. *International Journal of Environmental Research and Public Health, 16*(21), 4232.

UNDP. (2024). Urbanization in Pakistan. Retrieved from https://www.undp.org/pakistan/urbanisation-pakistan# (Accessed January 11, 2024).

Wasay, M., & Jabbar, A. (2009). Fight against chronic diseases (high blood pressure, stroke, diabetes and cancer) in Pakistan; Cost-effective interventions.

World Bank. (2024). Indicators. Retrieved from https://data.worldbank.org/indicator/ (Accessed January 11, 2024).

Zaidi, A. A., Ansari, T. Z., & Khan, A. (2012). The financial burden of cancer: Estimates from patients undergoing cancer care in a tertiary care hospital. *International Journal for Equity in Health, 11*(1), 1–6.

# Index

# About the Contributors

**Shehzad Ali** holds a Canada Research Chair in Public Health Economics and is the Associate Chair (Research) at the Department of Epidemiology and Biostatistics, Schulich School of Medicine and Dentistry, Western University, Canada. He is also a Visiting Associate Professor of Health Economics at the University of York (UK), an Honorary Fellow at Macquarie University (Australia), and an Affiliate/Adjunct Scientist at the Centre for Addictions and Mental Health (CAMH) and Bruyère Research Institute. Dr. Ali works at the intersection of health economics, equity, and policy, focusing on five key areas: health services performance indicators, integrating equity into economic evaluations using a distributional cost-effectiveness framework, health technology assessment, RCTs, and observational studies, and developing treatment-related algorithms to predict patient outcomes in clinical practice. Dr. Ali has served as principal or co-investigator and has held grants from major funding bodies in Canada (CIHR), the United States (NIH), the United Kingdom (NIHR), and Australia (NHMRC). He has published over 100 papers in peer-reviewed journals.

**Husan Bano Channar** is an Assistant Professor of Nursing at Peoples Nursing School at the Liaquat University of Medical and Health Sciences, Jamshoro. Husan is a PhD student at the Department of Physiology, University of Sindh, Jamshoro. Her PhD dissertation topic is "Factors and Determinants associated with Prevalence of Anemia among Adults in Karachi, Sindh, Pakistan." Husan has published some of her research in national and international journals. She has mentored several MS nursing students. Husan remained a member of the Pakistan Nursing Council for institute accreditation and a member of the Provincial Nurses Association Sindh.

**Abdullah Emran** has obtained an MPhil in Development Studies from the Pakistan Institute of Development Economics and holds a BS in Economics from the International Islamic University in Islamabad. His MPhil dissertation delved into the relationship between political regimes, institutions, and the development trajectory of Afghanistan. Abdullah's research interests primarily center around the role of institutions in the process of development in developing countries.

**Hafsa Hina** is an Assistant Professor and head of the School of Social Sciences at the Pakistan Institute of Development Economics. She holds a PhD in Economics. Her main area of research pertains to applied international macroeconomics, which analyzes trade imbalances, exchange rate monetary policy, and growth. She published her works in esteemed peer-reviewed journals, including *Pakistan Development Review*, *Complexity*, *PLOS*, *IEEE Journal*, and *Asia Pacific Journal*.

**Zulfiqar Ali Laghari** serves as Professor and Chairman of the Department of Physiology. Dr. Laghari obtained a PhD degree in developmental biology from Nottingham University, United Kingdom. He is also the founding chairman of departments like Public Health and Physiotherapy at the University of Sindh. Dr. Laghari has mentored several PhD and MS students and is continuing to do so. Dr. Zulfiqar remained office bearer of the Pakistan Physiological Society multiple times. Dr. Zulfiqar has authored several research publications in national and international journals.

**Muhammad Ashar Malik** is working as the Associate Dean of education at the Faculty of Arts and Sciences of the Aga Khan University, Karachi, Pakistan. He has a joint appointment with the Department of Community Health Sciences, Faculty of Health Sciences and Medical College, Aga Khan University. He has expertise in public health economics, social policies, equity and inclusion, and evaluation sciences. He holds an MA in Economics (University of Peshawar), a PG Diploma in Public Administration (IM Sciences, Peshawar), an MSc in Health Economics (University of York, UK), and a PhD in Public Health Economics (Erasmus University, The Netherlands). Ashar is involved in curriculum planning, management, and evaluation. He teaches at graduate and post-graduate-level in his area of expertise. He has published over two dozen research articles, a book on health policies in Pakistan, and two book chapters on ethics and economics, as well as pharmaceutical economics and economics of NCDs. He is a member of the Federal Ministry of Health's Technical Advisory Group on Immunization, the Academic Council of the International Society of

Pharmacoeconomics and Outcomes Research (ISPOR), and the World Health Organization's Technical Advisory Group on Climate Change and Health.

**Ayesha Nazir**, an MPhil graduate in Development Studies from the prestigious Pakistan Institution of Development Economics, is a passionate healthcare policy advocate inspired by personal experiences. She leverages her academic background to champion practical and effective healthcare policies. As an experienced educationist, administrative coordinator, and project manager, she balances her professional endeavors with motherhood and caring for her six-month-old child. With academic acumen, organizational skills, and a compassionate approach, Ayesha Nazir is poised to contribute to the healthcare sector significantly.

**Saman Nazir** is a committed Researcher whose work focuses on medical sociology and social stratification. She earned her PhD in Sociology from the University of North Texas and now serves as a Senior Researcher at the Pakistan Institute of Development Economics (PIDE). Her doctoral dissertation titled "Cesarean Section Delivery and Exclusive Breastfeeding in Pakistan: Emerging Challenges" delves into two crucial issues for maternal and neonatal health in Pakistan. Saman has collaborated on various studies, including those exploring consanguinity, educational assortative mating, fertility, and socioeconomic segregation in urban schools in Pakistan. Her research findings have been published in reputable peer-reviewed journals. Dr. Nazir has presented her research findings at prestigious conferences such as the American Sociological Association, Southwestern Sociological Association, and Mid-South Sociological Association. She was honored to receive the Fulbright Scholarship, a highly competitive award, which supported her PhD studies in the United States from 2015 to 2019. More recently, she led the successful acquisition of the Alumni Small Grant (ASG) for the research-based project "Pakistan for All." This initiative promotes co-existence and religious tolerance in Pakistani society, with a focus on children. Additionally, Dr. Nazir actively contributes to advancing public health initiatives as a member of the Pakistan U.S. Alumni Network (PUAN) Public Health Interest Group. Currently, Dr. Nazir is the principal investigator for a public health project titled "Assessing Public Toilets, Littering, and Spitting in Twin Cities: A Call for Healthcare Intervention," further demonstrating her dedication to improving public health outcomes in Pakistan.

**Halima S. Qureshi**, a seasoned consultant clinical psychologist since 2015 with a PhD in Clinical Psychology, is actively shaping the landscape of both clinical practice and academia. In addition to her expertise in clinical psychology, she has delved into social psychology, broadening her research scope. Her primary focus includes psychological interventions, non-suicidal self-injury, video gaming, and trauma. She has published her research in esteemed peer-reviewed journals. Since 2016, she has been imparting knowledge through training sessions and workshops, contributing to community initiatives combating mental health stigma. Halima has shared her insights as a psychology expert on national TV channels, highlighting her commitment to bridging the gap between research and practice. Her multifaceted contributions underscore her dedication to advancing the understanding of clinical and social psychology.

**Asad Saleem** is currently a Program Associate at Maan Education and Health Development (MEHD). Asad holds an MPhil in Development Studies from the Pakistan Institute of Development Economics. His MPhil thesis focused on local government, using health, education, water, and sanitation as indicators of development to assess Khyber Pakhtunkhwa's local governance performance. Asad is currently collaborating on various research projects related to public health.

**Ayaz Ali Samo** is currently serving as an Assistant Professor of Physiology at the Department of Physiology, University of Sindh. Dr. Ali obtained a PhD in Physiology from Beijing Normal University, China, in June 2018. He remained Vice President of the Pakistan Physiological Society from 2021 to 2023. His research focuses on Physiology, Epidemiology, and Public Health. He won two research grants from the Higher Education Commission, Islamabad. Dr. Ayaz supervises doctoral and master students. He has authored several publications in national and international scientific journals. Dr. Ali has visited the United States and China on academic exchange programs supported by the U.S. Consulate, Karachi, and the Ministry of Science and Technology, China.

**Arsalan Ahmed Uqaili** is an Assistant Professor of Physiology at the Department of Physiology, Liaquat University of Medical and Health Sciences, Jamshoro. After obtaining his Bachelor's in medicine, he did a Master's in Physiology at Isra University Hyderabad. He is a PhD candidate doing his dissertation on "Investigating the relationship between hematological markers and hepcidin levels in patients with Chronic Liver Disease." Dr. Uqaili Arslan has published some of his research in national and international journals.

**Mohammad Wasay** is currently a Professor (Alicharan endowed professor) of Neurology at Aga Khan University, Past President of the Pakistan

Society of Neurology and Pakistan Stroke Society, President of the Neurology Awareness and Research Foundation, Trustee and Chair of the specialty groups committee of World Federation of Neurology (WFN), Secretary of Environmental Neurology Specialty Group of WFN, Member, Global Policy Committee, World Stroke Organization (WSO), Editor—*Pakistan Journal of Neurological Sciences*, Chief Editor—*Jahan e Aasab* (Neurology public awareness magazine), Chair—Seed Grants Research Committee at Aga Khan University and Co-chair, NCD Think tank. Dr. Wasay received several national and international awards for educational, research, and advocacy activities, including the Teachers Recognition Award (American Academy of Neurology), Distinguished Teacher Award (Pakistan Society of Neurology), Outstanding Teacher Award (Aga Khan University), Gold Medal for Research (Pakistan Academy of Medical Sciences), and Advocacy Leader of the Year Award (American Academy of Neurology). He is serving as a fellow and Secretary of the Sind Chapter of the Pakistan Academy of Sciences. He was recently elected as a fellow of the World Academy of Sciences (TWAS). Dr. Wasay has published more than twenty-five research papers in peer-reviewed journals.

**Sumaira Yasmin** is a dedicated Educator and Researcher with a strong academic background. She holds an MPhil in Public Policy from the Pakistan Institute of Development Economics and a Master's in Economics from the Federal Urdu University, Islamabad. In addition to her studies in economics, Sumaira has pursued various courses in psychology and education, enhancing her interdisciplinary expertise. Her research interests focus on addressing critical public policy and healthcare issues. For her MPhil dissertation, Sumaira investigated the challenges of the Sehat Sahulat Program in Pakistan. She is part of the team collecting data on public health in the Twin Cities of Pakistan, furthering her contributions to the field.

**Fahd Zulfiqar** has a PhD in Anthropology, and his research interests are marginalization, political economy, sexual minorities, and exclusion. He also teaches at a post-graduate level. The courses he taught also have similar themes, such as human rights and development, gender and development, post-colonialism, and the political economy of development.

www.ingramcontent.com/pod-product-compliance
Lightning Source LLC
LaVergne TN
LVHW091530200926
848483LV00002B/355
*9781666962710*